London Burial Grounds

Isabella M. Holmes

ST. PETER'S, CORNHILL, IN 1817.

TABLE OF CONTENTS

INTRODUCTION

I. BRITISH AND ROMAN BURYING-PLACES
II. THE GRAVEYARDS OF PRIORIES AND CONVENTS
III. THE CATHEDRAL, THE ABBEY, THE TEMPLE, AND THE TOWER
IV. THE CITY CHURCHYARDS
V. LONDON CHURCHYARDS, OUTSIDE THE CITY
VI. PEST-FIELDS AND PLAGUE-PITS
VII. THE DISSENTERS' BURIAL-GROUNDS
VIII. BURIAL-PLACES OF FOREIGNERS IN LONDON
IX. HOSPITAL, ALMSHOUSE, AND WORKHOUSE GROUNDS
X. PRIVATE AND PROMISCUOUS CEMETERIES
XI. THE CLOSING OF THE BURIAL-GROUNDS AND VAULTS
XII. GRAVEYARDS AS PUBLIC GARDENS
XIII. THE CEMETERIES STILL IN USE
XIV. A FORECAST OF THE FUTURE

APPENDIX.

A. LIST OF BURIAL-GROUNDS IN EXISTENCE
B. LIST OF BURIAL-GROUNDS WHICH HAVE DISAPPEARED
C. CHURCHES AND CHAPELS WITHOUT BURIAL-GROUNDS, BUT WITH VAULTS UNDER THEM
D. HOW TO LAY OUT A BURIAL-GROUND AS A GARDEN
E. THE DISUSED BURIAL-GROUNDS ACT, ETC.

INTRODUCTION

IN looking one day at Rocque's plan of London (1742-5) I noticed how many burial-grounds and churchyards were marked upon it which no longer existed. I made a table of them, and traced their destiny, and the result of this research was printed in the First Annual Report of the Metropolitan Public Gardens Association, which was issued in 1884. I then went further, and commenced to draw up a list of all the burying-places, of which I could find any record, still existing, or that had ever existed in London. It was no easy task. A return drawn up by the late Sir Edwin Chadwick in 1843, for the use of the Parliamentary Committee which sat to consider questions relating to the sanitary condition of the labouring classes, contains a most valuable, though not perfectly complete, table of the graveyards in actual use at that date. Then there are the returns of the grounds closed by order in Council in 1853 and 1854, and still open for interments in 1855, which are also very useful. There is a return, dated June, 1833, purporting to show all the "Places of Burial belonging to each Parish or Precinct under the Authority of the Bishop of London," and all the "Places of Burial belonging to Dissenting Congregations within the Bills of Mortality," &c., with their size, and the annual number of burials in them. This, when I found it, I thought would be a great treasure, but I soon discovered such entries as the following: "Three letters have been addressed to the Officiating Ministers of the parishes of St. Benet, Gracechurch, St. Martin, Ludgate, and St. Margaret, Westminster, respectively; but no return has been received from either." "The united parishes of Allhallows, Bread Street, and St. John the Evangelist, not being under the authority of the Bishop of London, I have not any return to make." "I beg to add that there are several other places used as burial-grounds in this parish (Stepney) belonging to Jews, Dissenters, and others, of which I have no official cognizance, and to which, in fact, I have no access," &c. And with regard, generally, to the second part of the return, the following simple remark is made: "The Secretary of State is not able to ascertain the Places of Burial belonging to Dissenting congregations within the Bills of Mortality." In 1839 Walker described the condition of 47 of the most crowded metropolitan places of interment, and the Parliamentary Committee which sat in 1842 heard evidence about these and some others. In Maitland's "History of London" there is a list of 64 burial-places used in the year 1729, and not included in the Bills of Mortality. Some of these are outside London, and some are only vaults under buildings. I have also kept a list of about fifty books which I found of use, although in many of them only a few burial-grounds are mentioned or described. And this, with the addition of various ancient and modern maps and plans of London and its environs, is the material upon which I have had to work. But as it is never safe to take anything on trust, nothing but actual perambulations and inquiries on the spot could show the present size and condition of the burial-grounds, and even several that are marked on the ordnance maps have been built upon since they were published, as, for instance, the German ground in the Savoy, the additional ground to St. Martin's in the Fields, and Thomas' ground in Golden Lane, all of which have disappeared.

I have had some curious experiences while graveyard-hunting. At first I was less bold than I am now, and was hardly prepared to walk straight into private yards and look round them until asked my business and driven to retire. "My business" it is best not to reveal ordinarily. If one mentions that one is looking at a place because it was once a burial-ground the fact will generally be stoutly denied, and sometimes in good faith. But it is not unusual for an employé innocently to acknowledge that there are bones under the ground upon which he is standing, whereat his master, if he knew of it, would be very angry. For it must be remembered that it is to the interest of the owner of a yard to keep the circumstance of its having been used for interments in the background, and he is not pleased if, when he wants to put up a wall or enlarge a shed, he is stopped from doing so by the enforcement of the Disused Burial-Grounds Act of 1834, as amended by the Open Spaces Act of 1887.

I inquired of an old man once, in a court in Shoreditch, whether he remembered a graveyard existing by the workhouse.

"No," he said.

I noticed a newer part of the building, evidently a recently erected wing, and asked him how long it had been built.

"Oh, I moind," said he, "when they was buildin' that, they carted away a ton of bones." Here was the evidence I was seeking for.

One day a sleepy old Smithfield butcher, whose work-time was the night, and whose sleeping-time was the morning, was specially kept awake until 10 o'clock in order to see me, as he could remember the extent of a certain burial-ground before it was done away with. The information he was able to supply was very useful, but it was hard to keep him to the point, as the poor old man, once roused to remember the past, would persistently revert to the cottages which used to stand on the adjoining plot of land, and which ought, he said, to have come into his own possession if he had not been in some way defrauded out of his lawful inheritance.

It is often necessary, in order to see a graveyard, to go into one of the surrounding houses and ask for permission to look out from a back window. Such permission is sometimes refused at once, sometimes it is most kindly given. I remember arousing a divided opinion upon this matter by knocking at the door of one of the upper rooms in the almshouses in Bath Street. I wanted to see the ground used as a garden by the inmates of the St. Luke's Lunatic Asylum in Old Street, and which was at one time a pauper burial-ground for the parish. The old man did not at all like my invading his room, but the old lady was most affable, and had much to say upon the subject. At any rate I saw what I wanted, and made my mental report, but I left the old man grumbling at my unnecessary intrusion, and the old lady in smiles. I hope she did not suffer for her kindness.

If one asks to go into a burial-ground, it is generally imagined that one wants to see a particular grave. I have been supposed to have "some one lyin' there" in all quarters of the metropolis, and in all sorts of funny little places. I have been hailed as a sister by the quietest of Quakeresses and the darkest of bewigged Jewesses, by the leanest and most clean-shaven of ritualistic Priests, and by the bearded and buxom Dissenter. I remember, however, knocking at the gate of one Jewish ground which the caretaker was unwilling to let me enter. She asked me the direct question, "Are you a Jewess?" I had to say no, but happily I was armed with the name of a gentleman who had kindly told me to mention it in any such difficulty. It answered, and I was allowed in. One day I climbed a high, rickety fence in a builder's yard in Wandsworth in order to see over the wall into the Friends' burial-ground. No doubt the men in the place thought me mad,—anyhow they left me in peace.

I have often been assured that there is no possibility of a particular enclosure ever becoming a public garden by those who live, at a low rent, in the neighbouring cottage, on condition that they keep watch over the ground. Alas, before many months are over, they find that the wires have been pulled somehow or other, and that their precious yard is no longer available for their fowls to run in or for their clothes to dry in, but is invaded by their neighbours and their neighbour's unwelcome children. "They come four times a year to clear away the weeds." That is the sort of caretaking that some burial-grounds are subjected to; and on the other 361 days in the year all sorts of rubbish is deposited in them.

Twice I have had mud thrown at me, once by a woman in Cable Street, E., and once by a man in Silchester Road, W., but these were wholly unprovoked attacks, in fact mere accidental occurrences. For my general experience has been of the greatest consideration and politeness. I have never been out of my way for the sake of idle curiosity, but have not hesitated to go down any street or court or to knock at any door which was in my way, and I have never had cause to regret it. An appearance of utter insignificance and an air of knowing where you are going and what you want, is the passport for all parts of London; and I have seen young men and maidens, one moment indulging in the roughest play, the next moment step off the pavement to let me pass. The clergy and others always seem to think their own people the very worst. "You don't know what this neighbourhood is like," I have heard over and over again, and I am thankful I don't. But as far as a superficial knowledge of the streets goes they seem to be all much the same—north, south, east, and west—and their frequenters too. To the children, at any rate, one need never mind speaking. Poor little souls; they say "Miss," or "Mum," or "Missus," or "Teacher," or "Sister," or "Lady," but they never answer rudely.

Gravediggers and gardeners in cemeteries are generally communicative people, who do not at all mind stopping their work for a bit, and enlarging on the number of funerals, &c., which they daily witness. They speak of the actual headstones and monuments by the surnames engraved thereon, as, for instance, "Brown," "Smith," &c., and will point out a particular grave as "four behind Smith over there, Smith is the tall stone by the path; or if you look next to Wallace which has the shrub on it," and so on.

It is interesting to trace on maps of different dates the rise and fall of a graveyard. First there is the actual field, which on some particular day was acquired for the purpose. Then there is the burial-ground formed and in use. Then the plot appears to be vacant—put to no purpose, or used as a yard. Lastly buildings are on it, and the graveyard has quite disappeared. One difficulty to be encountered needs much study to overcome; it is the different names by which the same ground is called in different books or plans. For instance, Chadwick mentions in his list one called St. John's, Borough, whereas the proper name for this same ground is Butler's burial-ground, Horseydown. As another instance, and there are scores, it may be mentioned that the Peel Grove burial-ground was called in some returns the North-east London Cemetery, in others Cambridge Heath burial-ground, and in others Keldy's ground. Occasionally a graveyard is described as being "near the free school," or in some such vague terms, and it needs a knowledge of the districts and the buildings in them, past and present, to be able to locate some of these grounds which I have ventured to call "obscure."

Since 1883, as complete a list as I could make of the London burial-grounds has appeared in the Reports of the Metropolitan Public Gardens Association, and I have, from time to time, been asked for information about the more obscure ones. In the summer of 1894 the London County Council instructed its Parks Committee to make a return of all the burial-grounds existing in the County of London, with their size, ownership, and condition. Having been applied to for information and assistance, I offered to undertake the work. It involved some additional research at the British Museum, and a fresh perambulation. The offer being accepted I commenced the task in February, 1895, and sent in the return in June, accompanied by 60 sheets of the ordnance survey (25 inch to the mile), upon which the grounds were marked in colours, viz., those still in use blue, those disused green, those converted into public recreation grounds green with a red border. I gave the number existing in the County and City of London as 362, of which 41 were still in use, and 90 were public gardens and playgrounds. This did not include churches and chapels with vaults under them, but without graveyards. It must also be remembered that the area was strictly limited (as it is in this work) to that of the metropolitan boroughs, or the administrative County of London with the City. The cemeteries in the county do not represent all the parochial ones. There are, for instance, those of St. George's, Hanover Square, and Kensington at Hanwell, the Paddington Cemetery in Kilburn, the Jewish at Willesden, and very many more just outside the boundary, not to speak of a large number in what is called "London over the Border," which to all intents and purposes is still London, although separated by the River Lea, and governed by the West Ham Corporation.

The kindly notice taken of the return, which was published by the Council in October, 1895, has encouraged me to prepare the present volume, in which there is scope for a general view of the subject, for further historical details, and for particulars of those grounds which no longer exist.

The more public interest is brought to bear upon the burial-grounds, the more likely is it that they will be preserved from encroachments. The London County Council has special powers to put in force the provisions of the Disused Burial-grounds Act, and it has the record of their actual sites on the plans prepared by me. It is for the public to see that these provisions are carried out, not only for historical, sentimental, and sanitary reasons, but also because each burial-ground that is curtailed or annihilated means the loss of another space which may one day be available for public recreation; and considering that land, even in the poorest part of Whitechapel, fetches about £30,000 per acre, it is easily understood of what inestimable value is a plot of ground which cannot be built upon.

CHAPTER I

BRITISH AND ROMAN BURIAL-PLACES.

"Where now the haughty Empire that was spread

With such fond hope? Her very speech is dead."

WORDSWORTH.

EVERY chronicler of London history who can lay claim to be called an antiquarian, from Fitzstephen, Stow, and Pennant, to the Rev. W. J. Loftie and Sir Walter Besant, has tried to gather up the fragmentary evidence which from time to time has come to light, and to form some picture of the condition of London in the earliest times. Many have gone in largely for invention, and have weaved what they supposed to be circumstantial stories from discoveries of the most trivial kind, but these fictions are not worthy of repetition. As it is only with the evidences of the places of interment in London that this chapter has to deal, it is not possible to go into the question of the Roman roads, walls, villas, gardens and camps, of which traces have been found, although these relics really form the most interesting of the ancient remains, or "remarkables" as Maitland calls them, belonging to the several parishes.

A few tumuli scattered over London are supposed to mark the sites of British burial-places, Stukeley imagined he had discovered one by Long Acre, but the evidence is not trustworthy. Certainly there are some artificial mounds in Greenwich Park, which were opened in 1804 by the Rev. James Douglas, and found to contain spear-heads, beads, pieces of cloth, hair, &c., and there is the well-known one in Parliament Hill Fields, Hampstead, which the London County Council excavated in 1894. From the few broken pieces of human workmanship which were brought to light in this excavation, it was conjectured that the mound was an ancient British burial-place of the early bronze period, but no particular name can be associated with it. It is now railed round for its better protection, and planted with shrubs.

The Romans buried their dead outside their cities, often on each side of the highways immediately beyond the walls and gates, and they adopted this plan, to a certain extent, in Britain. But it must be remembered that Roman London, as first designed and built, was far smaller than that which is enclosed within the line of the city wall of which fragments still remain, and therefore some sepulchral monuments have been discovered inside this wall and its gates, as, for instance, near St. Martin's, Ludgate, in St. Paul's Churchyard, in Camomile Street and Lombard Street, and by the churches of St. Mary at Hill and St. Dunstan's in the East. Near Dowgate some excavations made by Wren brought to light what were then thought to be British graves, but as there were Roman urns at a still lower level the matter was rather difficult of solution.

THE TUMULUS AT HAMPSTEAD.

The largest number of sepulchral remains have been found on the east side of the City, commencing at Bishopsgate and Moorfields, and extending to Wapping on the south, and Sun Tavern Fields, Shadwell, on the east; and it is not improbable that a cemetery of considerable size occupied all this district in Roman times. In 1756 many earthen urns, containing ashes, burnt human bones, and coins, were dug up in a field "called Lottesworth, now Spitalfield," close to the present site of Christ Church, Spitalfields, together with some stone coffins and remnants of wooden ones which probably dated from British or Saxon times; and on many occasions during the last century, urns, lachrymatories, monumental stones, &c., were discovered in different spots in the district above mentioned. In many cases the monumental stones were erected to the memory of soldiers from various legions of the army, and on a few of them the inscriptions are still legible. Some of the Roman remains discovered in London are in the Guildhall Museum; the one represented in the accompanying picture, which was found near Ludgate, is with the Arundel marbles at Oxford. A few single graves have been identified among the traces of the gardens and villas which immediately surrounded the Roman Fort.

The following description of what Sir Christopher Wren found in St. Paul's Churchyard, on the north side of the Cathedral, is interesting. "Upon digging the foundation of the present fabrick of St. Paul's, he found under the graves of the latter ages, in a row below them, the Burial-places of the Saxon times—the Saxons, as it appeared, were accustomed to line their graves with chalk-stones, though some more eminent were entombed in coffins of whole stones. Below these were British graves, where were found ivory and wooden pins, of a hard wood, seemingly box, in abundance, of about six inches long; it seems the bodies were only wrapped up, and pinned in woollen shrouds, which being consumed, the pins remained entire. In the same row, and deeper, were Roman urns intermixed. This was eighteen feet deep or more, and belonged to the colony when Romans and Britons lived and died together." (From Wren's "Parentalia.") The remains found in the north-east corner of the churchyard were the best preserved.

ROMAN MONUMENT.

Some evidences of a Roman cemetery have also been discovered on the south side of the Thames, in Snow's Fields, Bermondsey, Union Street, Newington, and the burial-ground in Deverell Street. This district was probably the place of interment for those who lived in the small suburb which was growing up on the south side of the Bridge or Ferry. On Blackheath there have also been found traces of Roman burial, and in 1803 several urns were dug up in the Earl of Dartmouth's garden, but they were supposed by some authorities to be the remains of the Danes who were encamped in that neighbourhood.

Such are the very scanty traces that have hitherto been brought to light relating to the burial-places of those who were amongst the worthiest pioneers in the making of London, and who occupied it before the time of the Christians who founded the earlier priories and churches. For as soon as these Christian institutions were established, it became the practice to bury the dead inside them or around them, and the cloisters and burial-grounds of the priories, and the churchyards and vaults of the churches, took the place of the more distant cemeteries and the more scattered graves.

Roman London is buried with British, Saxon, and Danish London, far below the surface of nineteenth-century London, and Longfellow might have been writing its epitaph when he described the ruins under the sea—

[den from all mortal eyes

the sunken city lies;

cities have their graves!"

The dedications of the London churches mark historical periods, and there are a few names, such as St. Olave and St. Magnus, which are of Danish derivation, but of the Danish interments in London very few traces remain. Beyond the remnants found at Blackheath, and the belief held by some chroniclers that the church of St. Clement Danes was so named because it stood in a plot of ground where the Danes were buried, only one discovery of any importance has been made. On the south side of St. Paul's Churchyard, in digging the foundation for a new warehouse a few years ago, a relic was found with the following Runic inscription on it, which Mr. Loftie thinks must have belonged to an early stage of the Danish conquest, "Kina caused this stone to be laid over Tuki." A tradition used to prevail in Fulham that human remains, which have been discovered at different times in the neighbourhood of the river, were survivals of the Danish invasion, although the actual skeletons found there in 1809 (on the property of the Earl of Cholmondeley) seemed, from coins, daggers, &c., which were with them, to belong to the time of Charles I.

CHAPTER II

THE GRAVEYARDS OF PRIORIES AND CONVENTS.

"Gone are all the barons bold,

Gone are all the knights and squires,

Gone the Abbot stern and cold,

And the brotherhood of friars;

Not a name

Remains to fame,

From those mouldering days of old!"

LONGFELLOW.

FITZSTEPHEN'S statement that "there are in London and the suburbs 13 churches belonging to convents, besides 126 lesser parish churches," is not a very satisfactory one, as he does not proceed to name these several churches, or to tell his readers with what establishments they were connected. However, he was probably under the mark in putting the first figure at thirteen, for even in his time, and certainly very little later, there were many more than thirteen monastic and conventual buildings in London, and each had its church or chapel. The chief amongst these establishments which existed in London in the twelfth century, and which were made between that time and the dissolution of the priories in the days of Henry VIII., were:—

Inside the City Walls.

1. The Greyfriars or Franciscans, succeeded by Christ's Hospital.

2. The Blackfriars or Dominicans in the west.

3. The Crossed or Crutched Friars, by Fenchurch Street.

4. The Augustine Friars, by Broad Street.

5. St. Helen's Priory of Nuns, Bishopsgate Street.

6. The Priory of Holy Trinity, Aldgate.

7. The Priory and Sanctuary of St. Martin's le Grand.

8. Elsing Spital, London Wall.

9. The Priory of St. Augustine Papey.

10. St. James's Priory, the Hermitage in the Wall, Monkswell Street.

11. The Priory of St. Thomas Acon, Ironmonger Lane.

12. The Fraternities who had the care of St. Paul's Cathedral, including the brotherhood of All Souls, specially connected with the Charnel Chapel.

Outside the City Walls.

13. The Whitefriars or Carmelites, south of Fleet Street.

14. The Abbey and the Convent of Westminster.

15. A Brotherhood of St. Ursula at St. Mary le Strand.

16. A Brotherhood of the Trinity, without Aldersgate.

17. The Knights Templars, in the Strand.

18. The Priory of the Knights Hospitallers of St. John of Jerusalem, at Clerkenwell.

19. The Black Nuns of St. Mary's, Clerkenwell.

20. The Benedictine Priory of St. Bartholomew, with St. Bartholomew's Spital, West Smithfield.

21. The Carthusian Priory of the Salutation, subsequently the Charterhouse.

22. St. Mary Spital, without Bishopsgate.

23. The Nunnery of the Minoresses of St. Clare, the Minories.

24. The Cistercian Abbey of St. Mary of Grace, beyond the Tower.

25. St. Katharine's Hospital, by the Tower.

26. The Convent of St. Leonard, at Bromley-by-Bow.

27. The Priory of St. Mary Overie, Southwark, with a "House of Sisters."

28. Bermondsey Abbey.

29. The Nunnery of St. John the Baptist, Holywell.

30. The Convent of St. Mary Rounceval, Charing Cross.

A very complete list of the ecclesiastical institutions will be found in Brewer's "Beauties of London and Middlesex," vol. ii. p. 39.

Some of these brotherhoods were but small, and were mendicants; and they may not have had special burial-places of their own. In other cases burials may have only taken place in the priory churches, which were always much sought after for the purpose by outsiders, or in the cloisters. But most of the conventual establishments had a cemetery of considerable size—"the cloister garth," and peeps are given us now and then, by old writers, of the practices at the burial of the monks and nuns.

In the Church of the Crutched friars were two Dutch Fraternities, one of which was named in honour of the "Holy Blode of Wilsuak," and among their rules and orders is the following:—

"Also when any Brother or Suster of the same Bretherhede is dede, he or she shall have 4 Torchys of Wex of the Bretherhede, to bring the Body in Erthe: And every Brother and Suster shall come to his Masse of Requiem, and offer 1ᵈ and abide still to the Tyme the Body be buryed, uppon Pain of a l. Wex, yf he or she be within the Cite."

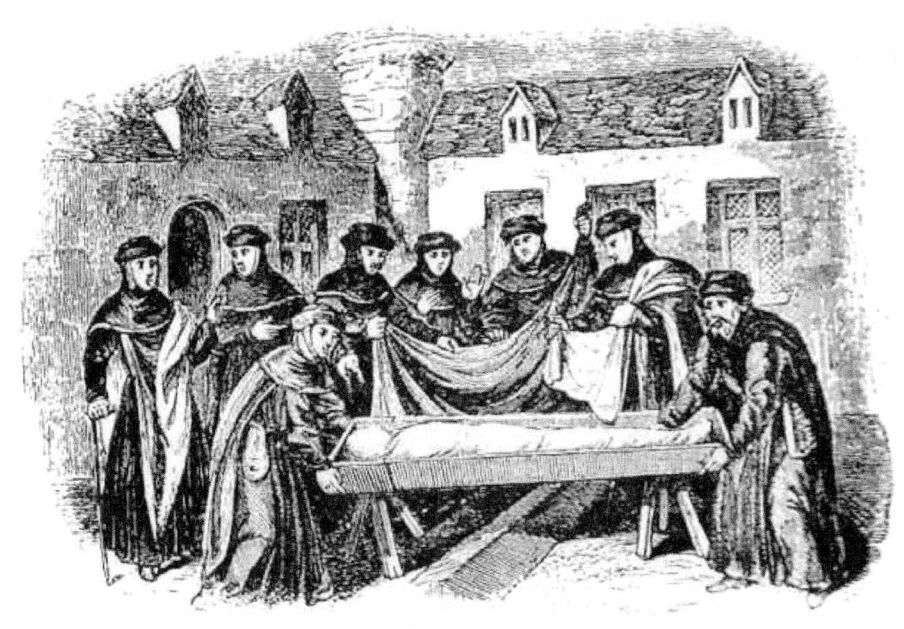

BURIAL OF A MONK.
(From a Harleian Manuscript).

Burials did not always take place in the evening, as might be imagined from the mention of torches and tapers, but often after mass, before dinner, and always with as little delay as possible. The written absolution was placed on the body of the monk or nun, and buried with it. Very solemn they seem to have been, these monastic funerals, especially when the body to be buried was that of an abbot, a prior, or a canon, with the procession of monks, the lighted tapers, the sprinkling of holy water, the chanting of psalms, the singing of the requiem mass, and the ringing of the bell. Strype gives a detailed account of the finding of four heads in pots or cases of "fine pewter," in a cupboard in the wall of the demolished building which belonged to the Black friars, when the rubbish was cleared away after the Great Fire of London. They were embalmed or preserved, and had tonsured hair. He imagined that they were the heads of "some zealous priests or friars, executed for treason ... or for denying the King's Supremacy; and here privately deposited by these Black Friars." It is probable that these heads were afterwards bought and taken to the Continent to be exhibited as holy relics. The City must have been a strange place in the thirteenth century, with the numerous churches and the very large priories and convents hedged in by narrow streets of wooden houses, where, even in those early days, men were busy, in their own several manners, in getting money. Neither the monks, nor the nuns, nor the mendicant friars were always exemplary in their behaviour, but at any rate the charitable works done at that time—the care of the sick, the prayers for the evil, the prayers for the souls of the dead, the building of the churches and the hospitals—were carried out by them, and we cannot imagine how we could have got on in our matter-of-fact generation without their efforts and their work. It is also pleasant to look back occasionally and to try and picture the life led in the more secluded priories outside the City, surrounded by fields and close to the Holy Wells, where there was time for prayer and meditation and good deeds.

"Yes, they can make, who fail to find,

Short leizure even in busiest days;

Moments, to cast a look behind,

And profit by those kindly rays

That through the clouds do sometimes steal,

And all the far-off past reveal."

Of the cloister garths there is very little which remains intact. The burial-ground of the Greyfriars is now the quadrangle of Christ's Hospital, but few traces of the old cloisters are left there. Of the grounds attached to Westminster Abbey I shall speak in the next chapter. That of St. Bartholomew's Priory, West Smithfield, was built upon many years ago. The site of the priory cemetery and that of the canons are marked on the accompanying plan, but

"Time has long effaced the inscriptions

On the cloister's funeral stones,"

and nothing is left to us except glimpses of the customs which used to take place there. The history of the establishment, founded by Rahere about 1113, is comparatively well known, owing to the recent efforts that have been made to restore what is left of the noble Norman Church. But there is not much remaining of what was once an extensive group of buildings except the choir of the original church, with its restored lady-chapel, crypt, and transepts. The nave has gone, and its site is marked by the churchyard, the bases of the pillars being buried among the bones. Leading out of the south transept is the "green-ground," another small churchyard, and a paved yard on the north side of the church was once the pauper ground.

According to a writer in the *Observator* of August 21, 1703, the cloisters of the priory and the space which still existed there became the resort of very low characters, "lords and ladies, aldermen and their wives, squires and fiddlers, citizens and rope-dancers, jackpuddings and lawyers, mistresses and maids, masters and 'prentices" meeting there for lotteries, plays, farces, and "all the temptations to destruction." Stow describes far more respectable gatherings in "the churchyard of St. Bartholomew," when the scholars from St. Paul's, Westminster, and other grammar schools used to meet for learned disputations, for proficiency in which garlands and prizes were awarded; but these meetings finally degenerated into free fights in the streets, and had to be discontinued.

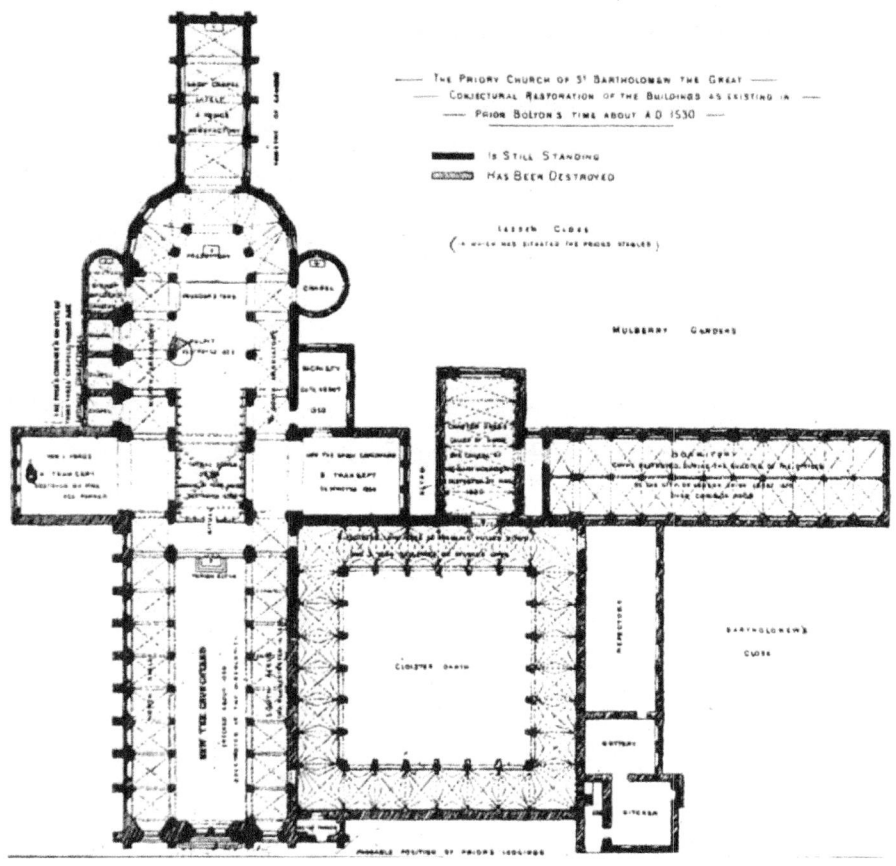

The Priory Church of St. Bartholomew The Great.

Some of the priory burial-grounds have survived in the parish churchyards, or at any rate parts of them have. The churchyard of St. Catherine Cree, in Leadenhall Street, is the successor of the burial-ground of Holy Trinity Priory, the church itself having been built in this cemetery. It was originally called Christ Church, which got corrupted to Cree Church, and so on. The churchyard is associated with the performance of miracle plays, moralities, or mysteries, and it was probably in this place that some of the latest of these shows were held. They are frequently mentioned by different chroniclers from the tenth to the sixteenth centuries. Such events as the Massacre of the Innocents, the Shepherds feeding their flocks on Christmas Eve, and the scenes in the history of St. Catherine, &c., were usually portrayed inside the churches; but Bishop Bonner put a stop to this practice in 1542, after which time stages were erected by strolling players in streets, by the wells, and in private houses. In London the churchyards seem to have been frequently used for the purpose, and in an old parish book belonging to St. Catherine's was the following entry, quoted in "Londinium Redivivum":—"Receyved of Hugh Grymes, for lycens geven to certen players to playe their enterludes in the churche-yarde from the feast of Easter, An. D'ni. 1560, untyll the feaste of Seynt Mychaell Tharchangell next comynge, every holydaye, to the use of the parysshe, the some of 27s and 8d." The miracle plays were a prelude to a more advanced form of dramatic representation, and after the establishment of the theatres we hear no more of them. The modern "flower service" originated, I believe, in the church of St. Catherine Cree, having been instituted by Dr. Whittemore.

S. EAST   S. WEST
VIEW OF THE CRYPT ON THE SITE OF THE LATE
COLLEGE OF S.t MARTIN LE GRAND.
Discovered in clearing for the New Post Office
THE CRYPT OF ST. MARTIN LE GRAND IN 1818.

Recent discoveries have shown that the priory cloister of the Augustine Friars was immediately to the north-east of the Dutch Church in Austin Friars. St. James's Priory, the Hermitage in the Wall, had a graveyard under the wall, on the other side of which was, and is, the churchyard of St. Giles', Cripplegate. Huge warehouses and offices now cover its site. The burial-ground of the Priory of St. Thomas Acon, in Ironmonger Lane, where pilgrims were buried who died on their visits to the chapel in honour of Becket, has also disappeared; but that of the priory of St. Augustine Papey survives in the little churchyard of St. Martin Outwich, in Camomile Street, which was presented to the parish by Robert Hyde in 1538, while the nuns of St. Helen's were probably buried in what is now St. Helen's Churchyard, Bishopsgate Street, which used to be, according to Stow, much larger.

No trace is left of the burial-places of the monks of Elsing Spital, the Crutched Friars, the White Friars, or the Black Friars, or of that of the splendid priory and sanctuary of St. Martin le Grand; they have gone with the buildings, of which only slight traces remain here and there, such as the porch of St. Alphege, London Wall, which belonged to Elsing Spital Priory. Probably they all had burying-grounds within their precincts. The crypt of St. Martin's was opened out in 1818, and a very perfect stone coffin found in it, when the present Post Office Buildings in Foster Lane were erected. The churches themselves were always much resorted to as places of interment by those who were not connected with the priories, especially the four magnificent churches, all of which are now gone, of the Greyfriars, the Whitefriars, the Blackfriars, and the Augustine Friars. The Dutch church is the successor to the nave of the last named. The site of the Greyfriars' church is occupied by the present church and churchyard of Christ Church, Newgate Street. Here were buried Margaret, second wife of Edward I., Isabella, Widow of Edward II., Joan Makepeace, wife of David Bruce, King of Scotland, and Isabella, wife of Lord Fitzwalter, the Queen of Man, besides the hearts of Edward II. and Queen Eleanor, the wife of Henry III., and, according to Weever, the bodies of "four duchesses, four countesses, one duke, twenty-eight barons, and some thirty-five knights," in all "six hundred and sixty-three persons of quality." Malcolm states that ten tombs and 140 gravestones (the fine monuments at the east end of the church) were destroyed and sold, in 1545, by Sir Martin Bowes, Lord Mayor, for fifty pounds.

I have given a list of the principal convents and priories outside the city. The site of St. Katharine's is buried in the Dock, and that of St. John the Baptist's, Holywell (by Curtain Road, Shoreditch), has also gone. The churchyards of St. Mary, Bromley, and St. Saviour, Southwark, are the survivals of the conventual burying-places; the cemetery of the nuns at Bromley was on the south side of the church, and upon its site Sir John Jacob built the Manor House, the bones being put under the house. But about two hundred years later (1813) the greater part of this site was again added to the churchyard, and re-consecrated. The burial-ground of Westminster Convent, with the Abbot's garden, have given place to the district and market of Covent Garden. The houses in White Lion Street and Spital Square are on the site of the cemetery or garth of St. Mary Spital. Here, after it ceased to be used for interments and before it was built upon, Spital Square was an open plot of ground with a pulpit in it and a house for the accommodation of the Lord Mayor and Corporation when they came on their annual visit to hear the "Spital Sermon." Of the priory church of the Knights Hospitallers of St. John of Jerusalem, in Clerkenwell, very few traces remain. The beautiful old crypt, lately cleared of coffins and restored, is older than the priory church (which was built over it), and dates from 1080 or 1090. The truly magnificent church was consecrated in 1185, the present structure occupying merely the site of the choir, the nave having probably extended the length of St. John's Square, and, together with the other buildings of the priory, it was pulled down at the Dissolution. The exact site of the cloisters and burial-ground is unknown. The present churchyard of St. John's is a small, narrow one at the eastern end, from which steps lead down into the ancient crypt. Here, between the years 1738 and 1853, about 325 bodies were buried, or rather the coffins were stacked, for they were above the floor. In 1893 a faculty was procured for their removal, and all the remains were reverently conveyed to Woking, a vellum document recording the fact being placed in the vestry of the church. The crypt is open to the public on the first Saturday in each month. Its complete restoration is still in hand. I am indebted to the kindness of Mr. H. W. Fincham for the picture of St. John's Crypt, and also for that of the garden in Benjamin Street, E.C.

The Nuns' burial-ground at Clerkenwell, and part of the beautiful cloister, existed until about one hundred years ago in the garden of the Duke of Newcastle's house, and its site is now occupied by the houses on the west side of St. James's Walk, a little north-east of St. James's Church. The Convent of St. Mary Rounceval was superseded by Northumberland House, subsequently pulled down when Northumberland Avenue was made; and the churchyard of Holy Trinity, Minories (now merely a part of the road) *may* be a relic of the Nunnery of the Minoresses of St. Clare. The Priory Church of St. Mary Overie (over the ferry) was purchased from the king by the parish in 1539, and has since been the parish Church of St. Saviour, Southwark, henceforth to be the Cathedral of South London.

CRYPT OF ST. JOHN'S, CLERKENWELL.

In the Crace Collection at the British Museum there is a plan, made by William Newton, purporting to show London in Elizabeth's time, in picture form. He marks the priories with their burial-grounds, but I doubt if it is very trustworthy. In Van den Wyngaerde's beautiful view (1550), reproduced by the Topographical Society in 1881, and the original of which is in the Bodleian Library, several of the conventual churches appear, not the least interesting being that of "S. Maria Spital."

The Cistercian abbey of St. Mary of Grace and the Carthusian priory of the Salutation were built on plague burial-grounds. (See Chapter VI.) The former has disappeared under the site of the Royal Mint, the latter survives in the Charterhouse. Probably they were very insanitary, but such, according to Dean Farrar, was the case with all the conventual establishments, and much accommodation was provided for sick monks.

Lastly we come to Bermondsey Abbey, the ancient and once famous settlement of Cluniac monks in the ea or eye (island) of a Saxon named Bearmund. Almost all traces of the abbey buildings have disappeared, though a good deal existed at the commencement of this century. There are some fragments of old windows and doorways among the shabby houses south of Grange Walk, and some pieces of the wall in the churchyard of St. Mary Magdalene. A considerable portion of the Abbey burial-ground was added to this churchyard in 1810. Amongst the benefactors of this establishment were William Rufus, Henry I., and King Stephen, and many eminent people were buried in the priory church, while much of great historic interest is connected with the history of Bermondsey Abbey.

The modern representatives of the ancient monasteries and nunneries lack the antiquarian flavour which is so attractive to us, and yet there is a certain interest attaching to them. But I have only to deal with their burial-grounds, and therefore need mention very few.

THE REMAINS OF BERMONDSEY ABBEY ABOUT 1800.

The third volume of Knight's "London" commences with the following words:—"It is a curious circumstance, and one in which the history of many changes of opinion may be read, that within forty years after what remained of the magnificent ecclesiastical foundation of the Abbey of Bermondsey had been swept away, a new conventual establishment has risen up, amidst the surrounding desecration of factories and warehouses, in a large and picturesque pile, with its stately church, fitted in every way for the residence and accommodation of thirty or forty inmates—the convent of the Sisters of Mercy." The writer of the article refers to the convent by the Roman Catholic Chapel in Parker's Row, built in 1838. The chapel, with a small graveyard given in 1833 or 1834, existed previously. The garden of the convent was used for burials until August, 1853, but there appear to be no gravestones in it, and it is a neatly-kept ground between two schools, whereas the graveyard on the east side of the church is untidy. Another disused burial-ground is behind the Roman Catholic Chapel in Commercial Road. Here the tombstones are laid flat, and the ground forms a garden of considerable size for the use of the priests.

On the north side of King Street, Hammersmith, just east of the Broadway Station, is the large red building known as the Convent of the Sacred Heart, a seminary and establishment erected by the late Cardinal Manning on the site of a Benedictine convent which was founded, according to some authorities, before the Reformation, and according to others during the reign of Charles II., and which included the Sisterhood of the English Benedictine Dames and a famous school, where many ladies of distinction received their early education. Brewer, in his "Beauties of London and Middlesex" (1816), thus describes the burial-ground of this convent: "The gravestones are laid flat on the turf, and the sisters are placed, as usual, with their feet to the east; the priests alone having the head towards the altar. There are several inscriptions on the stones, of which we insert the following specimen:—Here lies the body of The Right Reverend Lady Mary Anne Clavering, late Abbess of the English Benedictine Dames of Pontoise, Who died the 8th day of November, 1795, in the 65th year of her age." Cardinal Manning disposed of this little cemetery, which was by the lane on the east side, when erecting the present buildings. "It was dug up and done away with," according to the statement of one of the sisters at present in the convent.

But two similar burial-grounds are still to be found in this immediate neighbourhood, one is disused and the other is in use. The former is behind the Convent of the Good Shepherd in Fulham Palace Road, only about 14 by 12 yards in size, and closed a few years ago. The latter is at the extreme end of the garden of Nazareth Home in Hammersmith Road, under the wall of Great Church Lane. It is even smaller than the one in Fulham Palace Road, and has been in use for upwards of forty years, but as only the sisters are interred here it would appear to be still available for about another twenty years. The graves are in neat rows, a small cross is on each, with the name (or the adopted name) of the sister whose body lies beneath. It forms a little enclosure in the large space and garden behind the buildings of the Home, where many children are taught and many old people live. Another enclosure contains their poultry, and another a cow. The whole establishment is very interesting, and not the least interesting part of it is this little cemetery, of the existence of which, in all probability, very few of the inhabitants of the surrounding streets have any knowledge.

I have visited one other convent burial-ground, and in each case it is necessary to go through the ceremony of being peeped at through a grating, and, when admitted, passed along passages and through rooms while the doors are locked behind, and only granted permission to see what I want after some time of waiting and a large amount of explanation. I have been since told that I was singularly favoured by being admitted into the Franciscan Convent in Portobello Road, where the Mother Superior herself most kindly took me to see the little cemetery, explaining that it was "sanctioned by the Home Secretary,"—of which I was well aware. It is a charming little corner of a very pretty garden, a triangular grass plot edged with trees, not above a quarter of an acre in extent. It was formed in 1862 and first used in 1870, only five burials taking place in twenty-three years. It is, of course, merely for the interment of the nuns who, having given up the world and shut themselves into the convent, find their last resting-place within its precincts.

CHAPTER III

THE CATHEDRAL, THE ABBEY, THE TEMPLE, AND THE TOWER.

"The Saints are there—the Living Dead,

The Mourners glad and strong;

The sacred floor their quiet bed,

Their beams from every window shed,

Their voice in every song."

KEBLE.

THERE is one burial-ground in London which has received a large share of attention, and which has really been thought worthy of lengthy and detailed notices in histories of the metropolis—I mean St. Paul's Churchyard. The words convey a very distinct meaning to us now. They suggest Messrs. Hitchcock and Williams, and a number of other firms with large premises, a constant stream of vans, carts, omnibuses, cabs, and bicycles passing between Ludgate Hill and Cheapside or Cannon Street, and a neat garden with flower-beds, seats, and pigeons under the shadow of the great Cathedral—Wren's "monument"—which is so different from any other cathedral, and yet so suitable for the centre of the largest city in the world. Just as St. Paul's Cathedral was not always as it is now, so St. Paul's Churchyard is also vastly changed. Underneath the soil are the graves of Britons, Saxons, and Romans; and I have already referred to these, and have pointed out how far back into obscure history we can trace this particular graveyard.

Many books have been written about St. Paul's; Dugdale's is the best old history, and perhaps Dean Milman's is the best modern one. The stories of its foundation, of the shrine of St. Erkenwald, the disastrous fire of 1136, the Boy Bishops, the chained bibles and the commotion they aroused, the difficulties of the Reformation, and finally the other "Great Fire" of 1666, which led to the rebuilding of the Cathedral, not again as a Gothic structure, but somewhat after the style of St. Peter's at Rome, have all been told again and again. The crypt of the Cathedral was the parish church of St. Faith, and that of St. Gregory stood where the clock tower now is, at the west end. The site of St. Gregory's Churchyard is within the posts in front of the west door, where Queen Anne's statue stands, while the parish of St. Faith had a piece at the eastern end of the Cathedral, and, according to Newcourt, another piece was allotted to St. Martin's, Ludgate Hill. It is to Dugdale that we are chiefly indebted for a knowledge of what old St. Paul's, with its windows and monuments, was like—and a splendid church it must have been. He was an eminent antiquary who, thinking that the chief ecclesiastical buildings in England would suffer from the Civil War, made a most noble pilgrimage, and drew the monuments, copied the epitaphs, and took notes of the arms in windows, on walls, &c., in St. Paul's and Westminster Abbey first, and subsequently in Ely, Norwich, Peterborough, Lincoln, and a number of other cathedral, conventual, and parish Churches. The work he did at St. Paul's was of exceptional value, owing to the ravages of the Great Fire.

The Cathedral has been surrounded by such interesting buildings as a Bishop's Palace, the Chapter House and Library, a Bell Tower, several Chantries, a Charnel House, and St. Paul's School, founded by Dean Colet, and which, some years ago, was totally destroyed, reappearing as a meaty-red structure of huge dimensions (where the foundation scholars, or "fish," are in a small minority), in the uninteresting district of East Hammersmith, which is misnamed West Kensington.

St. Paul's Churchyard extended, especially on its northern side, farther than it does now. Part of it was known as Pardon Church Yard, or "Haugh," in which was a chapel founded by Gilbert Becket, rebuilt by Dean Moore in Henry V.'s time, and surrounded by a rich cloister with pictures of "The Dance of Death" painted by Machabre in it, somewhat like the ones still existing on the bridge at Lucerne, and with very fine monuments to those buried beneath. In 1549 the cloister, the chapel, the charnel house, the paintings, and the tombs were all cleared away by the Protector Somerset, the materials being used for his new mansion in the Strand, and the bones from the charnel house (Stow says one thousand cartloads) were reinterred in Finsbury Field. The churchyard seems to have been first entirely enclosed by a surrounding wall in 1285.

PAUL'S CROSS and Preaching there

Paul's Cross or preaching place, was erected in the form it appears in the plate, about the year 1449, by Thomas Kempe, then Bishop of London, on the site of a more antient cross, which had been destroyed by an earthquake in 1382. Its name first occurs in the year 1259, when Hen. III commanded the Mayor of London to oblige all the city youth of a certain age to take the oath of allegiance at Paul's Cross, to him and his heirs. From this period it was, for several centuries, used for almost every purpose political as well as ecclesiastical, and is continually noticed in history. It was destroyed by the Lord mayor of London, Isaac Pennington, in consequence of a vote of Parliament, in the year 1643.

PAUL'S CROSS.

But perhaps the most interesting object in the churchyard was Paul's Cross, which existed as far back as the reign of Henry III., if not earlier. From that time until 1643, when it was ruthlessly destroyed by order of Parliament, it formed a notable monument, round which the religious history of London and of England centred itself. Paul's Cross was an outdoor pulpit at the north-east corner of the Cathedral—"a pulpit cross of timber, mounted upon steps of stone covered with lead," from which "announcements and harangues on all such matters as the authorities in Church or State judged to be of public concern were poured into the popular ear and heart." It seems to have been used to preach sermons from as early as 1299, and men professing all shades of the Christian faith have discoursed there, miscreants have done penance there, bishops and clergy have renounced heresies, excited throngs have gathered round excited preachers, and tricks and delusions, called miracles, have been exposed there. Latimer and Ridley frequently occupied the pulpit, and "proclaimed to crowds of eager listeners that testimony which they both afterwards sealed with their blood." During the time of the reforming struggles of our Church the pulpit at Paul's Cross played an active part, and those who preached there in the reign of Mary had to be protected from the populace by the Queen's guard. In 1628 James I. came in state to hear a sermon from Bishop King, and Charles I. listened to another discourse from Paul's Cross in 1630. It is said that after its demolition an elm-tree marked its site, but even this has long since disappeared.

ELM ON SITE OF PAUL'S CROSS.

Yet the Churchyard was not only a religious centre, but was also a very worldly one. Many unseemly scenes used to take place there, and the ground was walled in because it was becoming the resort of those who did not behave themselves properly. The following account from Maitland gives us a sad, if a lively, picture of the times: "In the year 1569 a Lottery was set on Foot in St. Paul's Churchyard, where it was begun to be drawn at the West Door of the Church on the 11th of January, and continued incessantly drawing Day and Night till the 6th of May following." The Cathedral itself was put to a variety of unsuitable uses, and was made a judgment-hall for foreign heretics who were condemned to be burnt at Smithfield. The author of a tract written in the second half of the sixteenth century describes the south aisle as being used "for usury and popery, the north for simony, and the horse-fair in the midst for all kinds of bargains, meetings, brawlings, murthers, conspiracies; and the font for ordinary payments of money." Traffic in benefices was largely carried on there, and the middle aisle (Paul's Walk) was a rendezvous, every morning and afternoon, for a fashionable and eccentric medley. Thus was the chief temple in London treated as vilely as the Temple at Jerusalem, and there are those now living amongst us who wish to see our English churches used for secular purposes!

With one mighty blow the whole building was destroyed, and the beautiful Gothic Cathedral became a heap of cinders. It is told in "Parentalia" how, under the direction of Wren, the new St. Paul's arose like a phœnix from the ashes of the old church. From an interesting print of 1701 it appears that the churchyard was even then a fashionable promenade, but it is improbable that the building itself, in its new form, was ever subjected to such abuses as the old one had been. I have heard Wren's churches described as "religious rather than Christian," but as time goes on the architecture seems to be more appreciated. Wordsworth has said:—

"They dreamt not of a perishable home

Who thus could build,"

but he has also told us that the Cathedral is—

"Filled with mementoes, satiate with its past

Of grateful England's overflowing Dead"—

and herein lies its chief interest.

No one has done his duty by St. Paul's who has not been in the crypt. Dr. Donne's monument, which dates from before the fire, has been brought up and placed in the south aisle of the choir, amongst those of bishops and deans, but some fragments of other tombs from old St. Paul's are still in the crypt, besides many tablets and monuments of later date. There was for many years a prejudice against admitting memorial monuments in the Cathedral at all, but one being erected to the memory of John Howard, the reformer, the spell was broken. Several old stones on the floor of the crypt have no graves below them, those they commemorate having been buried outside in the churchyard, but now the few internments that take place are under the floor of the building, Sir Frederic (Lord) Leighton's being the newest grave. Here also lie Sir Nicholas Bacon, Sir Thomas Lawrence, Sir Joshua Reynolds, Sir Christopher Wren, Dean Colet, George Cruikshank, Opie, West, Turner, Lord Napier of Magdala, Lord Mayor Nottage (who died in office in 1885), Bishop Piers Claughton, and many other notable persons. There is one division where there are gravestones in memory of past vergers of the Cathedral. Directly under the dome are the remains of Nelson, in a coffin made from wood of the *Victory*, enclosed in a sarcophagus originally intended for Cardinal Wolsey, but put aside as he was not considered worthy of it, and subsequently brought out and altered to suit Lord Nelson. Close by is a larger sarcophagus containing the remains of the Duke of Wellington.

ST. MARGARET'S AND THE ABBEY CHURCHYARD ABOUT 1750.

The Churchyard is no longer a fashionable resort, but it has been a very useful one since 1879, and many are the visitors who may always be found sitting there, while the pigeons fly amongst the tall and smoky columns. The Rev. H. R. Haweis says the Cathedral should be washed. He is right, no doubt, but "stately Paule" still remains black.

Neither the graveyard of the Knights Templars, the great rivals of the Knights Hospitallers at Clerkenwell, nor the garth of the Abbey of St. Peter, have had a record so varied as that which clings round St. Paul's Churchyard. The Temple Church, especially the round portion of it, is most ancient and interesting, but it has been much injured by the modern representatives of the Templars who have denuded the walls of many rich old monuments. The part of the churchyard which is immediately round the church is closed and turfed and has some fine old stone coffins in it. The northern part is paved and gravelled and is added to the public thoroughfare, the chief object in it of general interest being the grave and monument of Oliver Goldsmith.

We go on, along the Strand, past Charing Cross, until we reach the "minster in the west," or the Collegiate Church of St. Peter, which was built in the Island of Thorney. It is probable that the whole space now occupied by the Abbey and St. Margaret's and their churchyards was at one time used for interments. At present the Abbey Churchyard and that of St. Margaret's (where at times a fair used to be held) are in one. They are neatly turfed and open to the public, and they form a simple but suitable base for the glorious old buildings which rise from them. On the south side of the Abbey are the large and small cloisters, with their grass plots and their ancient stones, while, according to Brayley, a part of Covent Garden Market is on the site of what used to be the burial-ground of the Westminster Convent. Portions of the cloisters are among the most ancient and interesting corners of the Abbey buildings, and the sight of them carries us back in thought to the days of the abbots and monks, who used to pace to and fro under the vaulted roof.

It is not, however, the burial-places outside the Abbey, but the church itself, round which the most thrilling associations gather. Here again the story has been often repeated, and if there are any of my readers (though I doubt if there can be one) who do not know what venerable tombs are contained there, they would do well to visit the Abbey, and not to rest until they have been carefully shown the treasures in Henry VII.'s Chapel. Beaumont sang—

"Think how many royal bones

Sleep within these heaps of stones....

Here's an acre sown indeed

With the richest, royallist seed."

From the shrine of Edward the Confessor and the tomb of Edward III. to the tablet in memory of Charles Dickens and the stone over the grave of Charles Darwin, they are one and all of the deepest interest, and it is perfectly needless for me to refer to the monuments here. Every Englishman is—or should be—proud of these relics, of the beautiful Chapel, the Poets' Corner, and the hallowed nave and aisles.

GREAT CLOISTER, WESTMINSTER.

It is true that there are too many monuments in Westminster Abbey; a memorial chapel in which some of them (especially the huge statues from the north transept) could be put, would be very advantageous. But, at any rate, they are not likely now to be much further added to, and from the old, royal tombs, there is not one fragment of mosaic or one splinter of stone which we should not grieve to lose. Sir Godfrey Kneller, the painter and the friend of Pope, did not wish to be interred in the Abbey because "they do bury fools there." But his monument is not missed amongst the tombs of England's greatest children, her kings and queens, her bishops and deans, her statesmen, her soldiers, her poets, her artists, and her philosophers. The whole building is one grand memorial. There may be "fools there," but they sink into utter insignificance, for "saints are there, the living dead."

The South East Prospect of the Chapel Royal of S$^{t.}$ Peter in the Tower.
ST. PETER'S CHAPEL IN THE TOWER ABOUT 1750.

To pass from the Abbey to the Tower is like passing from honour to shame, and yet amongst those who were imprisoned, executed, and buried in the great fortress and palace which became the state prison of England, many were innocent of the crimes for which they were punished, and many deserved to rest in Westminster even more than some of those who were interred there. There were four recognised burial-places connected with the Tower, the churchyard of St. Peter ad Vincula, the vaults under the church, the vaults "behind the church," and the outer graveyard. The last named was a narrow strip by the eastern wall, probably used for the burial of the humbler members of the numerous households which composed the Tower precinct. This ground was demolished when the Tower Bridge was made, being required for the wide approach thereto. It is also probable that burials took place in a somewhat promiscuous fashion in other parts of the fortress. We know, for instance, that the young Princes, after they had been smothered, were buried at the foot of the staircase of the White Tower, "meetly deep in the ground, under a great heap of stones," from whence their remains, or what was supposed to be their remains, were moved to Westminster Abbey in 1674 by Order of King Charles II.

In St. Peter's Church were buried the headless bodies of many a noble prisoner who was executed close by, with the remains of others who died during their confinement in the Tower—the Earl of Arundel, the Dukes of Somerset, Monmouth, Norfolk, and Northumberland, Queen Katherine, poor innocent Anne Boleyn, her brother, Lord Rochford, the Countess of Salisbury, Catherine Howard, and a great many more whose names are recorded in English history. The chapel is not as beautiful as it might be, and the graveyard attached to it is little more than a part of the great Tower courtyard, but the sad memories connected with it will always hallow this spot. In the quaint little church of Holy Trinity, Minories, supposed by some to be a survival of the Abbey of the Minoresses of St. Clare, there is still shown what is said to be the head of the Duke of Suffolk, the father of Lady Jane Grey. It is in a glass case, preserved like leather, some hair still clings to the scalp, while the false blow of the executioner can be clearly seen just above the place where the head was severed from the trunk. The verger keeps this marvellous relic locked up in a pew; it is a sort of detached fragment of the history of the Tower.

THREE COFFIN LIDS FROM THE TOWER.

I feel that I have done but very scant justice to those London burial-places which contain the ashes of the most illustrious dead. But I have no wish to go over ground already trodden by far worthier chroniclers than myself, and I therefore commend to all who desire to know more about the Cathedral, the Abbey, the Temple, and the Tower, the many excellent books which have been written upon their history, such as Dean Milman's "Annals of St. Paul's Cathedral," Dean Stanley's "Memorials of Westminster Abbey," and a number of more ancient and more modern works which especially relate to these buildings and to the monuments they contain. The Kyrle Society has recently published a capital little guide to the Cathedral, which can be bought with the tickets to view the crypt, the whispering gallery, &c., and which also serves as a handbook to the monuments in the nave and aisles.

"Death lays his icy hands on kings:

Sceptre and crown

Must tumble down,

And in the dust be equal made

With the poor crooked scythe and spade.

All heads must come

To the cold tomb,

Only the actions of the just

Smell sweet and blossom in the dust."

J. SHIRLEY.

CHAPTER IV.

THE CITY CHURCHYARDS.

"Such strange churchyards hide in the City of London."

DICKENS.

I HAVE already referred, in Chapter I., to the different areas occupied by the City of London at different periods. But the City, as we know it now, averages, roughly speaking, a mile and a half from east to west and three-quarters of a mile from north to south. It includes a considerable space outside the old wall, and the boundary line is very irregular, except on the southern side, where is the "silent highway." It is governed by the Corporation, and its ancient wards are represented by Aldermen, while the Lord Mayor commences his year of office by a public procession through the streets on November 9th, supported by his dignified companions, the Sheriffs.

The City of London is the Office of the World. Its highways represent untold wealth, and its byways reek with poverty and dirt; it contains the most bustling thoroughfares and the most retired corners; it is full of business and affairs up to date, and yet teeming with antiquarian interest, and relics of ancient history. As on one side of a busy road we have Cannon Street Station and on the other side the venerable "London Stone," so the City churches, with their old-world churchyards, are wedged in between huge modern warehouses, offices, and public buildings; "churchyards sometimes so entirely detached from churches, always so pressed upon by houses; so small, so rank, so silent, so forgotten—except for the few people who ever look down into them from their smoky windows. As I stand peeping in through the iron gates and rails I can peel the rusty metal off, like bark from an old tree. The illegible tombstones are all lopsided, the grave-mounds lost their shape in the rains of a hundred years ago, the Lombardy Poplar or Plane-tree that was once a drysalter's daughter and several common-councilmen, has withered like those worthies, and its departed leaves are dust beneath it.... Sometimes, the queer hall of some queer Company gives upon a churchyard such as this, and, when the Livery dine, you may hear them (if you are looking in through the iron rails, which you never are when I am) toasting their own Worshipful prosperity.... Sometimes, the commanding windows are all blank, and show no more sign of life than the graves below—not so much, for *they* tell of what once upon a time was life undoubtedly."

Poor little churchyards, they are so insignificant, and many of them are even more shrunken than when Charles Dickens visited them. Thus we hear of an injunction being sought for to restrain the would-be reformer from cutting off a two-foot-wide strip of St. Martin Orgar's ground to make a dry area behind the houses in Crooked Lane; and the Commissioners of Sewers possess the right, and sometimes use it, of curtailing a churchyard in order to widen a road. In 1884, for instance, they gave £750 for a piece at the eastern end of Allhallows' Churchyard, London Wall. The remainder of that little ground is now a public garden, laid out in 1894 by the Metropolitan Public Gardens Association, and is a quiet resting-place in the busy thoroughfare, with a piece of the ancient City wall still existing in it. Most of the churchyards "entirely detached from churches" are the sites of the burned buildings, which were used as burial-grounds for the amalgamated parishes—for the mournful calamity of 1666 visited the churches of London with "peculiar severity," 89 of them being destroyed, 51 of which were rebuilt by Wren and his followers, and 35 of which were not replaced. All the City churchyards are now protected from being built upon by the Disused Burial-grounds Act of 1888, but that Act has not yet been read to include the sites of the churches themselves which are from time to time removed, and which have all had interments in the vaults underneath them. The site of Allhallows' the Great, Upper Thames Street, was recently sold to a brewery company, but has not yet been built upon, because it is thought that an injunction will be served upon the builder and that it will be made a test case.

Of the burial-grounds attached to the Cathedral, the Temple, and the churches which are the survivals of the priories, I have already written; apart from these one of the oldest of the churches founded in the City is sometimes supposed to be that of St. Mary Woolnoth, Lombard Street. The present building, which is threatened by a railway company, is by Hawksmoor, but a church existed on the site in very early days. In St. Peter's, Cornhill, is a tablet, the authenticity of which is certainly open to grave doubt, recording the fact that a church was erected on this spot by Lucius in A.D. 179, but the genuine history of the foundation can only be traced as far back as 1230. The burial-ground of St. Benet Sherehog, in Pancras Lane, marks the site of a church dating from Saxon times, dedicated to St. Osyth,—Size Lane, which is close by, being a survival of the name. The City churches still standing, of which the whole or a part date from before the Great Fire, are St. Bartholomew's the Great; Allhallows', Barking; the Temple; St. Helen's, Bishopsgate Street; and St. Catherine Cree, Leadenhall Street, all connected with priories; and St. Bartholomew's the Less; St. Giles', Cripplegate; St. Olave's, Hart Street; St. Ethelburga's, Bishopsgate Street; St. Andrew's Undershaft, Leadenhall Street; and Allhallows', Staining, Star Alley.

The church of St. Bartholomew the Less, of which but a very small portion of the tower is ancient, is within the Hospital enclosure, and the churchyard is smaller than it was, some of it having been thrown into the paved courtyard. St. Ethelburga's churchyard is a quaint little courtyard with a few tombstones in it, only approached through the church and vestry. In St Andrew's Undershaft (or "under the maypole," which used to be suspended on the houses in St. Mary Axe) the monument of John Stow is to be found—poor Stow, whose survey of London is the foundation for all modern histories. The adjoining churchyard is very small. That of Allhallows', Barking, has lately been entirely covered with building materials, owing to the restoration of the church. It was, according to Stow, "sometime far larger."

The churchyard of St. Olave's, Hart Street (Dickens' St. Ghastly Grim), is an interesting one. The church itself is one of the most beautiful pieces of ecclesiastical architecture in London—a small Gothic building, admirable in its proportion. The old gate of the churchyard has skulls and cross bones on it, and in this ground were interred a vast number of the victims of the plague of 1665, which is said to have taken its origin in this parish in the Drapers' Almshouses.

ALLHALLOWS', STAINING, 1838.

Of the church of Allhallows', Staining, only the tower remains, in the centre of a neatly-kept little burial-ground. This was the model for the churchtower in "Old London" at the exhibition at South Kensington in 1886.[1] The churchyard of St. Giles', Cripplegate, the church which contains the monument to Milton, has a long and varied history. It is well known to antiquarians, as the valuable relic, the postern of the City wall, is situated in it. The story of this ground is one of additions and encroachments, and it has found a careful chronicler in Mr. Baddeley, a former churchwarden. The addition running south was called the "Green Churchyard," a name which we find repeated in other parishes—for instance, it was given to the higher portion of the churchyard of St. James', Piccadilly, and to the little piece by St. Bartholomew the Great, approached through the present south transept. The gravestones at St. Giles' have been laid flat, and the ground is neatly kept and generally open, but not provided with seats for the public. Until Michaelmas, 1640, "the military" used to be trained in this churchyard.[2]

1. In 1873 a crypt was made under the tower, in which were deposited the remains from Lambe's Chapel, St. James's in the Wall, Monkswell Street.

2. Malcolm's "Londinium Redivivum."

CRIPPLEGATE CHURCHYARD ABOUT 1830.

There were four churches in the City dedicated to St. Botolph, a pious Saxon who built a monastery, in 654, in Lincolnshire. It is a little curious that all the four churchyards are now public gardens—St. Botolph's, Bishopsgate; St. Botolph's, Aldgate; St. Botolph's, Aldersgate; and St. Botolph's, Billingsgate, The last-named church was not rebuilt after the Fire, and the site of one of its churchyards, the "lower ground," is now occupied by a new warehouse with red heads on the frontage, on the south side of Lower Thames Street. What remains of the "upper ground" is a small, three-cornered, asphalted court, open to the public, with seats, a drinking fountain, and a coffee stall. The charming little garden in Aldersgate Street includes three churchyards, that of St. Botolph, an additional one for St. Leonard's, Foster Lane, and an additional one for Christ Church, Newgate Street, which is at the western end, and was given to the parish in 1825 by the Governors of Christ's Hospital when the Great Hall was built and a small burial-ground at the north-west corner of the buildings could no longer be used. The Metropolitan Public Gardens Association laid out Aldgate churchyard in 1892; it is much appreciated, and is maintained by an annual grant from the charity funds of the parish. A melancholy incident took place here in September, 1838, when two men, a gravedigger and a fish-dealer, lost their lives in a grave by being poisoned with the foul air. The grave was a "common one," such as was often kept open for two months until filled with seventeen or eighteen bodies. It may safely be said that all the City burial-grounds were crowded to excess. Their limited area would invite such treatment, and it was only natural that the City parishioner should choose to be interred in the parish churchyard, unless the still greater privilege were afforded him of being buried in the vaults under the church. The other churchyards in the City which have been laid out for public recreation are those of St. Paul's Cathedral; St. Olave, Silver Street; Allhallows, London Wall; St. Katherine Coleman, Fenchurch Street; St. Mary, Aldermanbury; St. Sepulchre, Holborn; and St. Bride, Fleet Street; while the churchyard of St. Dunstan in the West, situated in Fetter Lane, is the playground of the Greystoke Place Board School; and that of St. James, Duke Street, is the playground of the Aldgate Ward Schools.

ST. MILDRED'S, BREAD STREET, ABOUT 1825.

Most of the remaining City churchyards are quiet little spaces, surrounded by huge warehouses. Many are only approached through the churches, and are invisible from the road. St. Mildred's, in Bread Street, is unfortunately used as a store-yard for ladders of all sizes, and it seems, from the accompanying illustration, to have been turned to account many years ago, while the very small piece that remains by the tower of St. Mary Somerset, Thames Street, where the Weavers of Brabant used to hold their meetings, is full of old iron, &c. One or two are private gardens, such as St. Michael's Churchyard, Queenhithe. Others have been paved and added to the public footway, such as that of St. Mary Abchurch, their extent being still visible. This is the Case with the churchyard of St. Michael Bassishaw, in Basinghall Street.

The ground is now part of the pavement, but the two large trees which grew in it are still flourishing. On the site of the churchyard of St. Benet Fink, in Threadneedle Street, is Peabody's statue. The untidy little yard in Farringdon Street, which is used as a volunteer drill-ground, was once an additional burying-place for St. Bride's, Fleet Street. It was given to the parish in 1610 by the Earl of Dorset, on condition that no more burials should take place in the southern part of the churchyard which was opposite his house. The house was destroyed by the Great Fire and the churchyard used again. The graveyard of St. Christopher le Stocks is the garden of the Bank of England, and Timbs states, although he does not vouch for the authenticity of the story, that the mould for the burial-ground of Whitfield's Tabernacle in Tottenham Court Road was brought from this churchyard, "by which the consecration fees were saved."

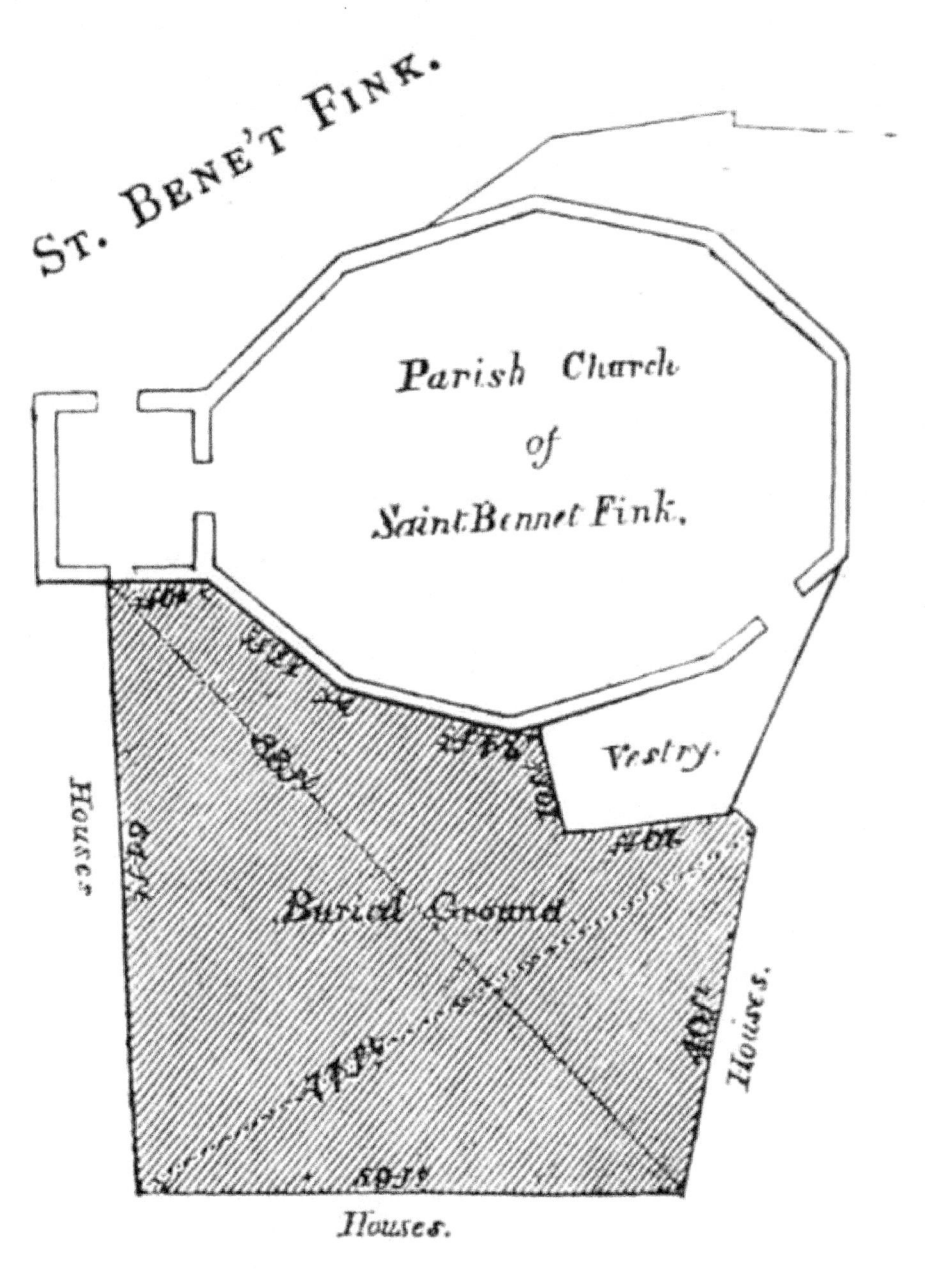

GROUND PLAN OF ST. BENET FINK IN 1834.

Of the City churchyards which have been completely annihilated, apart from other kinds of burial-grounds within this area, there must have been at least forty. And this destruction has been due to the dissolution of the priories, the formation of new streets, and the invasion of the railways. Norden mentions three churches in Farringdon Ward Within which have gone—St. Nicholas in the Fleshshambles (which was in Newgate Street), St. Ewans (south of Newgate Street), and St. Genyn within St. Martin le Grand. When Queen Victoria Street was made the churchyards of St. Mary Mounthaw, St. Nicholas Olave, and St. Mary Magdalen,

Knightrider Street, disappeared; that of St. Michael, Crooked Lane, a plot of land given by one Robert Marsh and consecrated in 1392, was sacrificed for King William Street; and that of St. Benet, Paul's Wharf (now the Welsh Church), where Inigo Jones was buried, for St. Benet's Hill. A complete list of them will be found in the Appendix. Cannon Street Station of the South Eastern Railway covers the churchyard of St. Mary Bothaw; and for Cannon Street Station of the District Railway that of St. John's, Cloak Lane, was destroyed, the human remains being "dug up, sifted, put in chests with charcoal, nailed down, put one on the top of the other in a brick vault and sealed up for ever, or rather till some others in time come to turn them out again." Part of the General Post Office is on the churchyard of St. Leonard, Foster Lane; the Mercer's Hall is on that of St. Thomas Acons, where the pilgrims were buried; the Mansion House Station is on that of Holy Trinity the Less; and the Mansion House itself is on that of St. Mary Woolchurch Haw, in which a balance used to stand "for the weighing of wool."

THE CHURCHYARD OF ST. BENET, PAUL'S WHARF, 1838.

    Most of the existing churchyards have but few tombstones left in them, several have none at all. But some of them can still boast of fine trees, which add much to the interest and picturesque appearance of the City streets, and I hope it may be a long time before those in Stationers' Hall Court, under which there were vaults belonging to St. Martin's, Ludgate, and in the churchyards of St. Peter Cheap, Wood Street, and St. Dunstan in the East, cease to grow and flourish.

    We want to see all of these little churchyards opened to the public and provided with seats. The Metropolitan Public Gardens Association is always ready to put them in order, but it is difficult to secure their maintenance. The parish funds which might be available for such a purpose have been so cut down and diverted by the Charity Commissioners that it is, in many cases, impossible for any provision to be made for the upkeep of the churchyard, small though the cost may be. But I trust that this difficulty may be, before long, removed, and then we may expect a great improvement in the condition of the City churchyards which have all been closed for burials for upwards of forty years, and which are so singularly well suited for conversion into "outdoor sitting-rooms" for those who can take a few moments of rest from their work in the surrounding offices and warehouses. And they are worthy of the utmost respect, for they contain the ashes of some of the noblest citizens of London, some of its greatest benefactors and its hardest workers, those who have helped, stone by stone, to raise the great city to the height to which it has attained in its influence in the world.

In 1668 the Lord Mayor "issued out a Precept, commanding, amongst other wholesome orders ... that the Inhabitants, Householders, and others concerned, should not throw or suffer any Ashes, Dirt, or other Filth, to be cast out ... before any Church or Churchyard ... upon pain of 20 shillings." But in 1896 we need visit very few of these same churchyards before we come to one in which rubbish of all kinds is allowed to accumulate and to remain. Yet they are sacred spots, consecrated ecclesiastically and historically, and instead of being permitted to sink into the oblivion of insignificance they should all be made beautiful in memory of the dead and for the benefit of the living, for in them are "the tombs of the wealthy and the humble heaps of the poor." The Old Society for the Protection of City Churches and Churchyards did something towards their preservation, and lately a new City Church Preservation Society has been formed, the Chairman of Council being Mr. H. C. Richards, M.P., and the Hon. Secretary the Rev. Rowland B. Hill. It has already displayed most praiseworthy activity, and is, at the present time, endeavouring to save the church of St. Mary Woolnoth, in Lombard Street (built by Hawksmoor) from being demolished for a railway station. There is a very small churchyard attached to this church.

And it may be interesting here to give particulars of a case in which the decision arrived at is valuable to those who are fighting the battle of protection. In the Session of 1881 the London School Board, through the Education Department, introduced a Bill, called the Elementary Education Provisional Order Confirmation Bill, for the purpose of acquiring compulsory powers over the burial-ground in Bream's Buildings, Fetter Lane, belonging to the church of St. Dunstan in the West, and which adjoins the Greystoke Place Board School. The rector and churchwardens, supported by the vestry of the parish, entered an opposition to the Bill, and appeared against it before the Committee of the House of Lords. Their opposition was entirely successful (and it must be remembered that the Disused Burial Grounds Act had not then been passed), and the London School Board was merely given a right of way to the school through the graveyard. The costs of the opposition amounted to £236 12s. 10d., which was charged upon the poor rate. The auditor disallowed the charge, but on appeal to the Local Government Board it was sanctioned.

CHAPTER V

LONDON CHURCHYARDS, OUTSIDE THE CITY.

"I will lay me in the village ground,

There are the dead respected."

H. K. WHITE.

THERE are few spots in England more peaceful, more suggestive, and more hallowed than our village churchyards, when they are treated with that reverence which is their due. I have many in my mind now, but I will try to think of one only "where the churchyard, grey with stone and green with turf, holds its century of dead," where "side by side, the poor man and the son of pride, lie calm and still." The church is grey and ivy-grown. Its broad tower, that has weathered many a storm, is half hidden amongst tall trees bursting into leaf, which hold, high up in their branches, the nests of the cawing rooks. Far below winds the gentle river, between wide stretches of meadow-land, and there is the old one-span bridge with the picturesque cottages of the village following each other down to it and up again, and in the background of the picture are the sheltering, sheep-covered hills. An old gabled parsonage adjoins the church, and the pathway which leads to it is through the peaceful sleeping-place of those whose tired bodies have been laid upon "the pillow of the restful earth." The birds are making music in the trees, the gentlest of vernal breezes stirs the air, and from the seat in the venerable porch I can look out upon that quiet scene in the "lengthening April day." Green grass, long and sweet, is growing amongst the "grey tombstones with their half-worn epitaphs," and is trying to hide the primroses and the early bluebell buds which are peeping from the ground, for there

"the flowers of earth

Their very best make speed to wear,

And e'en the funeral mound gives birth

To wild thyme fresh and violets fair."

It is so green and fresh, so calm and sweet a spot in which to await the resurrection morn, that we can understand what Keble felt when he said,

"Stoop, little child, nor fear to kiss

The green buds on this bed of death."

As there is "no fear in love," so there should be no "fear" in death, for death is but our translation into the presence of the greater love "which passeth knowledge."

Our London churchyards of to-day were once village churchyards, and were attached to quiet old churches which, with a few neighbouring houses, stood far away from the town and were encircled with fields. There are many now living who can remember walking from the City to St. Mary's, Islington, by a footpath through the meadows, and such was also at one time the case with Paddington, St. Pancras, Hackney, Shoreditch, Stepney, Bow, Bromley, Rotherhithe, Lewisham, Camberwell, Wandsworth, Battersea, and many other parishes. It is difficult to realise it now, and yet it is only in the present century that they have been merged into the great metropolis, and separated by many miles of houses from the hedges and fields. Nor is it long since the village stocks were moved from several of the churchyard gates.

Most of the original parish churches have been replaced, some of them more than once. The oldest ones now in existence are St. Saviour's, Southwark, Stepney, Bow, Chelsea, Fulham, the Savoy, Westminster (St. Margaret's), Lambeth, Deptford (St. Nicholas'), and

Putney, with the tower of old Hackney Church. Many of the others belong to the eighteenth century. In the tenth year of the reign of Queen Anne the number of houses in the districts adjacent to the City having increased so rapidly, it was enacted by Parliament that fifty new churches should be built "for the better Instruction of all in the Principles of Christianity," and for "redressing the inconvenience and growing mischiefs which resulted from the increase of Dissenters and Popery." In order to raise the necessary funds it was agreed to levy an additional duty of two shillings per chaldron "upon all Coals and Culm" that were brought into London, and two shillings per ton upon weighable coals for a term of 137 days, after which for eight years the duty was to be three shillings per chaldron and per ton. But although some old churches were rebuilt or repaired at that time, only ten new ones were erected, such as St. Anne's, Limehouse, St. George's in the East, St. Luke's, Old Street, and St. John the Evangelist's, Westminster.

ALL SAINTS, WANDSWORTH, ABOUT 1800.

Descriptions of the churchyards attached to these churches are not easy to find, nor were they of any great interest, except that many notable men were buried in them. Yet there is one point in connection with them that is interesting, and it is that although the churches are in the severe and sometimes almost grotesque style of architecture of Gibb, Hawksmoor, and others, yet in the eighteenth century it was customary to erect headstones over graves with elaborately carved designs. Eighteenth-century tombstones have hour-glasses, scythes, cherubs' heads—blowing or smiling or weeping—elaborate scenes, generally allegorical of the flight of time, and epitaphs upon which much thought and care were expended. With the nineteenth century the carved tombstones disappeared.[3] St. Paul's churchyard,

---

[3]. This subject has been carefully gone into by Mr. W. T. Vincent, who has quite lately brought out a book upon the designs on carved tombstones.

Deptford, contains many quaint specimens, and here also is a "shelter," the roof of which was the old pulpit sounding-board, But the older churchyards, those which may be more rightly described as the merged village churchyards, have been pictured from time to time.

EIGHTEENTH-CENTURY TOMBSTONE.

One of Mr. Loftie's original ideas is to describe London as known by Stow, Norden, and Shakespeare, who lived and wrote at about the same time, *i.e.*, 1600. I do not mean to say that he tells us what the burial-grounds were like in that day, for no historian of London ever seemed to think it worth while to do more than refer to one here and one there, or I should not have ventured to put forward this work at a time when we are satiated with histories of the metropolis; but I will, for a moment, adopt his plan. It is impossible to read *Hamlet* and the vivid description of the gravediggers who played at "loggats" with the skulls and bones, while they drank and sung, without coming to the conclusion that Shakespeare had witnessed the very same practices in the graveyards in his day as were exposed and stopped no less than two and a half centuries later, when "skittles" were played with bones and skulls at St. Ann's, Soho, and other churchyards. But I cannot entirely give up the idea that Shakespeare walked in some churchyards which awoke peaceful and reverent thoughts in his contemplative mind.

NINETEENTH-CENTURY TOMBSTONE.

Stow scarcely mentions the churchyards at all. He and his later editors give up many pages of his survey to inscriptions copied from monuments, some being from tombstones in the churchyards, but most being from the tablets in the churches, and he occasionally refers to the gift by citizens of pieces of ground for graveyards, these being mainly in the City itself. Perhaps, however, it may not be out of place to quote from one or two passages which give us an idea of the condition of the open land immediately adjoining the City, and which point to the fact that such parish churches as lay beyond this land must indeed have been rural and remote.

We read in the edition of 1633 that "filthie cottages" and alleys extended for "almost halfe a mile beyond" Whitechapel Church, "into the common field." He also refers to the fine houses, with large gardens, which were being built round the City, where former generations, more benevolently inclined, had erected hospitals and almshouses. He mentions the "wrestlings" that took place at Bartholomewtide by "Skinners Well, neere unto Clarkes Well." This Clarkes Well, or Clerkenwell, "is curbed about square with hard stone: not farre from the west end of Clarkenwell Church, but close without the wall that encloseth it." ... "Somewhat north from Holywell (Shoreditch) is one other well, curbed square with stone, and is called Dame Annis the cleere; and not far from it, but somewhat west, is also another cleere water, called Perilous Pond, because divers youths (by swimming therein) have been drowned." Stow most carefully enumerates the wells and conduits of the City and its surroundings, several being "neere to the Church." And it is a fact that many wells, conduits, and pumps in and around London were—and some still are—not only in close proximity to the churchyards, but actually in them. The water from St. Clement's Well and St. Giles' Well came through the burial-grounds. The site of the Bride's Well, which gave the name to the precinct and the hospital, is still marked by the pump in an alcove of the wall of St. Bride's Churchyard, Fleet Street. There was a pump by St. Michael le Querne and one in the churchyard of St. Mary le Bow, against the west wall of the church. There was a well in the crypt of St. Peter's, Walworth, a pump in Stepney Churchyard, and another in St. George's in the East, to which his parishioners used to resort for drinking water until the Rev. Harry Jones, during a cholera scare, hung a large placard on it, "*Dead Men's Broth!*" and Dickens used to picture the departed, when he heard the churchyard pumps at work, urging their protest, "Let us lie here in peace; don't suck us up and drink us!"

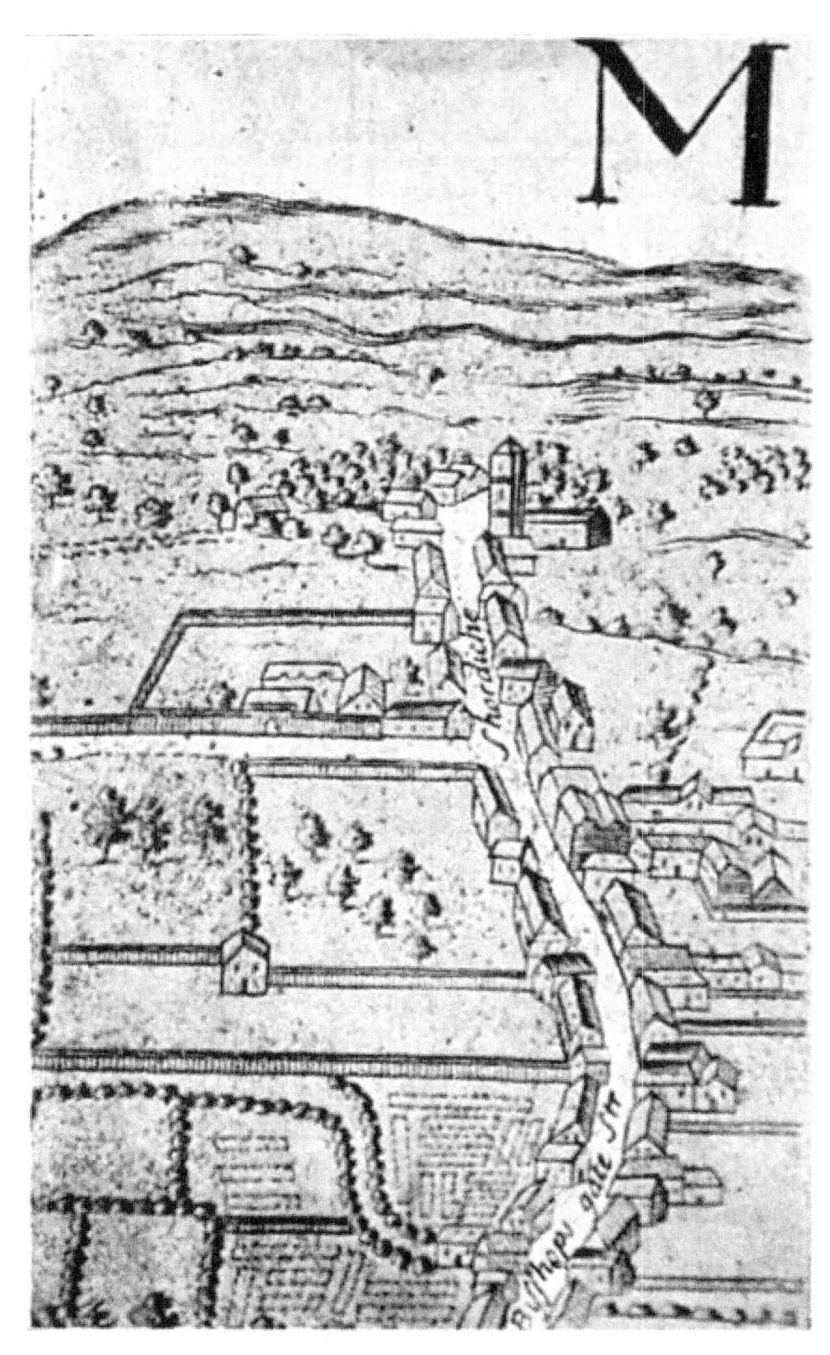

THE VILLAGE OF SHOREDITCH.
(From Aggas' Plan, 1560.)

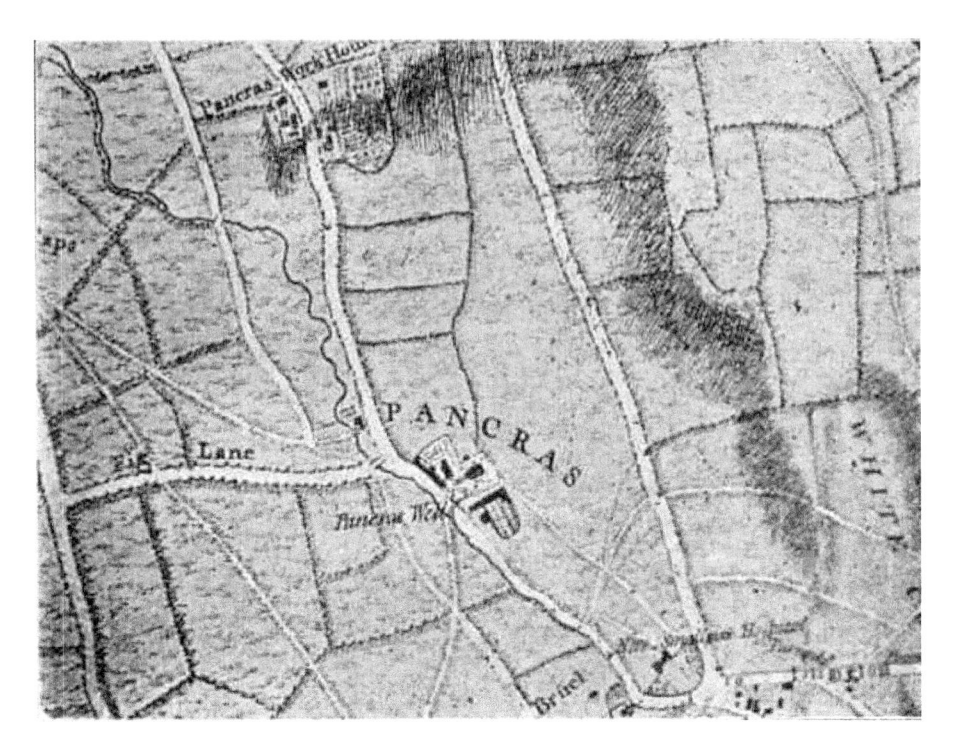

ST. PANCRAS VILLAGE.
(*From Rocque's Plan*, 1746.)

And Norden, what did he say? His plan of London, like the one by Aggas and later ones, gives us a picture of the remoteness of the outer parishes. Here is his description of old St. Pancras Churchyard: "Pancras Church standeth all alone, as utterly forsaken, old and wether-beaten, which, for the antiquity thereof, it is thought not to yield to Paules in London. About this church have bin many buildings now decayed, leaving poor Pancras without companie or comfort, yet it is now and then visited with Kentishtowne and Highgate, which are members thereof.... When there is a corpse to be interred, they are forced to leave the same within this forsaken church or churchyard, when (no doubt) it resteth as secure against the day of resurrection as if it laie in stately Paules." It would indeed be curious to see what Norden would think now of this churchyard, with the Midland Railway trains unceasingly rushing across it, and the "dome" and "trophy" of headstones, numbering 496, not to speak of the stacks and walls of them round about, which were moved into one part of the ground when the other part (Catholic Pancras) was acquired by the railway company. Poor Pancras is not forsaken now, it is in the midst of streets and houses, and what remains of the churchyard is full of seats and people.

This particular ground, with others in the same neighbourhood, were famed later on as the scenes of the operations of body-snatchers, as is evident from Tom Hood's rhyme, entitled "Jack Hall," from which one verse will be sufficient:—

"At last—it may be, Death took spite,

Or jesting only meant to fright—

He sought for jack night after night

The churchyards round;

And soon they met, the man and sprite,

In Pancras' ground."

When Jack Hall is himself dying, and twelve M.D.'s are round him, anxious for his body, he tells them:—

"I sold it thrice,

Forgive my crimes!

In short I have received its price

A dozen times."

Timbs in his "Romance of London" gives a detailed account of the first indictment for body-stealing—the act taking place at St. George the Martyr ground (behind the Foundling Hospital) in 1777. But it must be remembered that, although at one time body-snatchers or resurrection-men carried on a brisk trade, yet where one body may have been disinterred for hospital use one hundred were removed to make room for others.

The churchyards in London to which a somewhat rural flavour still clings are, perhaps, those in the extreme south east, such as St. Nicholas', Plumstead, and St. John the Baptist's, Eltham, which, together with Lee and Tooting Churchyards, are still used for interments, St. Mary's, Bromley-by-Bow (originally the chapel of St. Mary in the Convent of St. Leonard), with its beautiful altar tombs, and St. Mary's, Stoke Newington. There is something particularly picturesque about the last named, with the old church in its midst. Mrs. Barbauld lies buried here, and a lady whose death was caused by her clothes catching fire, upon whose tombstone this very quaint inscription was placed:—

"Reader, if you should ever witness such an afflicting scene, recollect that the only method to extinguish the flame, is to stifle it by an immediate covering."

All the parish churches had their churchyards, the only ones not actually adjoining them being those of St. George's, Hanover Square, St. George's, Bloomsbury, and St. George the Martyr, Queen Square, where the first body interred was that of Robert Nelson, author of "Fasts and Festivals." Some were added to many times, some have been seriously curtailed. The largest of the churchyards are Stepney, Hackney, and Camberwell. That of St. Anne's, Limehouse, had a strip taken off it in 1800, when Commercial Road was made, that of St. Paul's, Hammersmith, was similarly curtailed in 1884. The present churches of Hammersmith and Kensington are far larger than their predecessors, and therefore the churchyards dwindled when they were built. St. Clement Danes and St. John's, Westminster, once stood in fair-sized churchyards; now, in each case, there is only a railed-in enclosure round the church. But one of the most serious shortenings was at St. Martin's in the Fields. In fact, of those buried from this particular parish, few can have been undisturbed, except, perhaps, in the cemetery in Pratt Street, Camden Town, now a public garden, which belongs to St. Martin's. One of the parochial burial-grounds is under the northern block of the buildings forming the National Gallery, another one is lost in Charing Cross Road, while a third one (now a little garden) in Drury Lane was so disgustingly overcrowded that no burials could take place there without the disturbance of other bodies, which were crowded into pits dug in the ground, and covered with boards. But to return to the churchyard itself, the burial-ground immediately surrounding the church, where Nell Gwynne and Jack Sheppard were buried. A strip on the north side and a piece at the east end still exist, flagged with stones, and were planted with trees, provided with seats, and opened to the public by the Metropolitan Public Gardens Association in 1887. But once there was a large piece of ground on the south side, where now there is none, called the Waterman's Churchyard. Its disappearance is accounted for by the following inscription on a tablet on the church wall:—

> "These catacombs were constructed at the expense of the Commissioners of Her Majesty's Woods and Forests, in exchange for part of the burial-ground of this parish, on the south side of the church, given up for public improvements, and were consecrated by the Lord Bishop of London on the 7th day of June, 1831."

In *The Sunday Times* of June 12, 1831, these vaults are thus described:—

"The new vaults under St. Martin's burying-ground are the most capacious structure of the sort in London. They were opened on Tuesday, at the consecration of the new burial-ground. They consist of a series of vaults, running out of one another in various directions; they are lofty, and when lighted up, as on Tuesday, really presented something of a comfortable appearance." After relating something about the size and number of the arches, the quantity of coffins they would hold, &c., the description closes with these words: "Crowds of ladies perambulated the vaults for some time, and the whole had more the appearance of a fashionable promenade than a grim depository of decomposing mortality."

This account reminds me very much of the ceremony which took place after the opening of St. Peter's Churchyard, Walworth, as a garden, in May, 1895. The Rector had kindly provided tea in the crypt, a huge space under the church where gymnastic and other classes are held. This crypt used to be full of coffins lying about at random, with a well in the centre, but a faculty was obtained for their removal to a cemetery. The scene on the day to which I refer was a very gay one. Where, a few months previously, there had been coffins and dirt, there was a well white-washed building, lighted with plenty of gas, lace curtains between the solid pillars and low arches, a number of little tables with tea, cakes, &c., and many brightly-attired girls to wait on the visitors, who enjoyed their refreshment to the enlivening strains of a piano.

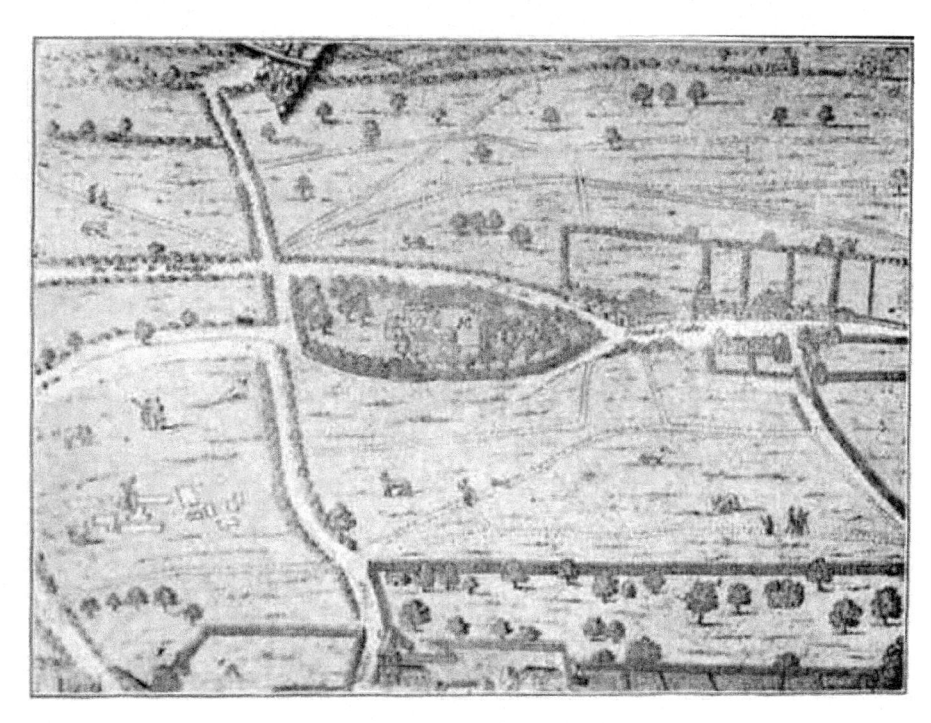

THE VILLAGE OF ST. GILES' IN THE FIELDS.
(From Aggas' Plan, 1560.)

The churchyard of St. Giles' in the Fields is a very interesting one. It might well be now called St. Giles' in the Slums, although of late years the surrounding streets have been much improved and the worst courts cleared away. Before there was a church of St. Giles' there was a lazaretto or leper hospital on the spot, and what is now the churchyard was the burial-ground attached thereto. As a parish the settlement seems to date from 1547, but the hospital was founded 200 years earlier, and was entrusted to the care of the Master and Brethren of the Order of Burton St. Lazar of Jerusalem, in Leicestershire. The churchyard, which holds many centuries of dead, was frequently enlarged, Brown's Gardens being added in 1628, until the parish secured an additional burial-ground, in 1803, adjoining that of St. Pancras. And yet it is barely an acre in extent. It is related in Thornbury's "Haunted London" that in 1670 the sexton agreed to furnish the rector and churchwardens with two fat capons, ready dressed, every Tuesday se'nnight in return for being allowed to introduce certain windows into the churchyard side of his house. But it could not have been a pleasant churchyard to look at. It was always damp, and vast numbers of the poor Irish were buried in it (the ground having been originally consecrated by a Roman Catholic), and it is hardly to be wondered at that the parish of St. Giles' enjoys the honour of having started the plague of 1665. And the practices carried on there at the beginning of this century were equal to the worst anywhere—revolting ill-treatment of the dead was the daily custom.

Now the churchyard is a public garden, Pendrell's tombstone being an object of historical interest, the inscription upon which runs as follows:—

"Here lieth Richard Pendrell, Preserver and Conductor to his sacred Majesty King Charles the Second of Great Britain, after his Escape from Worcester Fight, in the Year 1651, who died Feb. 8, 1671.

Hold, Passenger, here's shrouded in this Herse,

Unparalell'd Pendrell, thro' the Universe.

Like when the Eastern Star From Heaven gave Light

To three lost Kings; so he, in such dark Night,

To Britain's Monarch, toss'd by adverse War,

On Earth appear'd, a Second Eastern Star,

A Pope, a Stern, in her rebellious Main,

A Film to her Royal Sovereign.

Now to triumph in Heav'n's eternal Sphere,

He's hence advanc'd, for his just Steerage here;

Whilst Albion's Chronicles, with matchless Fame,

Embalm the Story of great Pendrell's Name."

This ridiculous epitaph belongs to the truly eulogistic group. It has its counterpart on a tombstone in Fulham Churchyard, erected to the memory of a lady, where the epitaph is "Silence is best," or in the following one from Lambeth:—

"Here lieth W. W.

Who nevermore will trouble you, trouble you."

Old Chelsea Church is noted for its monuments, many persons of distinction having been buried there, and in the churchyard is a great erection in memory of Sir Hans Sloane, but the ground is closed to the public, and the tombstones are sadly neglected. From a dramatic point of view the burial-ground attached to St. Paul's, Covent Garden, is most interesting, as it contains the graves of a large number of actors.

So many works have been written about monuments and epitaphs that it is not my intention to refer to many, but some are interesting as giving a peep into the life of those they commemorate. There are several in London which describe the number of times the deceased person was "tapped for dropsy." A tombstone at Stepney is in memory of one "Elizabeth Goodlad, who died in 1710, aged 99, and her twenty daughters." They must have been exemplary daughters not to have worn out their mother sooner! The Rev. Matthew Mead was also buried here, a most prolific writer of sermons and treatises on religion, including one with this quaint title, "The almost Christian tried and cast." Stepney Churchyard is very old; it is highly probable that there was a church there in Saxon times. The other churchyards in East London which can boast of considerable antiquity are Bromley, Bow, Whitechapel, and Hackney, although Sir Walter Besant, in his novel, "All Sorts and Conditions of Men," says that the churchyards in East London "are not even ancient." No doubt if he re-wrote that novel now he would alter many of his remarks. It is hardly possible to think that the eastern districts of London ever formed a "marvellous, unknown country," or that Rotherhithe needed any "discovery."

By the close of the last century and at the beginning of this one, the want of additional burial space was much felt in several parishes. Some had "poor grounds," and some, like St. James's, Clerkenwell, had a "middle ground," this particular one being now the playground of the Bowling Green Lane Board School, but the extra graveyards were all small and all crowded. The parishes of St. Margaret's, Westminster, St. James's, Piccadilly, St. Andrew's, Holborn, St. James's, Clerkenwell, St. Marylebone, and St. Mary's, Islington, secured additional burial-grounds in which chapels of ease were erected. These are Christ Church, Victoria Street, St. James's, Hampstead Road, Holy Trinity, Gray's Inn Road, St. James's, Pentonville Road, St. John's Wood Chapel, and the Chapel of Ease in Holloway Road, the ground surrounding which is one of the best kept churchyard gardens in London. Many of the district churches, built at the commencement of this century, also had graveyards attached. In Bethnal Green, for instance, not only is there the burial-ground of St. Matthew's, which was consecrated in 1746, and has vaults under the school as well as the church, but there are those of St. Peter's, St. Bartholomew's, and St. James' the Less, the two first being laid out as gardens, and the last being a dreary, swampy waste, containing about ten sad-looking tombstones and a colony of cocks and hens.

It is impossible, in a chapter already too long, to touch upon all the churchyards outside the City, but I must refer briefly to the four principal parish churches which have disappeared. The present building of St. Mary le Strand only dates from 1717; the original one stood in a "fair cemetery," much nearer the river, and was also called the Church of the Innocents. This ground was enlarged in 1355 by a plot 70 feet by 30 feet in size, but the church and churchyard disappeared about 1564 to make room for Somerset House. The church of St. John the Evangelist, Tybourn, was removed in 1400 by Bishop Braybrooke, and the first church of St. Marylebone was built to take its place. Provision was made for the preservation of the churchyard, but it also disappeared before long. It was near the site of the present Court House in Stratford Place, under which, and the older one, bones were dug up in 1727 and 1822.

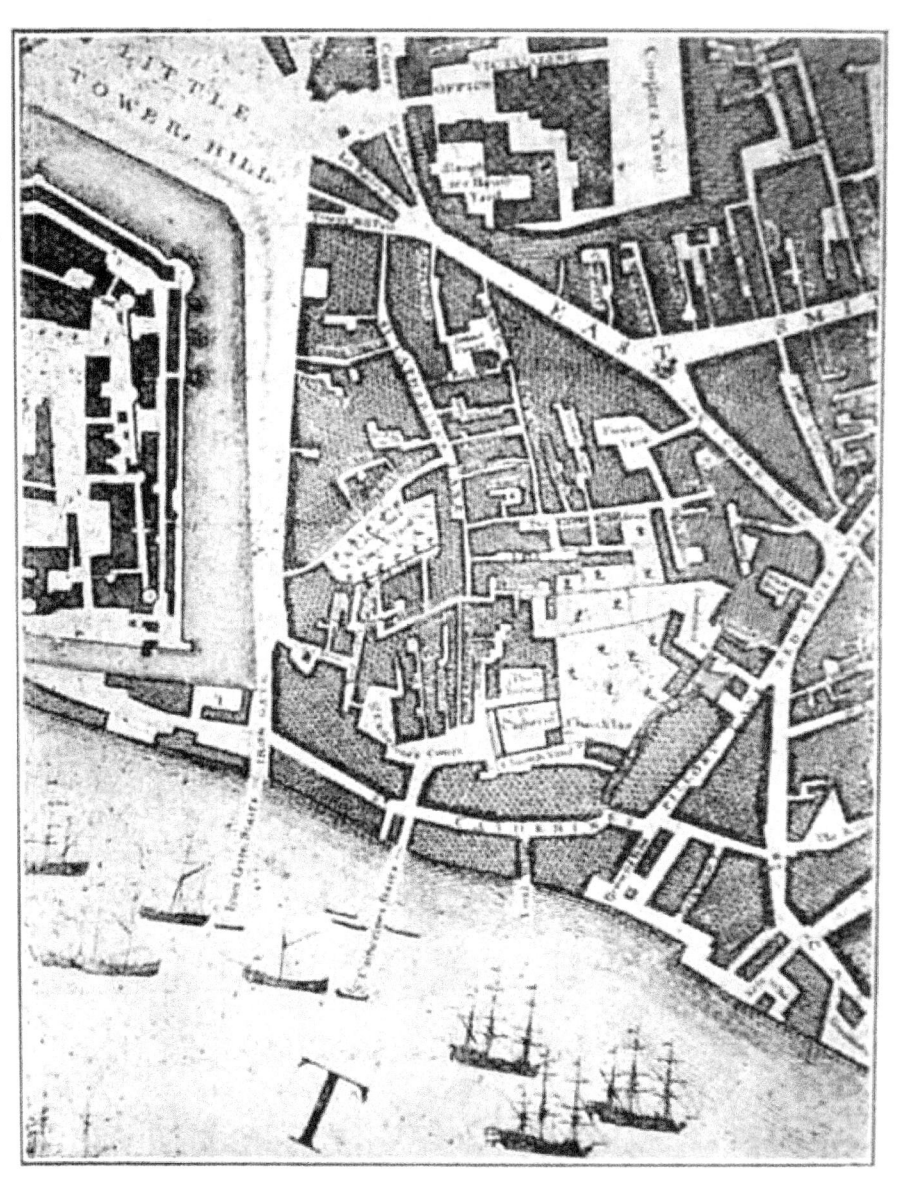

THE SITE OF ST. KATHARINE'S DOCKS.
(From Rocque's Plan, 1746.)

ST. MATTHEW'S, BETHNAL GREEN, 1818.

Tybourn Church was removed because it was in so lonely a situation, and yet so near the main road from Oxford to London, that robbers and thieves were always breaking into it to steal the bells, images, ornaments, &c. The Church of St. Margaret, Southwark, stood in the middle of the Borough High Street, with a much-used graveyard round it, which was enlarged in 1537. But it was in so inconvenient a place, and the ground was so much used for holding markets in, that it was removed about 1600, and the parish amalgamated with St. Saviour's. The old town hall took the place of the church, and the Borough Market is still held on or near the site of the churchyard. When St. Katharine's Docks were made, in 1827, St. Katharine's Church, the ruins of the hospital (dating from 1148), two churchyards of considerable size, and the whole parish,—inns, streets, houses and all, were totally annihilated. The church was a beautiful one; it has been described by Sir Walter Besant and other chroniclers, and must have been amongst the finest specimens of ecclesiastical architecture in London. The whole establishment was, to a certain extent, rebuilt near Regent's Park. It is said that a quantity of the human remains from the churchyard were used to fill up some old reservoirs, &c., in the neighbourhood; but, at any rate, it is a fact that they were distributed amongst the East-end churchyards, and several cartloads were taken to Bethnal Green and deposited in St. Matthew's ground, where the slope up to the west door of the church is composed of these bodies from St. Katharine's. There were originally steps leading to the entrance, but the steps are buried under this artificial hill, the ground having been raised several inches.

What may be called the parish churchyards in London, outside the City, number about seventy-two. Of these no less than forty are now being maintained as public gardens, and this does not include the additional parochial graveyards, nor those attached to district churches. A few, such as Streatham and Hampstead, are generally open to the public, but are not provided with seats, and one of the best kept is that of St. Bartholomew's, Sydenham, which, although not a public garden, is indeed "a thing of beauty." The old churchyard at Lee is also attractive, and contains tombs and effigies belonging to many families of note, including those of the Ropers, Boones, and Floodyers, and a monument to the memory of Sir Fretful Plagiary, of whom, notwithstanding the uncomfortable name with which he was endowed, his epitaph says, "He science knew, knew manners, knew the age."

CHAPTER VI

PEST-FIELDS AND PLAGUE-PITS.

"From plague, pestilence, and famine,

Good Lord, deliver us."

CONSIDERING that we have records of the visitation of London by direful plagues and pestilences at frequent intervals during ten centuries, and that these visitations always led to a mortality far in excess of the ordinary one, it is not to be wondered at that from time to time special burial-places had to be provided to meet the special need. In 664, during the time of the Saxon Heptarchy, London was "ravaged by the plague," and from that date forward it returned again and again, causing the kings, the courtiers and the richer citizens to be constantly fleeing for safety into the country, until the final and awful calamity of 1665. According to some authorities the plague has never re-appeared since then, although according to others a few cases occurred annually until the year 1679. But after that time, although there was a division for "the Plague" in the annual Bills of Mortality, there were no entries against it, and after 1703 we cease even to see the word recorded. In early days the visitations were so ordinary that, when mentioned in the histories of London, they are not taken much account of. Here is one record: "The plague making its appearance in France in 1361, the king to guard against the contagion spreading in London, ordered that all cattle for the use of the city should be slaughtered either at Stratford on one side the town, or at Knightsbridge on the other side, to keep the air free from filthy and putrid smells. This regulation was certainly wholesome; but the close dwellings of which the city then consisted, were always fit receptacles for contagious disorders; the plague accordingly came over, and in two days destroyed 1,200 persons." If an infectious disorder were to carry off 1,200 persons in two days in London now, when the population is counted by millions instead of by thousands, there would be a general panic, a special inquiry, and, perhaps, a Royal Commission.

In 1349 two large tracts of land were set aside for the interment of those who then died of the plague, and as their history is generally well known, I will give Noorthouck's somewhat concise account: "At length it (a great pestilence) reached London, where the common cemeteries were not capacious enough to receive the vast number of bodies, so that several well-disposed persons were induced to purchase ground to supply that defect. Amongst the rest, Ralph Stratford, Bishop of London, bought a piece of ground, called No-Man's-Land, which he inclosed with a brick wall, and dedicated to the burial of the dead. Adjoining to this was a place called Spittle Croft, the property of St. Bartholomew's Hospital, containing thirteen acres and a rod of ground, which was purchased for the same use of burying the dead by Sir Walter Manny, and was long remembered by an inscription fixed on a stone cross upon the premises. On this burial-ground the Charterhouse now stands. There was also another piece of ground purchased at the east end of the City, just without the wall, by one John Corey, a clergyman, for the same use; on which spot was afterwards, in this same reign, founded the Abbey of St. Mary of Grace, for Cistercian monks; it is now covered by the victualling-office and adjoining houses. It was asserted that not one in ten escaped this calamity, and that not less than 100,000 persons died in the whole." The next sentence is characteristic of the way in which, as I have already said, these visitations were treated. "Notwithstanding this sad misfortune, the city soon recovered itself, and advanced greatly in prosperity, as will appear by a charter it obtained in the year 1354, granting the privilege of having gold or silver maces carried before the chief magistrate." The translation of the Latin inscription on the stone cross on Sir Walter de Manny's ground is as follows:—

"A great plague raging in the year of our Lord 1349, this burial-ground was consecrated, wherein, and within the bounds of the present monastery, were buried more than 50,000 bodies of the dead, beside many others thenceforward to the present time: whose souls the Lord have mercy upon. Amen."

The space called No-Man's-Land was three acres in extent and was afterwards known as the Pardon Churchyard, being used for the interment of executed people and suicides. It was in use long after the Cistercian Monastery was built on the Spittle Croft. Wilderness Row, now merged into Clerkenwell Road, marks its site, while the gardens and courts of the Charterhouse, the Square, the site of a demolished burial-ground for the pensioners (Sutton's Ground), and the burial-ground which still exists at the north end of the precincts, are all part of the Spittle Croft and of the monastery burial-ground. There have already been attempts to do away with the Charterhouse, to substitute streets and houses for the old buildings, gardens, and courts, but happily it is not so easy as it once was to tamper with land consecrated for burials, even though that land may have been set aside 550 years ago. The "Victualling-office," which took the place of St. Mary's Abbey, was where the Royal Mint at present stands, and, if one may trust William Newton's plan, the abbey graveyard was where the entrance courtyard is now.

The numbers who died in subsequent visitations must have helped not a little to fill the parish churchyards, but it was not until the year of the Great Plague that there seems to have been any very general provision of extra ground, although the pest-house ground in the Irish Field, "nye" Old Street, was consecrated in 1662, especially for the parish of St. Giles, Cripplegate.

But the plague of 1665 taxed the resources, the patience, and the energy of the Mayor, magistrates, and citizens of London in a manner that was unprecedented. All through that fatal summer and autumn, and on into the commencement of the following year, did it play havoc with the people. In August and September it was at its height. The exact number of persons who died could not be known, for thousands of deaths were never recorded. Bodies were collected by the dead carts, which were filled and emptied and filled again from sunset to dawn, and no account was kept of the numbers thrown into the pits. At any rate, between August 6th and October 10th, 49,605 deaths were registered in the Bills of Mortality as from the Plague, and Defoe, whose "Journal of the Plague" gives every detail that any one can wish for, considered that during the visitation at least 100,000 must have perished, in addition to those who wandered away with the disease upon them and died in the outlying districts. "The number of those miserable objects was great. The country people would go and dig a hole at a distance from them, and then, with long poles and hooks at the end of them, drag the bodies into these pits, and then throw the earth in from as far as they could cast it, to cover them." It is pretty certain that many unrecorded burials took place in the fields of Stoke Newington.

London must have been a sad sight. All shows, pleasures and pastimes were stopped; people crowded continually into the churches, where dissenting ministers, notwithstanding the Act of Uniformity which was then in force, occupied the pulpits of deceased or absent vicars, and preached to the most attentive listeners; huge fires were always burning in the streets; children were kept out of the churchyards; the city was cleared of all "hogs, dogs, cats, tame pigeons and conies," special "dog-killers" being employed; and food and assistance was daily given to the most needy; while those who could afford to do so fled into the country, except a few devoted physicians, justices, and other helpers, including the Archbishop of Canterbury, the Earl of Craven, Monk (afterwards Duke of Marlborough), and Gilbert Latey and George Whitehead (Quakers).

The plague, introduced from Holland, first broke out in Long Acre, and gradually spread all over London. When it became impossible to bury in the ordinary way, huge pits were dug in the churchyards and bodies were deposited in them without coffins. The chief plague-pit in Aldgate Churchyard was about 40 ft. long, 15 or 16 ft. broad, and 20 ft. deep, and between the 6th and the 20th of September, 1,114 bodies were thrown into it. But it soon became necessary to make new burial-grounds and new pits for the reception of the dead, as the "common graves of every parish" became full.

THE PEST-HOUSES IN TOTHILL FIELDS.

There were pest-houses in the ground to the north of Old Street and in Tothill Fields, Westminster, to which infected persons were taken. They corresponded to the isolation hospitals of to-day. But they could only accommodate, at the most, 300 patients or so, and were wholly inadequate to meet the need. The pest-houses in Old Street, or rather Bath Street, were long ago destroyed; Pest-House Row and Russell Row used to mark their sites. But a portion of the pest-field exists in the garden behind the St. Luke's Lunatic Asylum, which was used as a burial-ground for the parish of St. Giles, Cripplegate, until the formation, in 1732, of St. Luke's parish, when it became the St Luke's "poor ground." The pest-houses in Tothill Fields were standing at the beginning of the present century. They were known as the "five houses" or the "seven chimneys," and were erected in 1642. The Tothill Fields, no longer being needed as a plague burial-ground, were subsequently built upon, but not until they had been used for the burial of 1,200 Scotch military prisoners with their wives. A considerable portion of the fields is, however, still open, and is known as Vincent Square, the playground of the Westminster School boys. Mackenzie Walcott, in his Memorials of Westminster, states that Harding's stoneyard in Earl Street is the site of the principal plague-pit. This, I believe, is now the yard of Her Majesty's Stationery Office, Waste Paper Department.

Defoe gives a very careful description of some of the plague-pits and burial-grounds which were made in his immediate neighbourhood. He mentions—

1. "A piece of ground beyond Goswell Street, near Mount Mill, ... where abundance were buried promiscuously from the Parishes of Aldersgate, Clerkenwell, and even out of the city. This ground, as I take it, was since made a Physick Garden, and after that has been built upon." Mount Mill was on the north side of Seward Street.

2. "A piece of ground just over the Black Ditch, as it was then called, at the end of Holloway Lane, in Shoreditch Parish; it has been since made a Yard for keeping Hogs, and for other ordinary Uses, but is quite out of Use for a burying-ground."

This Holywell Mount burial-ground has been "in use" again since Defoe's time, and was also used as a plague-pit before 1665. Originally the site of a theatre dating from the time of Shakespeare, and named after the neighbouring Holywell Convent in King John's Court, it afterwards became a burial-ground, famous as being used for the interment of a great many actors. There is a small part of it left, but at the outside not more than a quarter of an acre. It is behind the church of St. James', Curtain Road, and is approached by a passage from Holywell Row. A parish room has been built on it, and what remains is used as a timber yard. The piece between the parish room and the church is bare and untidy.

3. The third place mentioned by Defoe was at "the Upper end of Hand Alley in Bishopsgate Street, which was then a green field, and was taken in particularly for Bishopsgate Parish, tho' many of the Carts out of the City brought their dead thither also, particularly out of the Parish of Allhallows on the Wall."

He then goes on to describe how this place was very soon built upon, though the bodies were, in many cases, still undecomposed, and he states that the remains of 2,000 persons were put into a pit and railed round in an adjoining passage. New Street, Bishopsgate Street, now occupies the site of Hand Alley.

STEPNEY CHURCHYARD.

4. "Besides this there was a piece of ground in Moorfields," &c. Here he refers to the Bethlem burial-ground, which was not made at that time, but enlarged. Defoe finally mentions the extra grounds which had to be supplied in Stepney, then a very largely extended parish. They included a piece of ground adjoining the churchyard, which was afterwards added to it; and in 1886, in laying out this churchyard as a public garden, some human remains, without coffins, and very close to the surface, were accidentally disturbed at the south-western side of the ground. Another of the Stepney pest-grounds was in Spitalfields, "where since a chapel or Tabernacle has been built for ease to this great parish." I believe it to be St. Mary, Spital Square. Another was in Petticoat Lane. "There were no less than five other grounds made use of for the Parish of Stepney at that time, one where now stands the Parish Church of St. Paul's, Shadwell, and the other where now stands the Parish Church of St. John at Wapping." The churchyards of these two churches, the former of which is a public garden, and the latter of which is still closed, are therefore survivals of pest-fields. But there are three other places to account for which Defoe does not localise. One was possibly in Gower's Walk, Whitechapel, where human remains, without coffins, were come upon recently in digging the foundation for Messrs. Kinloch's new buildings. The remains were moved in boxes to a railway arch in Battersea in the winter of 1893-4. I saw this excavation myself, the layer of black earth, intermingled with bones, being between two layers of excellent gravel soil. One additional ground bought at the time of the Plague was on the north side of Mile End Road. By about 1745 it was used as a market-garden, and now the site is occupied by houses south of the junction of Lisbon and Collingwood Streets, Cambridge Road. Besides these it is certain that a large tract of land south of the London Hospital was also used for interments, and the Brewer's Garden and the site of St. Philip's Church were probably parts of this ground, which was known as Stepney Mount. On the north side of Corporation Row, Clerkenwell, in digging foundations for artisan's dwellings, a number of human remains were recently found. This site may have been a plague-pit, or it may have been a burial-ground for an old Bridewell close by, or an overflow from the graveyard in Bowling Green Lane.

The chief place of interment for those who died of the plague in Southwark was the burial-ground in Deadman's Place (now called Park Street). Here vast numbers of bodies were buried. The graveyard was afterwards attached to an Independent Chapel, and many eminent Dissenters were buried there, for it soon became a sort of Bunhill Fields For South London. Now the carts, the trucks, and the barrels in Messrs. Barclay and Perkins' Brewery roll on rails over the remains of the victims of the plague and the Dissenting ministers with their flocks.

THE SITE OF THE BREWER'S GARDEN ABOUT 1830.

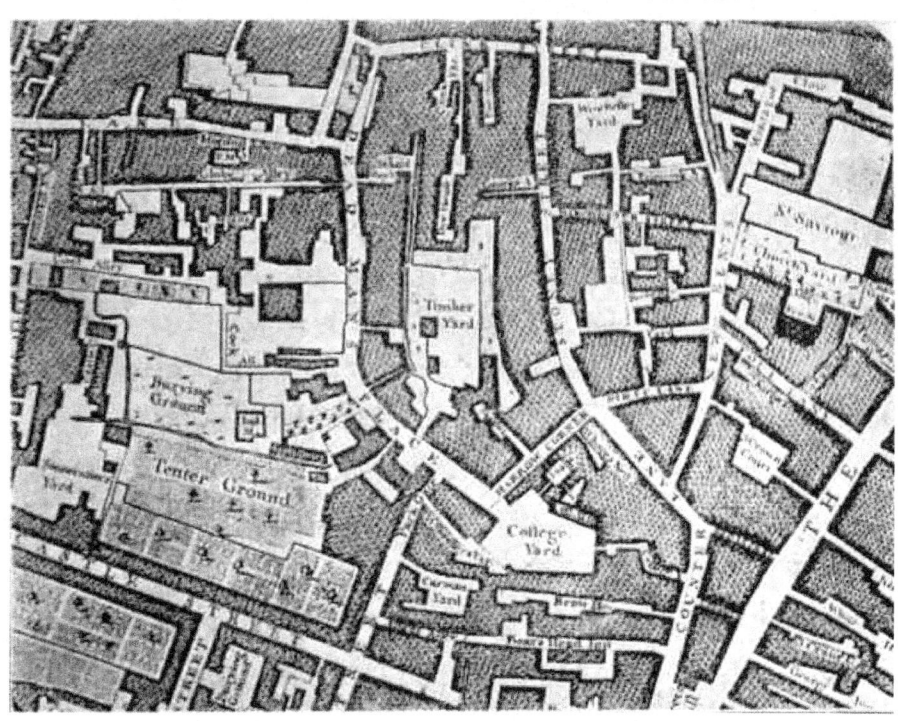

DISSENTERS' BURIAL-GROUND IN DEADMAN'S PLACE.
(From Rocque's Plan, 1746.)

But pest-fields were needed in the west of London, as well as in the north, south, and east, and in addition to Tothill Fields there was a large tract of land set aside near Poland Street, upon the site of which the St. James's Workhouse was subsequently built, a piece of the ground surviving still in the workhouse garden. Carnaby Market and Marshall Street were also built on the site about the year 1723, when three acres, known as Upton Farm, were given in exchange in the fields of Baynard's Watering Place (Bayswater), upon which Craven Hill Gardens now stands. There was a plague-pit near Golden Square, this district being all a part of the pest-field at one time.

The orchard of Normand House, by Lillie Road, Fulham, is said, by Mrs. S. C. Hall, to have been filled with bodies in the year of the Great Plague. The site of this orchard has almost gone; Lintaine Grove, and the houses on the north side of Lillie Road were built upon it. There is still a piece vacant, and for sale, at the corner of Tilton Street, about three-quarters of an acre in extent. Knightsbridge Green (opposite Tattersalls) was also used for the victims of the Plague, and those who died in the Lazar Hospital. Such are all the records of plague-pits and pest-fields which I think sufficiently authentic to record.

There used to be an additional burial-ground for Aldgate parish in Cartwright Street, E., consecrated in 1615. This, at the beginning of the present century, was covered with small houses, and on a part of the site the Weigh House School was built in 1846. The rookery was cleared by the Metropolitan Board of Works nearly forty years later, when Darby Street was made, and the vacant land was offered as a site for artisans' dwellings. I brought the case to the notice of the Metropolitan Public Gardens Association, and the Board was communicated with. At first it was denied that any part of the site had been a burial-ground, but excavations were made and human remains were found. Nor was this really necessary, for the workmen who had pulled down the houses, and the authorities at the school, were well aware of the fact, and knew of actual tombstones being unearthed, upon which a date as late as 1806 had been found. The Board of Works caused the plans for the surrounding new buildings to be altered, and what is left of the site of the burial-ground is now an asphalted playground adjoining the southern block. A certain gentleman afterwards wrote and circulated a pamphlet, in which he stated that the Metropolitan Board of Works had discovered one of the "seites" set apart in Whitechapel for a pest-ground in 1349, whereas the fact was that the Board had been driven, somewhat against its will, to preserve as an open space the site of a consecrated burial-ground belonging to the parish of St. Botolph, Aldgate. That it may once have been a part of a pest-field is likely enough, for they abounded in the district, but the age of the Aldgate ground was, I consider, sufficient to account for the driest of the dry bones found there.

Although the Plague has not re-appeared, there have been periods of great mortality from other diseases. Special provisions for burial had to be made at the time of the cholera visitations. In the outbreak of 1832, 196 bodies were interred in a plot of ground adjoining the additional burial-ground for Whitechapel (now the playground of the Davenant Schools). A large piece of ground by the churchyard of All Saints, Poplar, on the north side of the Rectory, was also used for the purpose, and the circumstance is recorded on the monument which stands in the middle of it.

The fact that the bodies in the pest-fields and plague-pits were usually buried without coffins, and were only wrapped in rugs, sheets, &C., has accelerated their decay, and it can no longer be thought dangerous when such pits are opened. Not that I wish in any way to defend the disturbance of human remains, for I hold that no ground in which interments have taken place should be used for any other purpose than that of an open space, and, apart from the legal and sentimental aspects of the question, human remains, in whatever state of decay they may be, are not fit foundations for buildings, nor is it seemly or proper to gather them up and burn them in a hole, or to cram them promiscuously into chests or "black boxes," to be padlocked and deposited in other grounds or convenient vaults. But the old plague-pits, the very crowded churchyards, and the private grounds where the soil was saturated with quicklime, the coffins smashed at once, and decay in every way hurried, are likely now to be less insalubrious than those grounds where lead and oaken coffins—specially intended to last for generations—are still in good preservation, and only occasionally give way and let out the putrifactive emanations.

CHAPTER VII

THE DISSENTERS' BURIAL-GROUNDS.

"Methodism was only to be detected as you detect curious larvæ, by diligent search in dirty corners."—GEORGE ELIOT.

FOREMOST amongst the burial-grounds devoted especially to Dissenters is Bunhill Fields,—not the New Bunhill Fields in Newington, nor Little Bunhill Fields in Islington, nor the City Bunhill Ground in Golden Lane, not the Quakers' ground in Bunhill Row—but the real, genuine, original Bunhill Fields, City Road.

The land on the north side of the City and south of Old Street was variously called the Moorfields, Finsbury Fields, the Artillery Ground, Windmill Hill, and Bone-hill or Bon-hill. In the year 1549, when the Charnel Chapel in St. Paul's Churchyard was pulled down, "the bones of the dead, couched up in a charnel under the chapel, were conveyed from thence into Finsbury Field, by report of him who paid for the carriage, amounting to more than one thousand cartloads, and there laid on a moorish ground, which, in a short time after, being raised by the soilage of the City, was able to bear three windmills." The number of windmills was, later on, increased to five, and they may be seen on many old maps of London. Heretics used to be interred in Moorfields, and bones from St. Matthew's, Friday Street, were moved to Haggerston, in fact several acres in this district were in use for the purpose of burying in.

The land north of the Artillery Ground was known as Bonhill or Bunhill Field, "part whereof, at present denominated Tindal's, or the Dissenters' great Burial-ground, was, by the Mayor and Citizens of London, in the year 1665, set apart and consecrated as a common Cemetery, for the interment of such corps as could not have room in their parochial burial-grounds in that dreadful year of pestilence. However, it not being made use of on that occasion, the said Tindal took a lease thereof, and converted it into a Burial-ground for the use of Dissenters." So wrote Maitland in 1756, but before that time a large plot was added on the north, and eventually the whole cemetery measured about five acres. There at least 100,000 persons found their last resting-place, including vast numbers of Methodist, Baptist, Presbyterian, and Independent ministers. In Walter Wilson's History of the Dissenting Meeting-houses, which might be more rightly called a history of dissenting divines, the burial of the ministers in Bunhill Fields is constantly mentioned, and the elaborate inscriptions from their tombs are given. These have, however, become much defaced, and numbers of them are now illegible. The ground belongs to the Corporation; it is not laid out as a garden, but paths have been made and seats placed in it, the gates being open during the day. The most frequented paths lead to the tombstones of John Bunyan, on the south side of the public thoroughfare in "Tyndal's Ground," and Daniel Defoe, on the north side, both being at the eastern end of the cemetery. Bunyan's tomb was restored in 1862 by public subscription, a piece of the original stone being now in the Congregational Church at Highgate. The monument to Defoe was raised in 1870 by a subscription in the *Christian World*. Amongst other celebrities buried here were Dr. Williams, the founder of the Library in Red Cross Street (now in Gordon Square), Susannah Wesley, mother of John and Charles, Isaac Watts, Sir Thomas Hardy of Reform Bill fame, and several members of the Cromwell family. The Corporation restored the tombstone of Henry Cromwell, which was found seven feet below the surface.

On the south side of the Thames the largest and most important of the Dissenters' burial-grounds was that attached to the Independent Chapel in Deadman's Place (now called Park Street, Southwark), originally a plague-ground, and very much used for the burial of the victims. Here many more ministers were buried, whose names are household words wherever Dissenters are gathered together. I cannot say what has become of their tombstones, but the site of the ground is now only one of the paved yards in Messrs. Barclay and Perkins' Brewery.

If the mantle of Bunhill Fields has fallen anywhere, I suppose that Abney Park Cemetery claims the distinction. It was first used in 1840, and has always been the favourite cemetery of the Dissenters, there being no separating line in it to mark off a consecrated portion. Its formation is also associated with the memory of Dr. Watts, who lived for some years, and who died, in the neighbourhood, at the house of his friend Sir Thomas Abney. There is a monument to him in the cemetery, although he was buried at Bunhill Fields, and there are many huge monuments to other eminent dissenting divines of latter days. The tombstones are crowded together as closely as it seems possible, and yet they are being constantly added to, although the greater part of this cemetery is already over-full.

UNION CHAPEL, WOOLWICH.

The first dissenting meeting-houses were in the City and its immediate neighbourhood. They were frequently but "upper rooms" in narrow courts, and had no graveyards attached to them. But when the persecution of the Dissenters, under the Act of Uniformity, was relaxed, meeting-houses and chapels sprang up in every part of London, and these, in some cases, had burial-grounds adjoining them. A few of the larger grounds, such as Sheen's, in Commercial Road, and the one in Globe Fields, were bought by private individuals and carried on as private speculations entirely apart from the Chapels. They are described in Chapter IX. But of the genuine Dissenters' graveyards *i.e.,* the little grounds attached to chapels and meeting-houses in London, there must have been at one time or another about eighty—there may have been more. This number of course represents but a very small portion of the meeting-houses themselves, which were in existence at the beginning of this century. The following remarks of the Rev. John Blackburn, one of the secretaries of the Union of Congregational Ministers, show how the respectable Dissenters repudiated the private burial-grounds: "I may with confidence disclaim the imputation that the graveyards of Dissenters were primarily and chiefly established with a view to emolument. Many graveyards that are private property, purchased by undertakers for their own emolument, are regarded as dissenting burial-grounds; and we are implicated in the censures that are pronounced upon the unseemly and disgusting transactions that have been detected in them.... By far the greatest portion of the persons buried in these grounds are not Dissenters at all.... The denomination to which I belong have about 120 chapels in and around London, and I believe there is not more than a sixth part of them that have graveyards attached."

In the returns of the Metropolitan burial-grounds which were made fifty or sixty years ago, those to whom the work was entrusted generally expressed their inability to find out the correct number of the Dissenters' grounds, and Walker wrote, "I have not been able to procure any satisfactory accounts of the numbers interred in burying-grounds unconnected with the Established Church. By some parties information was refused, by others the records of the place were stated to have been lost or neglected, and in some cases the parties most interested in suppressing, had alone the power to communicate." When I first began, twelve years ago, to make as complete a list as I could of the London burial-grounds, I wrote to the secretaries at the centres of the chief dissenting bodies, as I thought they might possess information about the burial-grounds of their own chapels. From the Congregationalists I had no reply; the Wesleyans kindly answered that they were endeavouring to procure the information, but it never came; the Baptists wrote two or three letters and took some trouble on my behalf, but they failed even to find the number of their grounds. I had, therefore, to seek my information in other ways.

The only body of Nonconformists that has kept a careful account of its graveyards is the Society of Friends. They also treated their grounds and the remains in them with greater respect (except in one notable case to which I shall refer), and they kept them neat and clean, and do so still. Walker recognised this fact as long ago as 1847. A statement respecting their graveyards was made by representatives of the Society to the committee which sat in 1843, showing that they still had considerable room in these grounds, and that they were careful not to allow less than 7 feet or 8 feet of earth above each coffin. The Friends attend to all matters connected with their meeting-houses and burial-grounds at their six weeks' meeting, and each of these grounds has been a Quakers' graveyard from the beginning, not changing hands, first belonging to one community and then another, as has been the case with so many of the chapel graveyards. The members of the Society have also exercised a most praiseworthy self-control by not wearing mourning, by avoiding useless expense at funerals, and ostentatious tombstones, memorials, or epitaphs. Until about fifty years ago no tombstones were used at all, as at Long Lane, S.E.; then they used small flat ones, as at Hammersmith and Peckham; and finally they adopted small upright ones, all the same shape, about a quarter of the size of the ordinary headstones in cemeteries. These may be seen at Ratcliff and Stoke Newington, the graveyard at the latter place, which surrounds the Park Street meeting-house, being still in use. I wish that every one who intends to erect a tombstone—and this is a note for Jews as well as Christians—would, before doing so, pay a visit to a Quakers' burial-ground, and ponder on the matter there. An interesting article on the Society of Friends has appeared in the *Times* of January 8, 1896, in which the following words are quoted, "The Quakers—the man and the Society—must move or perish." But I trust they may not move forward with the times in adopting more elaborate burial customs.

Four of the Quakers' graveyards have entirely disappeared. The burial-ground for the Friends of Westminster was in Long Acre, by Castle Street. It passed out of their hands in 1757, and was built upon. In rebuilding houses on the same spot, about four years ago, many human remains were disturbed. These were claimed by the Society, which was allowed to collect them and bury them at Isleworth. There was a little meeting-house with a burial-ground attached in Wapping Street, which seems to have been used until about 1779, but was then demolished, the worshippers moving to the meeting in Brook Street, Ratcliff. The other two burial-grounds which the Friends have lost were in Worcester Street and Ewer Street, Southwark. The latter, although it adjoined their Old Park Meeting (which the King took as a guard house), may never have been used by them. At any rate in 1839 it was in private hands, and eventually disappeared under the railway. The former, which dated from 1666, was very full, so that in 1733 the surface was raised above the original level. This was demolished when Southwark Street was made (1860); and the London Bridge and Charing Cross Railway also runs over its site. The Friends then moved the remains and a number of coffins to their ground in Long Lane, Bermondsey.[4]

4. A most interesting report upon this removal was made by the Surveyor to the six weeks' meeting, in which are contained some excellent remarks upon the futility of burying in lead coffins, nine of these being found in the ground. The graveyard had been disused since 1799.

The Quakers of the Bull-and-Mouth and Peel Divisions used a large ground near Bunhill Fields, between Checquer Alley and Coleman (now Roscoe) Street. It was acquired in 1661, and many times added to, and was used extensively by them at the time of the Great Plague, when they had their own special dead-cart. George Fox's body was carried here in 1690, an orderly procession, numbering 4,000 persons, following to the grave. In 1840 a school was built in it, and the rest of the tale it grieves me to tell. A part of the burial-ground exists now, not half an acre in area. It is neatly laid out as a sort of private garden. Five thousand bodies were dug up in the other part and buried, with carbolic acid, in a corner of the existing piece, and the site from which they were removed is now covered with a Board School, a coffee palace, houses, and shops, including the Bunhill Fields Memorial Buildings, erected in 1881.[5]

5. Although 12,000 Quakers were buried in the Coleman Street ground, including Edward Burrough and others who died as martyrs in Newgate Gaol, George Fox's grave was the only one marked by a stone,—a small tablet on the wall, with the simple inscription, "G. F." This attracted visits from country Friends in such numbers that a zealous member of the Society named Robert Howard "pronounced it 'Nehushtan,'" and caused it to be destroyed.

The remainder of the Friends' burial-grounds are intact. The one in Baker's Row, Whitechapel (acquired in 1687 and used by the Devonshire House Division), is now a recreation ground; and the one in Long Lane, Bermondsey, which was bought in 1697 for £120, has lately been laid out for the use of the public. In addition to these there are, in London itself, five little grounds adjoining meeting-houses in High Street, Deptford, in Brook Street, Ratcliff, in High Street, Wandsworth (given by Joan Stringer in 1697), by the Creek, Hammersmith, and in Hanover Street, Peckham Rye. The Society acquired the Ratcliff ground in 1666 or 1667, the land being originally copyhold, but enfranchised in 1734 for £21. All these grounds are neatly kept; the one in Peckham, which dates from 1821, is beautiful, and illustrates what can be done with a disused and closed graveyard, not even visible from the road, when it is treated with proper care and respect. Many of the burial-grounds just outside London have been sold with the meeting-houses.

There are not many Roman Catholic burial-grounds in London apart from those attached to conventual establishments. St. Mary's Church, Moorfields, has a very small churchyard and had two additional grounds, one in Bethnal Green which has disappeared, and one in Wades Place, Poplar, now used as a school playground. This is the case also with a Roman Catholic burial-ground in Duncan Terrace, Islington, which has been asphalted for the use of the boys' school, some tombstones and a figure of the Virgin Mary being in an enclosure on the north side. There is a very large ground dedicated to All Souls, by St. Mary's Church, Cadogan Terrace, Chelsea, and a small one by the church in Parker's Row, Dockhead, S.E., the garden here, which is now a recreation ground for the schools or the sisters, having also been used for burials. There is one in Woolwich, lately encroached upon through the enlargement of the school, where three lonely-looking graves are in a railed-in enclosure in the middle of a tar-paved yard; and there is also the ground behind St. Thomas's, Fulham, which is still in use.

FRIENDS' BURIAL-GROUND IN WHITECHAPEL.

But the burial-grounds adjoining Baptist, Wesleyan, Independent, and other Chapels, what shall be said of them? They have suffered terribly in the slaughter, and although many still exist, a very large number have entirely disappeared. Only three are open as public gardens—the Wesleyan ground in Cable Street, St. George's in the East, which was added to St. George's churchyard garden in 1875; the ground behind the Independent Chapel by St. Thomas' Square, Hackney; and the burial-ground adjoining Whitfield's Tabernacle, Tottenham Court Road, the subject of much litigation, which was opened in February, 1895, by the London County Council. The original chapel on this site was founded by George Whitefield in 1756, amongst his supporters being the Countess of Huntingdon, David Garrick, and Benjamin Franklin. One other graveyard was laid out as a garden, that adjoining Trinity Chapel, East India Dock Road, but it is now closed, no one at present undertaking its maintenance.

WHITFIELD'S TABERNACLE.

For the rest of the grounds, not only Methodist but also Congregationalist and above all Baptist, we must employ the "diligent search in dirty corners," but all the seeking in the world will not restore those that are gone—sold and built upon. The fates of some of them are recorded in Appendix B. The parishes south of the river seem to have been great strongholds of dissent. Woolwich, Deptford, Walworth, and Wandsworth are still full of chapels, many of which have burial-grounds attached. North of the Thames perhaps Hackney is richest in chapels and chapel graveyards, including the Unitarian in Chatham Place. Whitechapel also had a great many. But in the Borough and other parts of Southwark the little meeting-houses swarmed at one time, some of which, with their little burial-grounds, still exist. A few of the chapels now belong to the Salvation Army; one in York Street, Walworth, has lately been acquired as the Robert Browning Hall, and its burial-ground is to be a public garden; others in Peckham, Woolwich, and Hammersmith have been converted into schools (the two last named being board schools), their graveyards being the playgrounds; and many more have fallen from their first estate.

It might be instructive to those who are not well acquainted with South London to take a walk, in imagination, through Long Lane. It begins at St. George the Martyr, Borough, of "Little Dorrit" fame, where the churchyard is a public garden. Close by this, also on the north side of the lane, there used to be a Baptist Chapel in Sheer's Alley, with a burial-ground. Wilmott's Buildings occupy the site. Very little beyond is Collier's Rents. Here is a chapel which used to belong to the Baptists, but is now in the hands of the Congregational Union. Its dreary little graveyard is on the north side, behind a high wall. A little further on, and opposite, is Southwark Chapel (Wesleyan), built in 1808. It also has a graveyard, where the chief ornament is a hen-coop amongst the tumbling tombstones. A short turning to the north, Nelson Street, takes us to the disused burial-ground of Guy's Hospital; and before we come to the end of the lane there are three more grounds to be seen, that belonging to the Society of Friends, already mentioned in this Chapter, and one that adjoins it and is owned by the trustees of a neighbouring Baptist Chapel, which is very small and has a minister's vault in the middle. This ground originally belonged to the Independents of Beck Street, and its appellation when closed was the Neckinger Road Chapel burial-ground. Lastly we come to St. Mary Magdalene's, the parish church of Bermondsey, with a charming churchyard garden which includes a portion of the cemetery of Bermondsey Abbey. And yet Long Lane is only about half a mile in length!

It is a little curious to notice that in the next parish, Rotherhithe, there are no less than five churchyards, but not a single burial-ground belonging to the Dissenters.

When visiting the burial-grounds for the London County Council, I was much struck with three that seemed particularly neglected and untidy. These were the Baptist ground in Mare Street, Hackney, which was being used for the storage of old wood, furniture, and flower-pots; the ground behind the pretentious Congregational Chapel on Stockwell Green, where all kinds of dirty rubbish, paper, iron-building materials, the broken top of a lamp-post, &c., were lying about amongst the sinking graves; and a little ground in Church Street, Deptford, behind a chapel which belongs to a General Baptist (Unitarian) connection, whose creed I do not pretend to understand, but whose railings were so broken that a far larger visitor than I could have followed me through the gaps to behold broken tombstones, collections of unsavoury rubbish, and another specimen of the worn-out top of a lamp-post. There were many other very untidy grounds, such as those by the Wesleyan Chapel in Liverpool Road, King's Cross, and the Congregational Chapel in Esher Street, Lambeth; but I think the three I have mentioned above would have been—in the Spring of 1895, at any rate—awarded the first, second, and third prizes in a competition for neglect; and in January, 1896, I find these grounds are in much the same condition as they were then.

It is pleasant to turn to some of the chapel grounds which are well kept. The one which adjoins the Congregational Church in High Street, Deptford, is generally neat; so is the graveyard of the City Road Chapel, at any rate at its western end, where John Wesley's monument stands; and the same may be said of the portions that are left of the grounds adjoining Union Chapel, Streatham Hill, and the New West End Baptist Chapel in King Street, Hammersmith.

WESLEY'S MONUMENT IN THE GRAVEYARD OF THE CITY ROAD CHAPEL.

There was a large burial-ground behind a chapel in Cannon Street Road, E. The building passed into the hands of the Rector of St. George's in the East, but was afterwards pulled down, and one of Raine's Foundation Schools was subsequently erected on its site. The burial-ground, in which many Lascars[6] were interred, is now in three parts. One is a small playground for the school, the largest part is Messrs. Seaward Brothers' yard for their carts, and the third piece is a cooper's yard belonging to Messrs. Hasted and Sons. A similar kind of chapel in Penrose Street, Walworth, known for a time as St. John's Episcopal Chapel, is now the studio of a scenic artist, while the large burial-ground in the rear is the depôt of the Newington Vestry, and is full of carts, manure, gravel, dust, stones, &c.

[6]. These Lascars used to live in a court near by, and are said to have been locked in at night.

The East London Railway has swallowed up the graveyards by Rose Lane Chapel, Stepney, and the Sabbatarian or Seventh Day Baptists' Chapel in Mill Yard, by Leman Street; the Medical School of Guy's Hospital is on the Mazepond Baptist Chapel-ground; the site of one which adjoined the London Road Chapel, S.E., is now occupied by a tailor's shop, the next house being on the space where the chapel stood, and these two shops are easily picked out in the row as they are higher and newer than their neighbours on either side. A little Baptist graveyard in Dipping Alley, Horselydown, which had a baptistery in it, disappeared very many years ago; the site of the Baptist Chapel and burial-ground in Worship Street, Shoreditch, forms a part of the yard used as the goods depôt of the London and North Western Railway; a similar one in Broad Street, Wapping, is now, I believe, a milkman's yard, and was for many years previously the parish stoneyard; while the very crowded ground which used to be behind Buckingham Chapel, Palace Street, has a brewery on it. There is a little graveyard in front of Maberley Chapel, Ball's Pond (now called Earlham Hall), but the three tombstones that are left in it are not only put upon the north wall of the chapel, but have actually been painted with the wall.

I have mentioned that a few of the chapels have been replaced by schools, but I ought also to mention that the graveyards behind Abney Chapel, Stoke Newington, N., Denmark Row Chapel, Coldharbour Lane, S.E., and the chapel in Hanbury Street, Mile End New Town, E., were only closed for a very few years before school buildings were erected on them. A small yard remains of the last named, but practically nothing is left of the others. The site of the graveyard in the rear of the chapel in Gloucester Street, Shoreditch, has, together with that of the chapel itself, been merged into the premises of the Gaslight and Coke Company.

These are specimens of the uses to which the Dissenters' grounds have been put, and which we want to prevent in the future, for I hope that it may not be long before many of those that have not been entirely lost are "converted" into cheerful resting-places for the use of the living.

It is the question of their maintenance, when they are once laid out, that has hitherto caused so much difficulty, and this not only with the Dissenters' grounds, but also with the churchyards. Where the Vestry or District Board of Works will undertake to maintain a ground under the Open Spaces Acts it is simple enough, and in many cases this has been done most effectually. But some of these bodies will not accept the responsibility. The Corporation keeps up St. Paul's Churchyard and Bunhill Fields, and the London County Council maintains Whitfield's Tabernacle ground and ten graveyards which were laid out by the Metropolitan Public Gardens Association. It was with great difficulty and after a hard fight that the Earl of Meath managed to induce the Council to take over some of these grounds (and this only year by year), together with several squares and playgrounds, the maintenance of which was too heavy a burden upon the funds of a voluntary society. Of late years the Association has not laid out any burial-ground until its future maintenance is legally secured. A short time ago, soon after the publication of the return prepared by me for the Council, the Parks and Open Spaces Committee recommended that a conference should be held to consider some general scheme for the treatment of the burial-grounds which are still closed, their acquisition for the use of the public, and their maintenance, it being felt somewhat unjust that while some of the Metropolitan vestries and boards (such as St. Pancras and Hackney) were annually expending considerable sums in the upkeep of graveyard gardens, others (such as Rotherhithe and Limehouse) declined to do so. But the recommendation, when it came before the general meeting of the Council, was withdrawn for the time being, and the whole question remains in *statu quo ante*.

CHAPTER VIII

THE BURIAL-PLACES OF FOREIGNERS IN LONDON.

"The very names recorded here are strange,

Of foreign accent, and of different climes;

Alvares and Revira interchange

With Abraham and Jacob of old times."

LONGFELLOW.

IT is only natural that in London, to which so many from other countries have fled, and where so many foreigners have lived, worked, and died, there should be evidences left of their places of interment. Solitary cases of their burial among Englishmen are, of course, to be met with everywhere, and there are many such in the London graveyards. In Rotherhithe Churchyard is a well-known tombstone erected to the memory of Prince Lee-boo of the Pelew Islands, who died in 1784; in St. Ann's, Soho, there is a tablet to that of Theodore, the last King of Corsica; there is the grave of an Indian chief in the burial-ground of St. John's, Westminster, in Horseferry Road; and it is said that the first person interred in a part of Bishopsgate Churchyard was a Frenchman named Martin de la Tour, while this ground also used to contain a very old altar tomb with a Persian inscription round it to the memory of Coya Shawsware, a Persian merchant, who died in 1626. The edition of Stow's "Survey," published in 1633, contains a picture of this monument and an account of the funeral ceremonies which took place at the grave. Maitland also refers to it, but gives a totally different first name to the merchant. It is evident that for some time after his burial his son and other friends used to gather at the grave twice a day for prayer and funeral devotions, until driven away by the ridicule of the populace.

JEWISH CEMETERY, MILE END.

But there have been in London many special burial-grounds belonging to special groups of foreigners, and several of them remain. Foremost among these are the Jewish cemeteries.

Until the year 1177, the time of Henry II., the Jews in England were only allowed one burial-place. It was known as the Jews' Garden and was outside the wall of London by Cripplegate, several acres being devoted to the purpose—a neighbourhood subsequently known by the name of Leyrestowe. When other burial-places were permitted, this ground was built upon, but the remembrance of it still lives in the name of one street in the district, Jewin Street, reminding us of the time of the bitter persecutions which the Jews suffered, and which are chronicled, to our shame, in English history.

"Pride and humiliation hand in hand

Walked with them thro' the world where'er they went;

Trampled and beaten were they as the sand,

And yet unshaken as the continent."

In the first place it is to be noticed that the Jews, as a race, are particularly pledged to preserve their burial-places. This is not a law among them—so I have been told by the Chief Rabbi—but a binding obligation handed down from the most ancient times, and any disturbance of the burial-grounds which now exist is not permitted. No doubt it was totally beyond their power to prevent the "Jews' Garden" from being covered with streets, its very size and position rendered it practically impossible to preserve, and it was probably annihilated during one of those periods when the Jews were expelled from England. Another exception which proves the rule is at Oxford, where the Botanic Garden, which dates from 1622, was made on the site of the Jewish burial-ground.

They also strictly observed the sanitary laws respecting burial laid down for them, and their cemeteries have not been overcrowded. Burial is only allowed at 6 feet from the surface of the ground, and only one body is in each grave, one coffin not being placed above another; and this rule has been carried out in the Jewish burial-grounds in London—again with one exception.

In the very large, old graveyard in Brady Street, Bethnal Green (formerly called North Street), there are walls running through it, and the southern half is higher than the northern half, having quite a hilly appearance. The following is the explanation. This half of the ground was originally allotted to "strangers," Jews who belonged to no special congregation. About thirty years after it was full, a layer of earth, 4 feet in depth, was added to the ground, and it was used over again. As the coffins were again placed 6 feet from the surface, there still remained 4 feet of earth between them and the old ones beneath. As a result of this curious and interesting arrangement, there may be seen, in several cases, two gravestones standing up back to back, which represent the two graves below them. Here lie buried, with other members of the family, Nathan Mayer de Rothschild, the founder of the English house of Rothschild, Asher and Benjamin Goldsmid, and many another Jew famous on 'Change.

Within the Metropolitan area there are at present nine Jewish graveyards; there are others more lately acquired, and all still in use, at Willesden, West Ham, Edmonton, Plashet, and Golders Green, Hendon, The disused grounds which belong to the United Synagogue are those in Brady Street, Bethnal Green, E., Hoxton Street, N., Alderney Road, Mile End, E., and Grove Street, Hackney, E., and I cannot, unfortunately, call them well kept, but the neatest is the one in Alderney Road. In all of them the tombstones are upright, rather above the average size, and with inscriptions upon them which are almost invariably in Hebrew. The one in Hoxton is very small. It was originally formed for the use of the Hamborough Synagogue, Fenchurch Street, and was first used about the year 1700. All these grounds are old, part of the one in Alderney Road dates from about 1700, while the Brady Street Cemetery was formed in 1795. Many of the tombstones have at the top a representation of two outstretched hands with the thumbs joining, the symbol of descendants of Aaron, the High Priest. Others have a hand pouring water out of a flagon, and they are over the graves of the Levites whose duty in the synagogue is to pour water upon the hands of the Priests (the above-mentioned descendants of Aaron), who are nearly all named Cohen.

JEWISH CEMETERY IN FULHAM ROAD.

In Ball's Pond, Islington, is the small cemetery of the West London Congregation of British Jews, which is still in use. Here some very large and extravagant tombstones may be seen, and the ground is very neatly kept. In Fulham Road (Queen's Elm) is a dreary little ground belonging to the synagogue in St. Alban's Place, S.W. I believe an occasional interment takes place here in reserve plots, but the congregation has provided itself with another cemetery at Edmonton. I am indebted to the kindness of Mr. R. Proctor for the photograph of this graveyard. Some few years back, before the Disused Burial-grounds Act was in force, a row of shops was built on the west frontage of the ground, the one body lying in that part being removed to another place. No doubt the freehold worth of the land was considerable at that time, and therefore the congregation disregarded their scruples concerning this one deceased member. The graveyard can only be visited between certain hours on Sundays, but the rest of the Jewish cemeteries have resident caretakers. In Bancroft Road, Mile End, is another dreary place, which, although in so crowded a district, is still in use. When last I visited it I was told there was room for about four more graves! It belongs to the Maiden Lane Synagogue. None of these grounds, except that at Ball's Pond, have proper paths in them; they have been entirely filled with graves, between which a few narrow lines like sheep-tracks wind about the grass.

JEWISH BURIAL-GROUND BEHIND THE BETH HOLIM HOSPITAL, MILE END.

Lastly, there are the cemeteries of the Spanish and Portuguese Jews—one, closed for burials, behind the Beth Holim Hospital in Mile End Road, and one, nearly five acres in extent and still in use, just beyond the People's Palace. These are neatly kept, the former, or at any rate a part of it, being actually turned into a sort of garden for the patients in the hospital, with trees in it, paths and seats. The latter is bare of trees or shrubs, but is divided into plots, with paths between. In both of them the tombstones, unlike those in the other Jewish grounds, are flat, either slabs on the ground or low altar tombs; and in the large ground there are many children's graves, marked by much smaller altar tombs dotted amongst the large ones, which are very unique and interesting. The Hebrew inscription at the entrance tells us that this is "The House of the Living,"—"Beth Hayim." The cemetery was acquired in 1657, and contains the remains of the ancestors of Lord Beaconsfield, the Eardley family, Sampson Gideon, the Samudas, D'Aguilars, Ricardos, Lopes, and many others who trace their descent from Sephardi Jews.

Hitherto it has not been possible to secure any of the Jewish graveyards as public gardens, the feeling of the community is against it, but the day may yet come when the Council of the United Synagogue will allow the experiment to be tried.

JEWISH CEMETERY, MILE END.

The burial-ground of the Greeks in London is an enclosure in Norwood Cemetery, where some elaborate monuments may be seen. The Mohammedans can practise their rites at Woking.

There is no special place at the present time, I believe, where Danes and Swedes are buried, but their churches, with surrounding graveyards, were situated close together, in Wellclose and Prince's Square, E. The church in Prince's Square is still the Swedish church of London (Eleanora), and there is a notice at the corner of a turning on the south side of Cable Street, St. George's in the East,—"Till Svenska Kyrkan." Here, in a vault, are the remains of Emmanuel Swedenborg himself, while the garden contains many tombstones, especially an inner enclosure which was filled first. But the building now situated in Wellclose Square is no longer the Danish or Mariner's Church, the site is occupied by schools and mission buildings in connection with St. Paul's, Dock Street, the present seaman's church. Nor are there any tombstones in the garden, although it is certain that many Danes and many sailors were buried under the church, and in a surrounding graveyard, which was probably an inner enclosure like that in Prince's Square. Mention of it is made by Northook in 1773, and by Malcolm in 1803; and there is a picture of the church in Maitland's "History of London." The following account from the "Beauties of London and Middlesex (1815)" is also of interest:—"At the extremity of this parish is Wellclose Square, which has also borne the name of Marine Square, from the number of sea officers who used to reside in it. It is a pretty little neat square; but its principal ornament is the Danish church in the centre, in the midst of its churchyard, planted with trees.... This structure was erected in 1696, at the expense of Christian V., King of Denmark, as appears by the inscription: 'Templem Dano Norwegicum intercessione et munificentia serenissimi Danorum Regis Christiani Quinti erectum MDCXCVI.' Gaius Gabriel Cibber was the architect, who erected a monument within this church to the memory of his wife Jane, daughter of William Colley, Esq., and mother of Colley Cibber, the famous dramatist. The architect himself is also buried here." The Flemish burial-ground was in the district of St. Olave's, Southwark. It adjoined a chapel in Carter Lane, and before its demolition was used as an additional graveyard by the parishes of St. Olave and St. John, especially the former. When the railway to Greenwich was made this ground disappeared, and part of its site forms the approach to London Bridge Station.

A South View of QUEEN ELIZABETH'S FREE GRAMMAR SCHOOL in Tooley Street in the Parish of S^t. Olave, Southwark, *with a Plan of the adjacent Neighbourhood*

THE FLEMISH BURIAL-GROUND, CARTER LANE, ABOUT 1817.

In Milman's Row, Chelsea, there is a quaint and curious burial-ground belonging to the Moravians. The adjoining buildings have passed out of their hands, their present chapel being in Fetter Lane, E.C. In 1750 Count Zinzendorf purchased two acres of land (a part of the garden and stables of Beaufort House) of Sir Hans Sloane, about one acre of which was set aside for burials, and divided into four parts—the first for male infants and single brothers, the second for female infants and single sisters, the third for married brothers and widowers, and the fourth for married sisters and widows. The stones are flat on the grass and very small, not more than about 11 or 15 inches by 10 or 12 inches in size, and the ground was closed for interments about the year 1888.

There is no purely Dutch place of interment in London now. Besides the Dutch Church in Austin Friars (the survival of the priory of the Augustine Friars), which has lost its churchyard, they used to have a few chapels which seemed to change hands, sometimes belonging to Dutch and at other times to German congregations. Such was Zoar chapel, in Great Alie Street, Whitechapel, which is now a Baptist conventicle. It had a fair-sized burial-ground behind it at the beginning of the century, the site of which is covered by houses and a forge. One day recently I knocked at the door of this chapel, hoping to be allowed to look round it, in order to make sure that no part of the yard was left. The woman who opened it, when I politely asked if I might go in, said "No!" and slammed the door again at once. One meets with varied receptions in different places, Two German churches, with graveyards attached, were also in this neighbourhood—the Lutheran (St. George's), in Little Alie Street, and the Protestant Reformed Church, in Hooper Square. The latter has entirely disappeared, the railway covering its site. The former church still exists, with the little yard behind it, separated by a wall from the adjoining schoolyard, but the entrance from Little Alie Street has been bricked up.

The precinct of the Savoy had a distinctly foreign flavour about it, but the Savoy Chapel itself is now the only remnant left of the large group of buildings which were used at different times as palace, hospital, barracks, and prison, and finally demolished in 1877. The churchyard is probably even older than the church. It is now a neat little garden, in the possession of Her Majesty the Queen, as Duchess of Lancaster, and laid out, chiefly at her cost, for the use of the public. This is the burial-ground described by Dickens, in *All the Year Round*, with some of his tenderest touches, and of which he says: "I think that on summer nights the dew falls here—the only dew that is shed in all London, beyond the tears of the homeless." But the Savoy used to contain one, if not two, German chapels, besides a French Jesuit chapel and a meeting-place for Persian worship. The German church (wrongly called Dutch on Rocque's plan) had a burial-ground on its west side, which is marked on the ordnance maps, except the very latest, as it survived until 1876, when the human remains were removed to a cemetery at Colney Hatch. Now its site is covered by part of the new block of buildings which include the Savoy Chambers and the Medical Examination Hall. The Rev. W. Loftie's book, "Memorials of the Savoy," gives a full and interesting history of the Precinct, and is, as is usual with his works, compiled with care and truthfulness; but beyond simply mentioning the existence of the German burial-ground he has nothing to tell of it. We should have liked to know what the gravestones were like, and whether any persons of distinction were interred there.

We now turn to the French in London, and these have to be divided into the Roman Catholics and the Huguenots. No doubt Frenchmen and Frenchwomen have been laid to rest in the burial-grounds attached to all the Roman Catholic churches, and especially in All Souls Cemetery, behind the chapel of St. Mary, in Cadogan Place, Chelsea, which chapel was built by M. Voyaux de Franous, a French *Émigré* clergyman, and consecrated in 1811. Large numbers were also interred at St. Pancras, the eastern end of the old churchyard receiving, in consequence, the name of "Catholic Pancras." But this is the part which has been so much disturbed and appropriated by the Midland Railway Company, and what remains of it is some dreary, dark slips under the railway arches, and groups and hillocks of tombstones which were moved into the western part of the ground, where, amongst other illustrious graves, are those of Dr. Walker, of dictionary fame, Mary Woolstoncraft Godwin, and William Woollett, the engraver.

EAST HILL BURIAL-GROUND, WANDSWORTH.

About the year 1687 between thirteen and fourteen thousand French Protestants, driven from home by the intolerance of Louis XIV., settled in London, some in Spitalfields, others in the district of St. Giles' and Seven Dials, in Stepney, and in Wandsworth. There was a French church at Wandsworth, which subsequently fell into the hands of the Wesleyans, and the Huguenots who settled in this locality were chiefly engaged in trade as hatters. As a result of these settlements we find their graves in Bethnal Green Churchyard and other places, but especially in the East Hill burial-ground at Wandsworth, where many French Protestants of note were interred, and where there are some fine old headstones and altar tombs. It is a picturesque ground between the two roads, but, with the exception of a pathway through it, it is not open to the public.

Foreigners now have to be buried in the cemeteries, and many a strange service or ceremony has been held at the graveside of those who belong to other climes, especially, perhaps, in Kensal Green Cemetery, Norwood Cemetery, and the others that are non-parochial. The Jews and the Greeks are, I believe, the only communities of strangers who still keep up separate burial-grounds of their own in London.

CHAPTER IX

HOSPITAL, ALMSHOUSE, AND WORKHOUSE GROUNDS.

"Such ebb and flow must ever be,

Then wherefore should we mourn?"

WORDSWORTH.

WHEN the Greyfriars, or Christ's Hospital, was set aside for "poor children," and Bridewell for "the correction of vagabonds," St. Bartholomew's Hospital in the City and St. Thomas's in Southwark were devoted to the care of the "wounded, maimed, sick, and diseased"; and in these four benevolent institutions, which owe so much to the short-lived but truly pious King Edward VI., there was provision made for the burial of the dead. It must be remembered that the quadrangle of Christ's Hospital, which is still surrounded by cloisters, was the burial-ground of the Greyfriars, but apart from this, for the boys of the school or the officers or servants, there was a small plot of ground set apart as a graveyard at the north-west corner of the block of buildings. This was demolished when the great hall was built, in 1825, and if any of its site remains it is only a limited piece of the courtyard on the north side of the hall and the doctor's garden. A few tombstones are preserved in the passage leading to the doctor's house. At this time was formed the additional burial-ground for Christ Church at the western end of the churchyard of St. Botolph, Aldersgate Street. But the churchyard adjoining Christ Church, and even the cloisters themselves, were used from time to time by the Hospital, and it was the custom in the last century for a "blue" to be buried by torchlight. His schoolfellows passed through the venerable courtyards and buildings in procession, two by two, and sang a burial anthem from the 39th Psalm, which must have been a most solemn and touching sight, and was "particularly adapted to the monastic territory" of the Hospital. It will be a sad day when this noble old school is torn from its rightful home in the City of London, and when the boys receive a "modern" education in a trim, new building, and wear the dull tweed suit and the school cap dragged on at the back of their heads; and it is well to impress again and again upon the Charity Commissioners and the Almoners of the Hospital that a very considerable portion of the site will not be available for building upon, as it will come under the provisions of the Disused Burial-grounds Act. The same remark applies with even greater force to the neighbouring hospital, the Charterhouse, where all the gardens and courtyards, including the Square itself and the little burial-ground which is still recognisable as such, have been used at one time or another for interments. I have explained how this came about in a former chapter.

A CORNER OF CHRIST'S HOSPITAL, THE GREYFRIARS' CLOISTERS.

I think it probable that when St. Bartholomew's Hospital was far smaller than it is now, burials took place in the cloisters, or rather in the large space in the middle of which the western wing was built. In a very interesting old plan of the precincts, dated 1617, there is not only shown the "Church-yarde for ye poore" in two pieces, about where the west wing is now, but also a large ground which is named Christ Church Churchyard, to the south of this, but north of the City wall. The hospital later on used the Bethlem burial-ground, and the ground set aside eventually as the hospital graveyard (for the interment of unclaimed corpses), is in Seward Street, Goswell Road. This was first used about 1740, and, after being closed for burials, it was let as a carter's yard and was full of sheds and vans. Through the kindness of the Governors, it fell into the hands of the Metropolitan Public Gardens Association, and it is now a children's recreation ground maintained by St. Luke's Vestry. The burial-ground of St. Thomas's Hospital is at the corner of Mazepond; on part of it St. Olave's Rectory and Messrs. Bevington's leather warehouse were built; the remainder is leased to Guy's Hospital, and contains the treasurer's stables and an asphalted tennis-court for the use of the students. Guy's Hospital burial-ground is in Snow's Fields, Bermondsey, and is now a large builder's yard, but there is a reasonable hope of its being secured before long as a recreation ground. The "unclaimed corpses" from the London Hospital found their last resting-place very near home. In 1849 the whole of the southern part of the enclosure, quite an acre and a half, was the burial-ground, and here, although it was closed by order in Council in 1854, it appears that burials took place until about 1860, one of the present porters remembering his father acting as gravedigger. The medical school, the chaplain's house, and the nurse's home have all been built upon it, and it is sincerely to be hoped that no further encroachments will be permitted. The remaining part is the nurses' and students' garden and tennis-court, where they are in the habit of capering about in their short times off duty, and where it sometimes happens that the grass gives way beneath them—an ordinary occurrence when the subsoil is inhabited by coffins!

LONDON HOSPITAL BURIAL-GROUND.

Bridewell also had its burial-ground, where the lazy and evil were interred. It is at the corner of Dorset and Tudor Streets, near the Thames Embankment, and is an untidy yard, boarded off from the street with a high advertisement hoarding, and in the occupation of a builder.

The Bethlem burial-ground had a more interesting history. In 1569 Sir Thomas Roe, or Rowe, Merchant Taylor and Mayor, gave about one acre of land in the Moorfields "for Burial Ease to such parishes in London as wanted convenient ground." It was especially intended for the parish of St. Botolph's, Bishopsgate, and was probably used for the interment of lunatics from the neighbouring asylum, besides being used by St. Bartholomew's Hospital. It was enclosed with a brick wall at the persuasion of "the Lady his Wife," and she was buried there; and it was the custom upon Whit Sunday for the Lord Mayor and Aldermen to listen to a sermon delivered in this "new churchyard, near Bethlem." We read that in 1584 "a very good Sermon was preached ... and, by Reason no Plays were the Same Day (*i.e.*, Whit Sunday, as there used to be), all the City was quiet." But the Churchyard and the Asylum have disappeared, Liverpool Street Station having taken their place, and hundreds of the Great Eastern Railway goods vans daily roll over the mouldering remains of the departed citizens.

CHELSEA HOSPITAL GRAVEYARD.

Very different to the fate of these hospital burial-grounds is that of another one I will mention. Facing Queen's Road, Chelsea, is the long, narrow graveyard of the Chelsea Hospital. It is neatly kept, with good grass and trees. Here many a venerable pensioner has been laid to rest, and, although it can no longer be used for burials, it still serves to remind the living of their brethren who have gone before them. There are some fine monuments and epitaphs to very long-lived invalids, two aged 112, one 111, one 107, and so on, and it is one of those quiet and quaint corners of London which form so marked a contrast to the noisy streets close by. One pensioner, who died in 1732, named William Hiseman and aged 112, was "a veteran, if ever soldier was." It is recorded that he took unto himself a wife when he was above 100 years old. There is something very peaceful about these old men's graves; the grain gathered in by the "Reaper whose name is Death" was fully ripe:—

"It is not quiet, is not ease,

But something deeper far than these;

The separation that is here

Is of the grave; and of austere

Yet happy feelings of the dead."

On the south side of the Thames there are some other burial-grounds which should be mentioned here. Greenwich Hospital possesses no less than three cemeteries. In 1707 Prince George of Denmark gave a plot of ground for the purpose, measuring 660 by 132 feet. This is on the west side of the Royal Naval School. It is enclosed and full of tombstones. But in 1747 an extra two and a half acres, surrounding the old ground, were appropriated for interments. This space is well kept, containing some fine trees and only a few monuments. The gate from the school playground is generally open. Then there is the Hospital Cemetery in West Combe, nearly six acres in size, and first used in 1857. The burial-ground of God's Gift College (Dulwich) is at the corner of Court Lane. It dates from about 1700, and is a picturesque, well-kept little ground, with several handsome altar tombs in it. The cemetery of Morden College, Blackheath (founded for decayed merchants about 1695) also exists. It is about a quarter of an acre in size, with about eighty tombstones, but the graves have been levelled, and the ground, though still walled round, forms part of the College gardens.

VIEW FROM THE ALMSHOUSES, WHITE HORSE STREET, STEPNEY.

There were several almshouse graveyards in London, including the "College yard" for St. Saviour's Almshouses, Southwark, which is now a builder's store-yard in Park Street, and over which the London, Brighton, and South Coast Railway passes on arches, and one behind the Goldsmith's Almshouses, now covered by the artisans' dwellings on the west side of Goldsmith Row, Shoreditch. The frightfully crowded "almshouse ground" in Clement's Lane formed part of the site of the new Law Courts; while one in Crown Street, Soho, adjoining St. Martin's Almshouses, disappeared when the French Chapel was built, and has now been lost in Charing Cross Road. In order to enter the almshouses in White Horse Street, Stepney, it is necessary to pass through a graveyard, and it cannot be a lively outlook for the pensioners, who have gravestones just under their windows. It was connected with the Independent Chapel, and first used in 1781.

Perhaps the most interesting of these burial-grounds is one which belonged to the Bancroft Almshouses in Mile End Road. The fate of the asylum itself is well known; it has been replaced by the People's Palace, and the improvement from an antiquarian or architectural point of view is nil. The recent interest taken in the proposed destruction of the Trinity Hospital in Mile End Road points to the fact that the pendulum of public opinion is now swinging towards the preservation of historical buildings. The graveyard of Bancroft's Almshouses was a long strip on the eastern side. Part of it has been merged into the roadway. St. Benet's Church (consecrated in 1872), Hall, and Vicarage were built upon it, and the bones of the pensioners are under the Vicarage garden. The northernmost point of the graveyard is enclosed and rooted over, and forms a little yard where flag-staffs, &c., are stored. But between this and the wall of the Vicarage there is a piece open to the road, with some heaps of stones in it and rubbish. There are, at any rate, four gravestones left, against the wall, and there may be others behind the stones; but I daresay it is only a very small proportion of those who pass in and out of the Palace who have ever noticed this relic of the Bancroft Almshouses.

In a large number of the London parishes it was necessary to have "poor grounds," *i.e.*, graveyards where bodies could be interred at a trifling cost or entirely at the cost of the parish; for, notwithstanding the great dislike of the poor to "a pauper's funeral," and the efforts they will make to avoid it, there always have been cases in which no other sort of funeral can be arranged. Some of the "poor grounds" were attached to the workhouses, others were merely a part of the parish churchyards, while others again were older additional burial-grounds secured by the parishes before the days of workhouses.

The workhouse of St. Andrew's, Holborn, was in Shoe Lane, and in the adjoining graveyard the unfortunate young genius, Chatterton, was buried. This ground gave way to the Farringdon Market, which, in its turn, has been supplanted by a new street called Farringdon Avenue. The workhouse ground of St. Sepulchre's, Holborn, together with another additional graveyard belonging to the parish, was in Durham Yard, and the sites of both of them have disappeared in the goods depôt of the Great Northern Railway. The burial-grounds by the workhouses of Shoreditch, St. Paul's, Covent Garden, and St. Giles (in Short's Gardens) have also disappeared; so also has the one allotted to the use of St. James' Workhouse in Poland Street, which was a part of the old pest-field, although a remnant of the pest-field exists still as the workhouse garden. The original Whitechapel Workhouse was built in 1768 on a burial-ground, and then a plot of land immediately to the north was set aside for a poor ground, and consecrated in 1796. This in turn became the playground of the Davenant Schools, one of which (facing St. Mary's Street) was built in it. A recent addition to the other school has also encroached on the burial-ground. In 1832 196 cholera cases were interred in an adjoining piece of ground, which was probably what is now used as a stoneyard, and is full of carts. The workhouse graveyard, belonging to St. Clement Danes, was in Portugal Street. The workhouse itself was re-adapted and re-opened as King's College Hospital, but the burial-ground was used until its condition was so loathsome, and the burning of coffins and mutilation of bodies was of such every-day occurrence, that it must have been one of the very worst of such places in London. It is now the garden or courtyard and approach, between the hospital and Portugal Street. The burial-ground attached to the Workhouse of St. Saviour's, Southwark (which may have been the old Baptist burial-ground in Bandy Leg Walk which existed in 1729) has a curious history. The workhouse was supplanted by Winchester House, the palace of the bishops when South London was in their diocese, the old Winchester House, nearer the river, having been destroyed. This in time became a hat manufactory, the burial-ground remaining as a garden situated between the building and Southwark Bridge

Road. Finally, the site was secured by the Metropolitan Board of Works for the Central Fire Brigade Station, and what is now left of the burial-ground is the garden or courtyard between the new buildings which face the road and the old house behind them. If the paupers and the bishops and the factory hands did not succeed in frightening away the ghosts of the departed, they must have a sorry time of it now when the call-bells from all parts of London bring out the engines and the men who fight the flames.

Of the parochial "poor grounds" not adjoining workhouses a few are worth noticing. St. Saviour's, Southwark, in addition to the workhouse ground, the College or Almshouse ground, and the churchyard itself, which was from time to time added to, curtailed and used for markets, possessed still another graveyard, the famous Cross Bones ground in Union Street, referred to by Stow as having been made "far from the Parish Church," for the interment of the low women who frequented the neighbourhood. It subsequently became the parish poor ground, and after having been in use, and very much overcrowded, for upwards of 200 years, it was closed by order in Council dated October 24, 1853. In a report upon the state of this ground the previous year, it is stated that "it is crowded with dead, and many fragments of undecayed bones, some even entire, are mixed up with the earth of the mounds over the graves," and it "can be considered only as a convenient place for getting rid of the dead, but it bears no marks of ever having been set apart as a place of Christian sepulture." The Cross Bones ground passed out of the hands of the rector several years ago and was sold as a building site, but building operations were opposed and stopped. Schools were erected in it before it was closed for burials. It has been the subject of much litigation, and it now stands vacant, waiting for some one to purchase it as a playground, and used in the meantime as the site for fairs, merry-go-rounds, and cheap shows.

The "poor ground" for the parish of St. George the Martyr, Southwark, is a square plot of land, now a little public garden, in Tabard Street. It was originally the burial-ground of the adjoining Lock Hospital before that building was removed in 1809 to Knightsbridge, whence, later on, it was again removed to Harrow Road. It is said by some that the little cemetery was even older than the hospital, and may have been used for interments during no less than eight centuries. The Cripplegate "Poor ground," or the "upper churchyard of St. Giles," was in Bear and Ragged Staff Yard (afterwards called Warwick Place) out of Whitecross Street, and was first used in 1636. It was very much overcrowded, so much so that it was more than once shut up for a few years as full, but always re-opened again. A part of the site is now occupied by the northern half of the church of St. Mary, Charterhouse, and by its mission-house, there being only a tar-paved pathway round these buildings to represent the rest of the ground. The church was built in 1864. There are human remains within six inches of the surface of the ground, several having been dug up and put in a vault which is under the mission-house, and the entrance to which is closed with a very large flat stone, bearing the date of 1865. The mission-house is giving way already, and it has large cracks in it, for a vault of this kind is not a good foundation.

The parish of St. James', Clerkenwell, had a very small "poor ground," in Ray Street, which was bought in 1755 for £340, and was consecrated eight years later. It was 800 square yards in area, and was approached through a private house occupied by a butcher, "who had his slaughter-house and stable at the back, and immediately adjoining the burial-ground." In about the year 1824 it was found that several bodies had been exhumed and placed in the stable; this caused a scandal in the neighbourhood, and the man and his business were ruined. When Farringdon Street and the Metropolitan Railway were made, the site of the ground in Ray Street, together with Ray Street itself, entirely disappeared; and the "sleepers of the railway are laid over the sleepers in death." The burial-ground had already been done away with, the Clerkenwell Commissioners, according to Pinks, having taken it for public improvements, when they collected the remains into one spot and erected a plain mausoleum over them.

In early days it seems to have been the custom for patients entering the large hospitals to pay a sum of money down for possible funeral expenses, except in cases of sudden accident. Later on a security given by a householder was considered sufficient, but now no such arrangement is needed. The sum demanded at St. Bartholomew's was 17s. 6d., and at Guy's £1 was paid. At Westminster Hospital and at the Lock (Hyde Park Corner), from which some patients may have been buried in what is now called Knightsbridge Green, no security was asked; but at the Bethlem Hospital an entrance sum of £100 had to be paid for board, funeral expenses, &c. In case of death at a London hospital at the present time, the friends or relations of the deceased are expected to remove and bury the body, and this has often led to a good deal of difficulty, one body being claimed by various people, because the person who buries it can often secure the insurance money. Bodies which are now unclaimed (and at St. Bartholomew's there are about eight in a year) are buried in a cemetery at the cost of the hospital.

CHAPTER X

PRIVATE AND PROMISCUOUS CEMETERIES.

"Praises on tombs are trifles vainly spent,

A man's good name is his best monument."

Epitaph on Pindar's monument in St. Botolph's, Aldersgate Street.

THERE are two chief senses in which the word "private" may be taken. It denotes what belongs to a particular person, family, or institution apart from the general public—thus we say a "private chapel," a "private drive," and so on. It also means that which has been set into being by a private individual, and which is, therefore, a private speculation. Into these two classes I can divide the graveyards which are to be dealt with in this chapter.

The Romans preserved the right of erecting tombs in their country residences. Their very stringent laws prevented them from burying the dead inside the cities (except certain classes of privileged persons), but as long as the interment took place outside the walls, it seems, at one time, to have mattered little where a tomb was set up. This practice was put a stop to in the time of Duillius, and sepulchres were no longer allowed in fields and private grounds, as it was found that the custom was tending to diminish the area of land available for cultivation.

I think that such a practice was never general in London or the surrounding district, but there are a few cases in which something of the sort took place. In Wood's "Ecclesiastical Antiquities" it is stated that there was a cemetery at Somerset House, Strand, for the Catholic members of Queen Henrietta Maria's household (1626). It is certain that the vaults under the palace chapel were used, as they were closed for interments in 1777 (fourteen burials having taken place in fifty-seven years), and if there was also a cemetery, the use of which was in this way restricted, it may fairly be called private. It is possible however that this may have been a part of the original churchyard of St. Mary le Strand. The site has now disappeared, the present building of Somerset House being far more extended than was the old one.

Another curious private ground, also used by Romanists, was the garden of Hundsdon House, the French Embassy, in Blackfriars. In 1623 the floor of a neighbouring Jesuit chapel gave way, and about 95 persons were killed. Stow says that 20 bodies (of the poorer people) were buried on the spot. Malcolm states that 44 were buried in the courtyard before the Ambassador's house, and 15 in his garden. Brayley's version is that some were buried in a burying-place "within the Spanish Ambassador's house in Holborn," and that two great pits were dug, one in the forecourt of the French Ambassador's house, 18 feet by 12 feet, where 44 were interred, the other in the garden behind, 12 feet by 8 feet. Wood gives the number of those buried in these pits as 47. It was, at any rate, a curious and summary way of disposing of the bodies of those who had so suddenly lost their lives.

I only know of one burial-ground in London which is so strictly private as to have only one grave in it. In Retreat Place, Hackney, a quiet corner near the Unitarian Church, there is a row of twelve almshouses, founded by Samuel Robinson in 1812, "for the widows of Dissenting ministers professing Calvinistic doctrines." In front of this establishment is a neatly-kept grass plot, and in the centre of it is a large altar tomb—not erected for the use of the ministers' widows, but containing the mortal remains of Samuel Robinson, who died in 1833, and of his own widow who survived him three years. For my own part I should prefer the enclosure without the grave, but perhaps the widows like to be daily reminded of their benefactor.

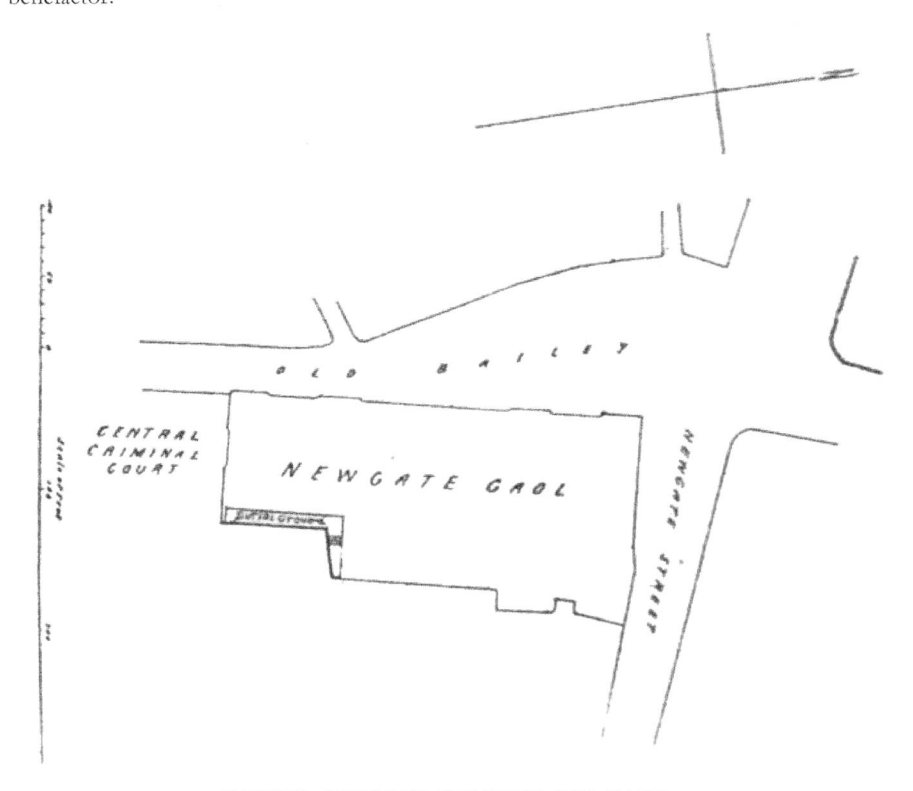

BURIAL-GROUND IN NEWGATE GAOL.

There are, no doubt, many private gardens and yards in London in which burials have taken place, surreptitiously if not openly. Only recently an undertaker was remanded for having been in the habit of temporarily depositing the bodies of stillborn infants in his own back premises until such time as there should be enough to make it worth while for him to give them a decent burial. But, numerous as these instances may be, it is difficult to get any record of them.

Convent burial-grounds are very private, but of these I have already spoken in Chapter II. In Millbank Penitentiary a space, 432 square yards in extent, was set aside as a graveyard, in which there was ordinarily rather over one burial per month. There is a picture of it in Griffith's "Memorials of Millbank," but no description. This particular plot of ground is to be preserved as an open space when the new buildings are erected on the site of the prison; it will probably belong to the London School Board. Newgate burial-ground is still in use. It is a passage in the prison, 10 feet wide and 85 feet long, in which are interred, with a plentiful supply of quicklime, the bodies of those who are executed within the walls. This reminds me of the gallows which stood for so many years at the Tyburn turnpike, the site of which is still marked by a stone in the Bayswater Road, a few yards west of the Marble Arch. Those who were executed here (there were 24 in 1729) were buried on the spot, and this extraordinary burial-ground was situated at the point now occupied by the house at the corner of Edgware Road and Upper Bryanston Street.[7] Mr. W. J. Loftie entirely discredits this story, and says that one jawbone is all that was ever found to represent human remains on this site. On their way to the gallows the poor criminals received a present of a large bowl of ale, called St. Giles' bowl, from the lazar hospital of St. Giles, which was situated close to where the church now stands. And thus they were refreshed on their last sad journey.

7. Smith's "St. Marylebone."

By the close of the last century the London churchyards, and the additional burial-grounds provided by the parishes, were becoming so overcrowded, that it occurred to some adventurers to start cemeteries as private speculations; and it was greatly owing to their existence and to their abuse that the agitation arose which finally led to the passing of the "Act to amend the Laws concerning the Burial of the Dead in the Metropolis," under which the metropolitan burial-grounds were closed. The speculation was found to be a successful one, and was imitated in different parts of London, until by the year 1835 there must have been at least fourteen burial-grounds in London carried on by private persons, besides some additional chapels with vaults under them conducted in the same way. A few of these grounds originated in connection with neighbouring places of worship, but were subsequently bought by private persons. In Central London there were (1) Spa Fields, Clerkenwell; (2) Thomas' burial-ground, Golden Lane; (3) the New City Bunhill Fields, or the City of London burial-ground, Golden Lane. In North London there was (4) the New or Little Bunhill Fields, Church Street, Islington. In East London there were (5) Sheen's burial-ground, Whitechapel; (6) Victoria Park Cemetery, Bethnal Green; (7) the East London Cemetery or Beaumont's ground, Mile End; (8) Globe Fields burial-ground, Mile End Old Town; (9) the North-east London Cemetery, or Cambridge Heath burial-ground, or Peel Grove burial-ground, or Keldy's Ground, Bethnal Green; (10) Gibraltar Walk burial-ground, Bethnal Green; (11) Ebenezer Chapel ground, Ratcliff Highway. And in South London (12) Butler's burial-ground, Horselydown, or St. John's; (13) the New Bunhill Fields, or Hoole and Martin's ground, Deverell Street, New Kent Road; and (14) a ground in Ewer Street, Southwark.

The charges made for interments in these places were generally slightly lower than in the churchyards, in order to attract customers, and those who officiated at the funerals were, in many cases, not ministers of religion at all. In Butler's burial-ground, for instance, the person who read the burial service (of the Church of England) wore a surplice, but he was merely an employé of the undertaker, who also acted as porter. In Hoole and Martin's ground a Mr. Thomas Jenner was employed to officiate at funerals for £20 a year. He also read the burial service of the Church of England, but he was by trade a shoemaker, or a patten-maker, whose shop was close by. The owners of these private grounds were naturally tempted to crowd them to excess, and it is impossible to think of what took place in some of them without shuddering. No doubt practices as vile, as unwholesome, and as irreverent were carried on in many of the churchyards; but the over-crowding of the private grounds is so associated with the idea of private gloating over private gains that it is more repulsive.

One of the most notoriously offensive spots in London was Enon Chapel, Clement's Lane. The chapel was built, and the vaults under it were made, as a speculation by a dissenting minister named Howse. The burial-fees were small, and the place was resorted to by the poor, as many as nine or ten burials often taking place on a Sunday afternoon. The space available for coffins was, at the highest computation, 59 feet by 29 feet, with a depth of 6 feet, and no less than 20,000 coffins were deposited there. In order to accomplish this herculean task it was the common practice to burn the older coffins in the minister's house, under his copper and in his fireplaces. Between the coffins and the floor of the chapel there was nothing but the boards. In time the effluvium in the chapel became intolerable, and no one attended the services, but the vaults were still used for interments, so that "more money was made from the dead than from the living"—a state of affairs which existed in many of the private burial-places of the metropolis. As I shall have to refer again to the condition of these grounds in speaking of the closing of graveyards in London, I will not enlarge upon it any further here, except to quote from the evidence brought before the Select Committee which sat in 1842 to consider the question of Interment in Towns, respecting the Globe Fields burial-ground in Mile End, which is merely one example out of sixty-five examinations.

William Miller, called in and examined.

"1615. CHAIRMAN. What is your occupation?—A jobbing, labouring man, when I can get anything to do."

"1616. Have you been a gravedigger in Globe Fields. Mile End?—Yes."

"1617. Is that a private burying-ground?—Yes."

"1618. To whom does it belong?—Mr. Thomas Tagg."

"1620. Have many pits been dug in it for the depositing of bodies previously interred?—Yes."

"1621. Where did they come from?—Out of the coffins which were emptied for others to go into the graves."

"1623. Were the coffins chucked in with them?—No; they were broken up and burnt."

"1624. Were they bones, or bodies, that were interred?—Yes; the bones and bodies as well."

"1625. Were they entire, or in a state of decomposition?—Some were dry bones, and some were perfect."

"1627. What did you do with them?—Chucked them into the pit."

"1628. What sort of pit?—A deep, square pit, about four feet wide and seven or eight feet deep."

"1629. How many bodies did you chuck in?—I cannot say, they were so numerous; each pit would hold about a dozen."

"1630. How many of these pits did you dig?—I suppose I dug a matter of 20 myself."

"1632. How near to the surface of the earth did these dead bodies or bones come?—Within about two feet."

"1638. What is the size of this ground?—It is rather better than half an acre."

"1639. How many bodies are buried in that ground within a year?—I cannot say; I suppose there are 14,000 have been buried in that ground."

"1640. How long has it been open?—Since the year 1820."

"1641. Do you recollect any circumstance which occurred there about the month of October, 1839?—Yes."

"1642. Will you state it to the Committee?—Some boys were at work there; a policeman on the railroad happened to see them in the act of taking some bones out of baskets, and got a policeman in the police force of the metropolis, and sent him in and seized the boys with a bag of nails and plates of the coffins, going away to sell them, and going to sell the bones."

"1643. To what purpose are the bones applied?—I do not know."

"1644. What is done with the wood of the coffins?—Burnt for their own private use."

"1645. By whom?—By the sexton."

"1648. MR. COWPER. Is it burnt in the sexton's house?—Yes."

"1649. SIR WILLIAM CLAY. What was done with the iron or metal handles of the coffins?—They were burnt on the coffins when I was there, and were thrown out among the ashes about the ground anywhere."

"1653. MR. AINSWORTH. Who performs the burial service over the dead?—A gentleman of the name of Cauch."

"1654. Does he reside there?—No, he resides opposite."

"1655. What is he?—I do not know that he is anything; he has formerly been a shoemaker."

"1656. Does he put on a gown when he buries the dead?—Yes, a surplice."

"1657. What service does he read?—The regular Church service."

"1665. CHAIRMAN. Were you in the habit of performing this grave-digging without the use of spirits?—No; we were obliged to be half groggy to do it, and we cheered one another and sung to one another."

"1666. You found the work so disgusting you were obliged to be half drunk?—Yes."

And so on. Many of the revelations made to this committee are so revolting that they are best forgotten. It is, perhaps, only fair to say that this particular man's evidence was contradicted by Mr. Thomas Tagg, the owner of the ground, but it was subsequently corroborated by other and disinterested witnesses.

PEEL GROVE BURIAL-GROUND, BETHNAL GREEN.

VICTORIA PARK CEMETERY BEFORE BEING LAID OUT.

The fate of these fourteen grounds has been a varied one. Thomas's has gone, and its site is occupied by a large building, chiefly a shoe factory, on the north side of Playhouse Yard, and immediately to the west of the church known as St. Mary's Charterhouse. Sheen's is now the yard of Messrs. Fairclough, carters, off Commercial Road, and there are some stables and sheds in it. It was, some few years back, a cooperage. Peel Grove burial-ground is smaller than it was, and what is left is a builder's yard about an acre in extent, the remainder of the space having been built upon. The very small ground by Ebenezer Chapel, near St. George's in the East, is also a timber-yard, the chapel itself having long since fallen into disuse. Over half of the Globe Fields ground the Great Eastern Railway runs; the remainder is a bare yard, with several miserable tombstones in it and quantities of rubbish. It is fast closed behind an iron gate of colossal proportions, and it daily becomes more neglected and untidy. Little Bunhill Fields in Islington is divided into several parts; one division belongs to the General Post Office, and contains parcels-carts, &c., other pieces are let or sold as builders' yards or are lying vacant. New Bunhill Fields, near New Kent Road, has been through many vicissitudes. It was very much overcrowded with bodies, and in the vault under the chapel burials used to take place "on lease," *i.e.* £1 would be paid for a coffin to be deposited for six months, after which time no inquiries were to be made. As soon as the ground was closed for burials it became a timber-yard, and the chapel in it was used as a saw-mill. Now the sawing goes on in an adjoining shed, and the chapel belongs to the Salvation Army, the graveyard being still covered with high stacks of timber. The City of London ground, in Golden Lane, which was only used for about twenty years, is divided. The part situated in the parish of St. Luke's belongs to Messrs. Sutton & Co., carriers, and is full of carts, the greater part of it being roofed in. The part situated within the city boundary forms the site of the City Mortuary and Coroner's Court, with a neatly-kept yard between the two buildings. Gibraltar Walk burial-ground, Bethnal Green Road, has only had small slices cut off it and doled out as yards, &c., for the surrounding houses. The main portion is a neglected jungle, forming a sort of private garden to the big house which opens on to it, and in which the owner of the ground lives. In order to see Butler's burial-ground it is necessary to go down Coxon's Place, Horselydown, where two yards will be found. One is a small builder's yard, with "Beware of the Dog" on the gate. Once I doubted the existence of the dog, and pushed open this gate, but he was there in full vigour, and I speedily fled. The adjoining yard, which is much larger, is Messrs. Zurhoost's cooperage, and is full of barrels. There were vaults used for burials under three or four of the houses. They can still be seen, and are now, apparently, dwelling-places for the living. The graveyard in Ewer Street has disappeared under the London Bridge and Charing Cross Railway.

The East London Cemetery, in Shandy Street, Mile End, is a recreation ground chiefly for children. So is Spa Fields, Clerkenwell, which was one of the most crowded burial-grounds in London, after having been a fashionable tea-garden, and before being used as a volunteer drill-ground. Both these grounds were secured and laid out by the Metropolitan Public Gardens Association, and are maintained by the London County Council. Such is also the history of Victoria Park Cemetery, a space of 11½ acres, and by far the largest of the private venture burial-grounds. In this ground it was stated that, on every Sunday in the year 1856, 130 bodies were interred. After years of negotiation and much difficulty, the Metropolitan Public Gardens Association secured it, and converted it from a dreary waste of crumbling tombstones and sinking graves into a most charming little park for the people of Bethnal Green. It was opened by H.R.H. the Duke of York in July, 1894, and the County Council maintains it, having re-christened it Meath Gardens.

VICTORIA PARK CEMETERY WHEN FIRST LAID OUT.

It need hardly be pointed out that in very few of the spaces I have just described are any tombstones to be found. To a casual observer they are utterly unrecognisable as burial-grounds, and it is many years since such relics can have existed in them. When, for instance, a burial-ground becomes a builder's yard, tombstones are very much in the way, and they are soon converted into paving-stones. Some years ago a few inscriptions were still legible on the stones which paved the passage to Spa Fields from Exmouth Street, but by this time even these must be worn away. But if it is denied by the owners of these yards that they are burial-grounds there is one method of proving it which soon dispels all doubt, and that is by digging down into the soil. It will not be necessary to make any deep excavation before the spade turns up some earth mixed with human remains, which, once seen, are always recognisable.

Archbishop Herring adopted this plan, as he was anxious to know if any burials had taken place in what was always known as the "burying-ground" of Lambeth Palace, on the north side of the chapel, by the site of the smaller cloisters. In fact he had the whole space dug over, but without success, for no signs of human remains were found; and it is probable that the interments which took place within the palace were all under the chapel.

CHAPTER XI

THE CLOSING OF THE BURIAL-GROUNDS AND VAULTS.

"These laugh at Jeat, and Marble put for signs,

To sever the good fellowship of dust,

And spoil the meeting. What shall point out them,

When they shall bow, and kneel, and fall down flat

To kiss those heaps which now they have in trust?"

GEORGE HERBERT.

BY the commencement of the present century the minds of thoughtful men on the Continent, in America, and in England, began to be exercised about the overcrowded state of the graveyards in the towns, and their very unwholesome effect upon those who lived near them.

We owe the agitation which finally led to the closing of the London graveyards mainly to the untiring zeal of a surgeon of Drury Lane, George Alfred Walker. His work lay amongst the poor of that district, and he was led to believe that the frequent occurrence of what he called typhus fever, and similar maladies, was due in great measure to the large number of overcrowded burial-grounds which existed in the neighbourhood. He made a very careful study of the subject, he gathered information from France, Germany, and other countries, he visited a large number of the worst graveyards in London, and made searching inquiries respecting them. Having become familiar with the practices that were carried on in these places, he brought out a book dealing with the whole question in the year 1839, the title-page of which fully explains its purpose. It is as follows:—

"GATHERINGS FROM GRAVEYARDS,

PARTICULARLY THOSE OF LONDON.

With a concise History of the modes of Interment among

different Nations from the earliest periods,

and a detail of dangerous

and fatal results

produced by the unwise and revolting custom

of inhuming the dead in the midst of the living.

By G. A. WALKER, Surgeon."

The question was taken up from purely philanthropic motives. Walker was not connected with, or interested in, any particular Cemetery, but he was "fully convinced of the necessity for *legislative interference* to destroy the present dangerous system."

He had precedents to go upon, for as early as the year 1765 a decree was made by the Parliament of Paris, closing all cemeteries and churchyards within the city, and providing for the formation of eight cemeteries in the suburbs; and in 1774 a further decree was made prohibiting the re-opening of vaults, similar action being subsequently taken in other French towns. Nor was France alone to be admired. Precautions of the same kind were adopted from time to time in Rome and other cities of Italy, in Denmark, in New York, and even in Dublin; but the London burial-grounds still continued to be in constant use.

Walker collected details of many cases of death and illness directly attributable to contact with human remains in a state of putrefaction. It was certain that gravediggers held their lives in their hands. The more experienced of them, when they "bored" or "tapped" coffins, immediately fled to a distance, and remained away until they considered that the harmful exhalations would have been sufficiently distributed into the air for them to continue their unpleasant work in comparative safety. Another custom was to burn papers, &c., in graves and vaults, while some men were in the habit of holding rue and garlic in their mouths. But they generally suffered from bad health, were frequently seriously ill, and sometimes died from the direct effects of the poison they had inhaled. They were also much addicted to drink, and very many were accustomed to say that they could not do their work without the help of spirits.

After making the following general statement, Walker carefully described between forty and fifty of the most crowded of the metropolitan burial-places, and especially those in his own district: "Although willing to admit that the neighbourhood of slaughter-houses—the decomposition of vegetable substances—the narrowness of the streets, and the filth and poverty of some of the inhabitants, greatly contributed to the furtherance of the mischief (typhus fever), I felt convinced that the grand cause of all the evil was the immediate proximity of the burial-places, public as well as private." It is quite unnecessary to repeat the descriptions, they are much alike; I will only give one as a specimen, which is free from obnoxious details.

"*St. Ann's, Soho.*—There is only one burying-ground belonging to this parish; it is walled in on the side next to Prince's Street; close to this wall is the bone house; rotten coffin wood and fragments of bones are scattered about. Some graves are only partly filled up, and left in that state, intended, probably, for paupers. The ground is very full, and is considerably raised above its original level; it is overlooked by houses thickly inhabited. The inhabitants of the neighbourhood have frequently complained of the past and present condition of this place. The numbers of dead here are immense."

Some of his descriptions were thought at the time to be exaggerated, but they were fully corroborated in the evidence given before the Parliamentary Committee which sat in 1842.

Such a note as the following is instructive: "Ground in immediate proximity to this place" (Bermondsey Churchyard) "is advertised to be let on lease for building purposes." And yet some of the very burial-grounds themselves have since become the sites for streets and houses!

It would not be fair to give the reader the impression that Walker was the first to speak of the unwholesome condition of the London graveyards. Here is a quotation from a sermon preached by Bishop Latimer in 1552: "The citizens of Naim had their burying-places without the city, which, no doubt, is a laudable thing; and I do marvel that London, being so great a city, hath not a burial-place without: for no doubt it is an unwholesome thing to bury within the city, especially at such a time, when there be great sicknesses, and many die together. I think verily that many a man taketh his death in St. Paul's Churchyard, and this I speak of experience; for I myself, when I have been there on some mornings to hear the sermons, have felt such an ill-savoured, unwholesome savour, that I was the worse for it a great while after; and I think no less—but it is the occasion of great sickness and disease." And from his time onwards allusions were made, in sermons and discourses, by ministers and physicians, to the dangers of contact with decaying animal substances.

CHURCHYARD OF ST. ANN, SOHO, IN 1810.

To turn from London for a moment. It is stated in Roger's "Social Life in Scotland" that when Queen Mary visited Dundee in 1594 she found that "the deid of the Naill burgh is buryit in the midst thereof, quhairin the common traffic of merchandise is usit, and that throw occasion of the said burial, pest, and other contagious sickness is engenderit." The evil was remedied by granting to the burgh as a place of sepulchre the site of the Greyfriars Monastery.

Sir Christopher Wren, when considering the question of the rebuilding of London after the Great Fire, made some very wise remarks upon the question of intramural interments. He wished to see suburban cemeteries established, and burials in churches and churchyards discontinued, partly because he considered the constant raising of the level of a churchyard rendered the church damp and more liable to premature decay. But Wren's plans for rebuilding the city were not carried out; they were approved by the King and Parliament, but disapproved by the Corporation; and this scheme of his respecting the practice of burial fell through with the rest. The churches were rebuilt on the old sites, the churchyards were again used, and the sites of several of those churches which were not rebuilt became additional burial-grounds for the parishes. And yet, in the return published in 1833, it is curious to find that only one place is described as being "very full of bodies," the churchyard of St. John's, Clerkenwell. There was no great desire on the part of those connected with the parishes to increase their burial accommodation.

Walker stuck to his ground manfully. He gathered round him a few of the leading men of the day, who formed themselves into a Society for the Abolition of Burials in Towns, and he delivered a series of able lectures upon the subject and continued to make inquiries and to expose practices carried on in various grounds. Spa Fields, for instance, was taken as a specimen, and a pamphlet was issued showing how it was the custom to burn bodies behind a brick enclosure, and how the gravestones were moved about to give an appearance of emptiness in certain parts of the ground. It was computed that, by burning coffins, mutilating remains, and using vast quantities of quicklime, at least 80,000 corpses had been put in a space fitted to hold 1,000.

In 1842 and 1843 a Royal Commission was sitting upon the question of the Health of Towns and the Sanitary Condition of the Labouring Classes, and a Select Committee was appointed "to consider the expediency of framing some Legislative Enactments (due respect being paid to the rights of the Clergy), to remedy the evils arising from the Interment of Bodies within the Precincts of large Towns, or of Places densely populated." The following were the members of the Committee: Mr. Mackinnon (Chairman), Lord Ashley, Colonel Fox, Mr. Thomas Duncombe, Mr. Evelyn Denison, Sir William Clay, Sir Robert Harry Inglis, Mr. Ainsworth, Mr. Beckett, Lord Mahon, Mr. Cowper, Colonel Acton, Mr. Kemble, Mr. Vernon, and Mr. Redhead Yorke; and they sat from 17th of March till 5th of May, 1842, and conducted sixty-five examinations. Amongst the witnesses who gave evidence were clergymen, dissenting ministers, medical men, including Sir Benjamin Brodie and Mr. Walker, sextons, gravediggers, residents in the neighbourhood of burial-grounds and others, with the Bishop of London (C. J. Blomfield). I have already quoted from these evidences in the previous chapter, and they do not vary very much. I will only therefore give a few extracts from the Report of the Committee:—"After long and patient investigation, Your Committee cannot arrive at any other conclusion than that the nuisance of Interments in large Towns, and the injury arising to the Health of the Community from the practice, are fully proved.... No time ought to be lost by the Legislature in applying a remedy.... The Evidence has also exhibited the singular instance of the most wealthy, moral, and civilised community in the world tolerating a practice and an abuse which has been corrected for years by nearly all other civilised nations in every part of the globe." Then follow resolutions respecting the provision by parishes, either single or amalgamated, of cemeteries; the fees which it would be desirable to charge; the due consideration to be shown to those who desired burial in unconsecrated ground; the exceptions to be made in the cases of some family vaults, of the Cathedral and the Abbey, and of certain cemeteries which had recently been formed, &c., with the final remark: "That the duty of framing and introducing a Bill on the principles set forth in the foregoing Resolutions, would be most efficiently discharged by Her Majesty's Government, and that it is earnestly recommended to them by the Committee." And yet it was not until 1852 that Mr. Mackinnon's Bill was introduced and the Act of Parliament was passed, entitled an Act to Amend the Laws concerning the Burial of the Dead in the Metropolis, commonly known as the Burials Act, 15 and 16 Victoria.

Then the Home Secretary was besieged with memorials and letters from those who resided in various parts of London, praying for the Act to be put in force in the burial-grounds in their own neighbourhoods, besides applications for permission to open cemeteries on the outskirts of the town. The same dreary and miserable stories of the overcrowding of graveyards and the indecent practices carried on in them were again brought to light, and it must not be supposed that the grounds in the west of London were any better than those in the centre, the east, or the south. The description given by the memorialists (five medical men) of the burial-ground belonging to St. George's, Hanover Square, which is situated on the north side of Bayswater Road, together with the letters written about it, could hardly be exceeded. And yet this ground was, or rather is, in a fashionable neighbourhood, close to the Marble Arch, and surrounded by houses let at very high rentals. It is certain that it was a common custom to move freshly-buried bodies from the more expensive part of the ground to the cheaper part, used for paupers and others, thus making room for more graves for which the higher fees were paid. Lawrence Sterne, who wrote "The Sentimental Journey," was buried here. I hope his remains did not have an unsentimental one.

From west, east, north, and south the same lament was heard, and the same petition came from other cities and towns in England. It was a common topic for the newspapers and journals, and it is hardly possible to look through any of them, published between 1850 and 1855, without finding references to the graveyards, or notices of their being closed by order in Council. An anonymous poem called "City Graves," appeared in *Household Words* on December 14, 1850. It has seven verses, of which I will give three:—

"Within those walls, the peace of death—

Without, life's ceaseless din;

The toiler, at his work, can see

The tombs of his mouldering kin;

And the living without grow, day by day,

More like the dead within.

"I saw from out the earth peep forth

The white and glistening bones,

With jagged ends of coffin planks,

That e'en the worm disowns;

And once a smooth round skull rolled on,

Like a football, on the stones.

"Too late the wished-for boon has come,

Too late wiped out the stain,—

No Schedule shall restore to health,

No Act give life again

To the thousands whom, in bygone years,

Our City Graves have slain!"

On the 13th of January, 1853, Islington Churchyard was closed for burials, and from that time forward the notices were issued for the cessation of interments in vaults and graveyards all over London; and the list which was printed of all the burial-grounds in London still open for interments on January 1, 1855 (and in many of these only the existing vaults were to be used), was quite a short one. By that date eight of the large cemeteries had been opened and were in use.

When once closed for burials the question naturally arose as to what was to be done with the grounds. The following clause was inserted into one of the Burial Acts (18 and 19 Vict.):—

"18. In every case in which any order in Council has been or shall hereafter be issued for the discontinuance of burials in any churchyard or burial-ground, the Burial Board or Churchwardens, as the case may be, shall maintain such churchyard or burial-ground of any parish in decent order, and also do the necessary repair of the walls and other fences thereof, and the costs and expenses shall be repaid by the Overseers, upon the certificate of the Burial Board or Churchwardens, as the case may be, out of the rate made for the relief of the Poor of the parish or place in which such churchyard or burial-ground is situate, unless there shall be some other fund legally chargeable with such costs and expenses."

Here at once comes in the difficulty of ownership or guardianship, and it is not always understood by the rector or vicar of a church that he, during his incumbency, has the sole right of using any grounds enclosed within the churchyard fence or wall, and that these grounds are not, as is frequently supposed, under the joint control of the incumbent and churchwardens. This is clearly set forth in the following quotations from the book of Church Law, 4th edition, page 322:—

"By his induction into the real and corporeal possession of his benefice in general, a Rector or Vicar becomes invested, in particular, with freehold rights in all the land and buildings which are enclosed within the churchyard fence or wall."

"The rights thus acquired carry with them the exclusive right of access to the Church, and also (saving any established right of way) to the Churchyard, so that no one can lawfully exclude him from them, nor enter them of their own right, but only by his permission, so long as Incumbent."

Yet it is the Burial Board or the churchwardens who are to see that a burial-ground or a churchyard is kept "in decent order," and to repair the walls and fences; and if a churchyard is not kept in such order, or is used as a storing yard or for any other unsuitable purposes, both the incumbent and the churchwardens are evidently in fault. But although there have been some cases of gross neglect the London churchyards have, on the whole, been kept fairly well as far as the walls or fences and the tombstones are concerned. A few have certainly degenerated into little less than rubbish heaps, but others have been maintained with great care. The Burial Boards have been conscientious in this respect pretty generally over London, but there are not very many disused burial-grounds under the control of the Burial Boards. A few churchyards, chiefly in the City, have been curtailed for the widening of roads, or altogether sacrificed for railways or new streets; a few additional parochial burial-grounds have also disappeared, and a few, but very few, have been misappropriated and let or sold as builders' yards, &c. The case was, however, far different, where an unconsecrated burial-ground was in private hands or belonged to three or four chapel trustees, for then the temptation to raise money on it was very great. Nearly all the private grounds and a large number of the Dissenters' grounds were turned to account, as I have already shown in Chapters VII. and X.

BATTERSEA CHURCHYARD ABOUT 1830.

So the churchyards remained, useless, closed and dreary, no one went into them, the children gazed through the palings and their parents deposited wastepaper, dead cats, rotten food, old clothes, &c., in them, and it was twenty years after they had been shut up before any of the disused graveyards were converted into public gardens. It must, of course, be borne in mind that, when first closed, these grounds were very unwholesome, but twenty years did, at any rate, a good deal towards ameliorating their condition, and now that another twenty years have passed we may safely say that no evil effects can accrue from letting people walk about in them, people, that is, who already live with these grounds in their midst. And there is no more sure way of hastening their improvement than by importing fresh soil and planting trees, shrubs and flowers.

ST. JAMES'S, PENTONVILLE, IN JANUARY, 1896.

The closing of the burial-grounds included the closing of the vaults. There is hardly a church in London, and but few chapels, with a graveyard attached, which had not also vaults used for interments under the building, and there are many churches and chapels which had vaults but not graveyards.

The earliest burials took place in the churchyards, the south side being always the favourite. It seems originally to have been customary to bury only stillborn infants, felons and suicides on the north side of the building. It became a fashion of later times to bury in or under the church, and the first place used was the porch. But when once the custom was established the inside of the church became the privileged place, and the most honoured dead were laid nearest the altar. The ancient crypts, such as those at St. Bartholomew's and Clerkenwell, were not, I imagine, originally intended for burying in, although coffins were put in them later on. But the vaults, such as those under the City churches and the parish churches outside the City, were expressly made for the purpose, a few having been used for beer or wine instead of bodies.

Many vaults were private, such as "Lady Jersey's Vault" and "Holden's Vault," both in St. Bride's, Fleet Street, and in this same church there is a "Doctor's vault." St. Clement Danes and other churches have a "Rector's vault," and St. Saviour's, Southwark, can boast of a "Bishop's vault." The bodies from under some of the City churches which have been pulled down were moved to others; the coffins from St. Michael, Crooked Lane, were divided between St. Edmund King and Martyr and St. Mary Woolnoth, and those that went to the latter place have had a second removal, the vaults having to be cleared out a few years ago. In many places there were vaults under the vestries, the adjoining schools, almshouses, the sextons' houses, &c., and at Lambeth, among the places of interment closed by order in Council, was a "vault under the station-house." A list of the London churches and chapels which were provided with burial-vaults, but not with graveyards, will be found in Appendix C. It is not unlikely that many of these will have, in time, to be cleared out. In some cases the coffins or remains have already been collected and reinterred in cemeteries, the one at Woking having been especially favoured. They are very liable to become a nuisance, and are far more dangerous to the living than the human remains under the plots of ground open to the air.

CHAPTER XII

GRAVEYARDS AS PUBLIC GARDENS.

"Some young children sported among the tombs, and hid from each other, with laughing faces. They had an infant with them, and had laid it down asleep upon a child's grave, in a little bed of leaves.... Nell drew near and asked them whose grave it was. The child answered that that was not its name; it was a garden—his brother's. It was greener, he said, than all the other gardens, and the birds loved it better because he had been used to feed them."—*From the "Old Curiosity Shop,"* DICKENS.

THE late Sir Edwin Chadwick, in the Report which he drew up in 1843 (ten years before the burial-grounds were closed), wrote the following significant words:—"The only observation I at present submit upon the space of ground now occupied (as burial-grounds) is that it would serve hereafter advantageously to be kept open as public ground." Happily he lived long enough to see some of these very graveyards upon which he had reported converted into open gardens. Their conversion and their preservation have gone hand in hand. Partly to facilitate their being acquired as open spaces an Act was framed, by the passing of which it became illegal to build on any ground that had been set aside for interments. And there could be no better way of securing the preservation of a burial-ground from encroachment or misuse, than by laying it out and handing it over to a public body to be maintained for the benefit of the public under the Open Spaces Act. Once given to the people, the people are not likely to give up an inch of it again without a struggle.

By the year 1877 seven disused burial-grounds in London had been converted into public gardens; those of St. Botolph's, Bishopsgate, St. George's in the East, and the Wesleyan graveyard adjoining (forming one ground), the additional ground for St. Martin's in the Fields in Drury Lane, St. John's, Waterloo Bridge Road, and St. Pancras' old churchyard, with the adjoining graveyard belonging to St. Giles' in the Fields (forming one ground). These may be called the five pioneer gardens. But St. Botolph's was closed again for several years, and St. Martin's for a short time, and St. Pancras' and St. Giles' had to have much more done to them before they became attractive open spaces, so that the one which really stands out as the recreation ground that has had the longest existence is St. George's, for this has been in constant use for twenty years. The Rev. Harry Jones, in his books, "East and West London," and "Fifty Years," describes the difficulties he went through to get the vestry to agree to the scheme, and to secure a faculty for laying out the ground. He and his co-workers were in the Consistory Court for two days, but they succeeded in the end, the wall between the churchyard and the Nonconformist burial-ground was done away with, and a most valuable new thoroughfare was opened out from Cable Street to St. George's Street (Ratcliff Highway). Thus a precedent was created, and the way was made easier for others, including the Dean and Chapter of St. Paul's, to lay out their churchyards. Since that time, 1875, the part adjoining the church has also been opened, the whole ground being about three acres in area, and it is always bright and neat and full of people enjoying the seats, the grass, the flowers, and the air.

CHURCHYARD OF ST. GEORGE'S IN THE EAST.

Mr. Loftie has written: "Of St. George's in the East there is not much to be said." He refers to the church, but even this, one of Hawksmoor's chief works, is rather too lightly disposed of. Of the parish there is indeed much to tell. No other church in London can boast of nineteenth-century riots continued Sunday after Sunday for eighteen months, necessitating the presence of police in the sacred building. No other parish ever contained a Danish and a Swedish church, with the bones of Emmanuel Swedenborg. St. George's is in touch with all corners of the globe, for the London Docks contain countless stores of treasures from the east and the west, the north and the south. Here several of the chief of those commonly known as the "broad churchmen" of the day have served as curates; and here the famous life of Father Lowder was lived for twenty-four years, while the famous church of St. Peter's, London Docks, arose in the southern part of the parish,—Father Lowder, of whom the Rev. Harry Jones, in a memorial sermon, has said: "He was simply fearless.... He ever meant what he said, and said what he meant.... The mention of him meets the most sacred moods of the soul." And the pioneer garden is still unique in being an amalgamation of a churchyard and a dissenting burial-ground. How different it is from what it was once like may be gathered from the following description in *Household Words* of November 16, 1850: "The graveyard was dank and clayey, and air blew coldly through the masts and rigging of the shipping moored in the Thames and the Docks." The curate comes to the parish, the curate who eventually built Christ Church, Watney Street, dispirited and discouraged. He had fancied it was to St. George's, Hanover Square, he was going! And "the occasional funeral duty of the country was changed for the constant day by day, week by week, repetitions of a gorged London graveyard," to which "the close courts and poverty-stricken streets of his parish sent every year many hundred tenants." Then the churchyard, like all the others in London, was closed, and became the usual useless cat-walk, with high walls around, and blackening tombstones, until the day when those negotiations began which resulted in the present charming garden. And this is a story which has now been repeated in every division of London.

In the year 1882 the Earl of Meath (then Lord Brabazon) started the Metropolitan Public Gardens Association. It began on this wise. The Kyrle Society and the National Health Society had each an Open Spaces sub-committee, Miss Octavia Hill, of the Kyrle Society, having always been a prominent supporter of the movement for promoting open spaces, "outdoor sitting-rooms" she called them, in poor districts. But the funds of these committees were very small, and the work they could accomplish, except in the matter of influencing public opinion, very limited. They made grants of seats to a few churchyards which were being laid out, and joined in deputations to public bodies respecting open spaces, &c. Lord and Lady Brabazon had laid out the churchyards of St. John, Hoxton, and St. Mary, Haggerston, and had taken much interest in the formation of other grounds, such as the

Brewers' Garden at Stepney, which mainly owed its existence to the Rev. Sydney Vatcher, present vicar of St. Philip's; and Lord Brabazon felt that there was room and need for a separate association for preserving, acquiring, and laying out open spaces, and for promoting similar objects. He therefore invited representatives of the Kyrle and National Health Societies, and others interested in the matter, to meet him and to discuss the advisability of sinking their own committees in a new and separate body, or rather of amalgamating their efforts in the same direction. The National Health Society only too gladly acquiesced, and from that time forward passed on all work connected with open spaces to the new body, Mr. Ernest Hart, Chairman of their Council, becoming the first vice-chairman of the Metropolitan Public Gardens Association. There are now eighteen. But Miss Octavia Hill held back. And this is the reason why there is still an Open Spaces branch of the Kyrle Society, and why on the title-page of the annual reports of the Gardens Association the words "In connection with the National Health Society," are always inserted. The following graveyards have been laid out as gardens by the Kyrle Society in London—St. Peter's, Bethnal Green, E., St. George's, Bloomsbury, W. C. (the Metropolitan Public Gardens Association giving £100 towards the laying out of each of these), St. George the Martyr, Bloomsbury, W.C., and the burial-ground of St. Nicholas', Deptford, in Wellington Street, S.E.—four very useful grounds.

CHURCHYARD OF ST. BOTOLPH, ALDGATE.

The new association was formed in November, 1882, and soon flourished amazingly. By the end of 1895 it had carried through upwards of 320 successful undertakings, had 60 other works on hand, and had made offers and attempts, without success, respecting about 200 schemes. But the indirect work of the Association has also been most valuable; the tone of public opinion on the subject of open spaces has entirely changed during the past twelve years, and this is due, in great measure, to the untiring exertions of the Earl of Meath and his co-workers. New Acts of Parliament, including the Disused Burial-grounds Act, have been passed, useful clauses have been inserted in the Open Spaces Acts, and several Bills threatening open spaces have been opposed and extinguished. The Association has worked with the Commons Preservation and Kyrle Societies to forward many most important schemes; it has secured, after much labour, the opening on Saturdays of upwards of 200 Board School playgrounds, and its influence upon the work of the public bodies has been wonderful. It is, for instance, scarcely too much to say that a week seldom goes by without some communication passing between the Association and the London County Council.

But my subject is graveyards only, and the following is a list of those that have been laid out as recreation grounds and opened by the Metropolitan Public Gardens Association since the Spring of 1885:—

1. St. Bartholomew's Churchyard, Bethnal Green, E.
2. The East London Cemetery, E.

3. Holy Trinity Churchyard, Rotherhithe, S.E.
4. St. Paul's Churchyard, Shadwell, E.
5. Spa Fields, Clerkenwell, E.C.
6. St. John at Hackney Churchyard, E. (a part).
7. St. Mary le Strand Ground in Russell Court, W.C.
8. St. James's Churchyard, Bermondsey, S.E.
9. Holy Trinity Churchyard, Mile End, E.
10. St. Martin's in the Fields Churchyard, W.C.
11. St. George's Churchyard, Camberwell, S.E.
12. St. Dunstan's Churchyard, Stepney, E.
13. St. Anne's Churchyard, Limehouse, E.
14. Trinity Chapel-ground, Poplar, E.
15. St. Alphege Churchyard, Greenwich, S.E.
16. Seward Street Burial-ground, E.C.
17. St. James's Churchyard, Ratcliff, E.
18. St. Botolph's Churchyard, Aldgate, E.
19. St. Ann's Churchyard, Soho, W.
20. Shoreditch Old Ground, Hackney Road, E.
21. Christ Church Churchyard, Spitalfields, E.
22. All Saints' Churchyard, Poplar, E. (a part).
23. St. Botolph's Churchyard, Bishopsgate, E.C.
24. St. Katharine Coleman Churchyard, E.C.
25. St. Olave's Churchyard, Silver Street, E.C.
26. Victoria Park Cemetery, or Meath Gardens, E.
27. Allhallows' Churchyard, London Wall, E.C.
28. St. Mary's Churchyard, Bow, E. (a part).
29. St. Peter's Churchyard, Walworth, S.E.
30. St. Mary's Churchyard, Woolwich, S.E.[8]

[8]. The laying out of four more churchyards is in hand.

The other grounds laid out by the Association have been squares, vacant sites, and churchyards not used for interments. In addition to these, grants have been given, amounting to many hundred pounds, towards the laying out of some fourteen graveyards, and seats, &c., for another twenty-eight, besides which the Association has secured the opening of many more and has saved others from being built upon.

One year the income of the Association amounted to over £11,000. This was due to a shower of wealth from the Mansion House Fund for the Employment of the Unemployed. The Earl of Meath, at the Mansion House Committee, boldly promised, with a smiling face and a sinking heart, that if a grant were made to it the Association would find labour at once and use up the money in wages. I remember being sent for to Lancaster Gate in this emergency. It was no easy matter then and there to provide the work, and the money could not be spent on materials. But within a few weeks hundreds of men were employed, and their food arranged for into the bargain. This process was repeated the following winter (1887-8), but since then the Mansion House Funds have been smaller and their distribution far more careful, while the Association has had to depend for its income upon the subscriptions and donations of its members and friends.

There are now within the metropolitan area ninety burial-grounds actually dedicated to the public as recreation grounds, and being maintained as such under the Open Spaces Act of 1881, or by trustees, or under agreement with the vicar, &c., including four that are Board School playgrounds. To those who remember these places before they were converted the transformation is wonderful. One Sunday in the year 1878, the Rev. H. R. Haweis told his congregation at St. James's, Westmoreland Street, that in a hasty walk through their own parish burial-ground in Paddington Street, Marylebone, he had met "orange-peel, rotten eggs, cast-off hair-plaits, oyster-shells, crockery, newspapers with bread and meat, dead cats and five live ones," and that on the grave of one Elizabeth Smith, "in the very centre of the churchyard," he found "twelve old kettles, two coal-scuttles, three old hats, and an umbrella." Some of the congregation doubted it, but they went to look, and found it true. This particular ground was laid out as a garden by the St. Marylebone Vestry in 1886, the Association providing £200 and the wages of the labourers. I remember, in a paper I wrote some ten years ago, describing a similar ground (and there were, and still are, many such in London)— I think it was St. James's, Clerkenwell. This is also now a neat garden, towards the laying out of which, in 1890, the Association gave £50 and several seats.

A CORNER OF ST. JOHN'S GARDEN, BENJAMIN STREET.

I have already referred, in previous chapters, to some of the more interesting of the graveyards which have been laid out as open spaces. There is a very charming little garden in Benjamin Street, near Farringdon Road, which belongs to the parish of St. John's, Clerkenwell. It was consecrated in 1755 by the Bishop of Lincoln, acting for the Bishop of London, having been conveyed to trustees as an extra parochial burial-ground, the site being a gift to the parish by the will of Simon Michell, who died in 1750. After being closed for burials it fell into the hands of a member of the Clerkenwell Vestry, and was covered with workshops and rubbish until the then Rector, the Rev. W. Dawson, instituted proceedings against him, secured the land, laid it out by public subscription (in 1881), and maintained it at his private expense. It is now in the hands of trustees, and the Holborn District Board of Works and the Clerkenwell Vestry contribute towards its upkeep. Several other gardens in London have had a somewhat similarly checkered history. The burial-ground in Hackney Road belonging to Shoreditch has a quaint old building in it, once the parish watch-house, and used as a temporary hospital at the time of the cholera visitation. A new-gateway has lately been made at St. James's, Ratcliff, leading into the churchyard garden, erected as a memorial to the late vicar, the Rev. R. K. Arbuthnot, who spent very many years in the parish and died in harness. A special service was held on November 30, 1895, when the choir walked in procession through the grounds, the ceremony ending by the singing of the Rev. H. R.

Haweis's hymn, "The Homeland." The gate was dedicated by the Rural Dean, Prebendary Turner, present Rector of St. George's in the East, and opened by Sir Walter Besant. Greenwich and Woolwich Churchyards, which were laid out by the Association, the cost of the latter being borne by Mr. Passmore Edwards, are both fine gardens, Woolwich is especially attractive, as it stands high above the river, with an extensive view. H.R.H. the Duke of Cambridge opened Greenwich Churchyard, and H.R.H. the Duchess of Fife opened that of Woolwich. St. James's Churchyard, Bermondsey, was extensively used for airing clothes before the Association laid it out.

In this matter of the conversion of churchyards into public gardens there has, indeed, been a wonderful change in public opinion. It used to be necessary to visit the clergy and to ask them to allow the grounds to be laid out, with the result, usually, that the request or offer was declined. But a new race of clergy seems to be springing up, and such men as the present Rectors of Woolwich, Walworth, and Bethnal Green no sooner came into possession of their livings than they wrote to the Association, begging that their churchyards might be taken in hand. The new Rector of Bethnal Green, already well known as the "head" of Oxford House, not only asked the Association to lay out his churchyard but also made a Christmas present of it to the Vestry, and ere long it will be a most useful open space. And this has happened in very many places, most of the parish churchyards being new public gardens, except Camberwell, Rotherhithe, Battersea, Clapham, Wandsworth, Kensington, Wapping, Homerton, and a few others; but there are still several district churchyards which it would be very advantageous to lay out.

To return to some of the quainter spots. In the burial-ground of St. George the Martyr, Bloomsbury, there stands a private gentleman's dissecting-room. Hackney Churchyard includes the ground surrounding the tower of the older church (St. Augustine's), while Bermondsey Churchyard includes the cemetery of the Abbey. The little playground in Russell Court, Drury Lane, which was a graveyard attached to the parish of St. Mary le Strand, is immortalised as "Tom all alones" in Dickens' "Bleak House." This was "that there berryin' ground," where, said poor Jo, "'they laid him as was werry good to me'"—the place "with houses looking on on every side, save where a reeking little tunnel of a court gives access to the iron gate....

"'He was put there,' says Jo, holding to the bar and looking in.

"'Where? Oh, what a scene of horror!'

"'There,' says Jo, pointing, 'over yinder—among them piles of bones, and close to that there kitchen winder! ... Look at the rat! Hi! Look! There he goes! Ho! into the ground.'"

When the Association got hold of it, it was little else than a heap of decaying rubbish thrown from the surrounding houses, and the carcases of eighteen cats were removed at once. It is now an asphalted recreation ground, and is often crowded with children using the swings and the seats. But it has lately lost its characteristic appearance, the surrounding houses have been pulled down, and it is at present "opened out." The "kitchen winder" no longer leads into a kitchen, though the iron gate is still in its original state, with the worn step upon which Lady Deadlock's life was brought to a close.

It must not be supposed that there has been no opposition to the conversion of graveyards into public gardens. Many owners have refused to allow it, and from time to time (though the times are now getting very few and far between) letters have been written to the newspapers pointing out the danger of admitting the public into them. But the burial-grounds are there—in the midst of crowded streets—whether we like them or no, and they become far more wholesome when fresh soil is imported, good gravel paths made, and the ground drained, and when grass, flowers, trees, and shrubs take the place of the rotting rubbish. A certain gentleman, somewhat well known, wrote on several occasions to the *Times*, arguing against the laying out of churchyards, and saying that a "blue haze" hung about a square in New York which once was a burial-ground. But no blue haze hangs about our gardens in London, children are born and bred by the hundred in those very kitchens whose "winders" look upon them, and they are of the utmost value as open spaces in all parts of the town.

THE CHURCHYARD OF ALLHALLOWS, LONDON WALL.

On the other hand, every consideration should be shown for those whose objections to the transformation have been on sentimental grounds. In Appendix D will be seen the steps to be taken for laying out and throwing open to the public a disused churchyard or burial-ground, and from this those who are not already aware of it may notice two points—first, that any person interested in any particular tombstone has the right and the power to prevent such tombstone from being moved; second, that the inscriptions on the stones, and their exact positions in a ground to be laid out, are preserved in perpetuity in the office of the Registrar of the Diocese; whereas the actual inscriptions themselves on the tombstones, whether a ground is closed, or open, are daily becoming more defaced, and when it is closed there is no such record of them and no guarantee that they may not be broken, shifted, or stolen. Nor must it be imagined that the tombstones in all graveyard gardens have necessarily to be moved. It is only where they are standing so thickly that the ground cannot be laid out otherwise. In some places, such as Spa Fields, not a single gravestone existed when it came into the hands of the Association; in others, such as St. Mary le Strand, there were only a few and these already on the walls; while in others, again, such as Holy Trinity, Rotherhithe, there were so few that it was not necessary to get a faculty to remove them, but they were left *in situ*. There is rather an amusing tombstone at All Saints', Poplar. It stands tall and solitary in the middle of a path, which could not be diverted because of other stones; and when the path was made this particular monument was left in the very centre. I think the best way of disposing of tombstones is by putting them against the walls, even if it necessitates two or three rows. They are very dismal standing in groups, as at St. James's, Hampstead Road, and the wall of headstones at St. Luke's, Chelsea, is by no means attractive. Nor are the "dome" and "trophy" at St. Pancras, to which I have already referred. In St. John's Garden, Horseferry Road, they are cemented into an even row against the wall, and look as if they would last for ever.

I would not say that a converted graveyard is a better garden than a converted square, but yet there is something more interesting about it—it is so very human; and where there are monuments to notable persons (which naturally are undisturbed) they form something with an historical flavour about it which is attractive to look at. At Paddington Churchyard, for instance, there is the grave of Mrs. Siddons, in front of which it is said that Miss Mary Anderson, during her first tour in England, was often seen to stand.

"Isn't it foine!" said a ragged little urchin to me on the day when that particular ground was thrown open to the public. He was simply bursting with delight at having a garden to go into. I answered that I thought it was. This reminds me of another little denizen of the slums, at Lincoln's Inn Fields. He was inside—I had just left the ground after the opening ceremony. He peeped through the railings, overflowing with smiles; "You can come *in*, Miss," he said. I was not a Miss, but I thanked him for the information.

IN THE GRAVEYARD OF ST. JOHN'S IN HORSEFERRY ROAD.

Apart from the question of the moving of tombstones, there are many people who think it irreverent for a ground once used for burial ever to be used for recreation; they do not like the idea of people walking about over the graves. This feeling is worthy of all respect. It is found largely developed among the Jews, and has prevented them, hitherto, from allowing any of their graveyards to be laid out as public gardens. There are other people—and I am thankful that I do not come across them—who would like our churches turned into theatres and our churchyards into "Tivolis." They do far more harm to the cause of open spaces than do those who are slow to adapt themselves to modern ideas. But as far as my experience goes, I have found that the people who chiefly object to the conversion of burial-grounds into gardens are those who stay at home. They have in their mind's eye a picture of a well-kept cemetery, where burials take place every day, or of a sweet village churchyard, where the grass is soft and green and the graves are peaceful and undisturbed. One of the last things that I should ever wish to see is a village churchyard turned into the village recreation ground; and it was sad to find as I did a short time ago, that a certain rural churchyard in West Middlesex was being used as a drying-ground for clean clothes. But the London disused graveyards are *so* different, that I believe it is only necessary to take these objectors (though they will never come) into a neglected ground, to point out to them the sinking graves, to help them to pick their way so that they may avoid the dirty rubbish lying about, and the pitfalls into which they may stumble, in order to convince them that the ground, if turned into a public garden, would be treated with more reverence and in a more seemly manner. Then show them a graveyard garden; let them sit there for a bit to watch the people who come in and out, the men who have a brief rest in the middle of the day, the women who can snatch a few moments from their crowded and noisy homes, the big children with the "prams," and the little children they have in charge—and the change in the minds of the objectors will be complete.

The laying out of the churchyards is being carried out in many large towns besides London, though the initiative came from the metropolis. Liverpool, Leeds, Birmingham, Glasgow, and other places are adopting the plan, and in Norwich there is a young and flourishing Open Space Society which has already done much in this direction. As the City of Norwich contains about fifty churches, nearly all of which have churchyards, the Society has its work cut out for it, in this one way alone, for a good many years.

My impression is that amongst the London burial-grounds which are still closed and useless, there are fewer very untidy ones than there used to be. The agitation that has led to the laying out of 80 or 90 as public recreation grounds has also had a beneficial effect upon those which are not yet laid out. If this is the case it is very satisfactory, and it is an indirect result of the labours of the members of the Metropolitan Public Gardens Association, and of others who have interested themselves in the matter, which should be a cause for thankfulness and encouragement.

CHAPTER XIII

THE CEMETERIES STILL IN USE.

"With thy rude ploughshare, Death, turn up the sod,

And spread the furrow for the seed we sow;

This is the field and acre of our God,

This is the place where human harvests grow."

LONGFELLOW.

BESIDES the churchyards of Tooting, Plumstead, Lee, and Eltham, that are still available for interments, and some others, such as Charlton and Fulham, where burials in existing graves or vaults are sanctioned on application to the Home Secretary, ten burial-grounds, which can hardly be called cemeteries, are still being used in London. These are the South Street or Garratt's Lane ground at Wandsworth, consecrated in 1808, where widows, widowers, and parents of deceased persons already interred there can be buried, and the Holly Lane ground in Hampstead, which was consecrated in 1812, and is occasionally used; the graveyard by the Friends' Meeting-House in Stoke Newington, those in the convents in King Street, Hammersmith, and Portobello Road, and one in Newgate Gaol (to all of which I have referred); and a burial-ground crowded with tombstones behind St. Thomas' Roman Catholic Church in Fulham, where new graves are still dug, although there appears to be no room for more monuments, and although densely-populated streets are on every side. The other three are Jewish grounds, one in Ball's Pond, N., and two in Mile End, E., and they are described in Chapter VIII.

It will be noticed that when the Act was passed, under which the metropolitan burial-grounds were to be closed, seven of the new cemeteries were already in use, and while the burial-grounds were being closed, other cemeteries were being started.

The Act for the formation of Kensal Green Cemetery was passed in 1832, after unremitting efforts on the part of Mr. G. F. Carden. It is situated by the Harrow Road, not far short of Willesden Junction, and when first made was practically in the country. Now it is in the midst of large colonies of small houses. It has, as is usual, a consecrated and an unconsecrated portion, with a chapel in each. Its establishment led the way to the formation of other cemeteries, but most of the later ones were acquired by the parishes, not started by companies.

Several of the large cemeteries which have thus sprung into existence are just outside the metropolitan area, but the following are within the boundary of the County of London, and are tabulated in the order in which they were established:—

	NAME OF CEMETERY.	SIZE IN ACRES.	DATE OF FIRST INTERMENT.
1.	All Souls' Cemetery, Kensal Green, W.	69¼	1833
2.	The South Metropolitan Cemetery, Norwood, S.E.	40	1838
3.	St. James' Cemetery, Highgate, N.W.	38	1839
4.	Abney Park Cemetery, Stoke Newington, N.	32	1840
5.	Brompton Cemetery, or the West London, or London and Westminster Cemetery, W.	38	1840
6.	All Saints' Cemetery, Nunhead, S.E.	50	1840
7.	City of London and Tower Hamlets Cemetery, South Grove, Mile End, E.	33	1841
8.	Lambeth Cemetery, Tooting Graveney, S.W.	41	1854
9.	Charlton Cemetery, S.E.	8	1855
10.	St. Mary's Cemetery, Putney, Putney Lower Common, S.W.	3	1855
11.	Woolwich Cemetery, Wickham Lane, S.E.	32	1856
12.	Camberwell Cemetery, Peckham Rye. S.E.	29½	1856
13.	Greenwich Hospital Cemetery, Westcombe, S.E.	6	1857
14.	Deptford Cemetery (St. Paul's), Lewisham, S.E.	17	1858
15.	St. Mary's Roman Catholic Cemetery, Kensal Green, W.	30	1858

16.	Lewisham Cemetery, S.E.	15½	1858
17.	St. Mary's Cemetery, Battersea, S.W.	8½	1860
18.	Fulham Cemetery, S.W,	12½	1865
19.	Hammersmith Cemetery, Fulham, S.W.	16½	1869
20.	Lee Cemetery, Hither Green, S.E.	10	1873
21.	Hampstead Cemetery, Fortune Green, N.W.	19¼	1876
22.	Wandsworth Cemetery, Magdalen Road, S.W.	12	1878
23.	Plumstead Cemetery, S.E.	32¼	1890
24.	Greenwich Cemetery	15	
	Total	608¼	

Some of these cemeteries have been added to since they were first formed, and, considering the rate at which they are being used, they will all need to be enlarged in a very few years—that is if the present mode of interment continues to be the ordinary one.

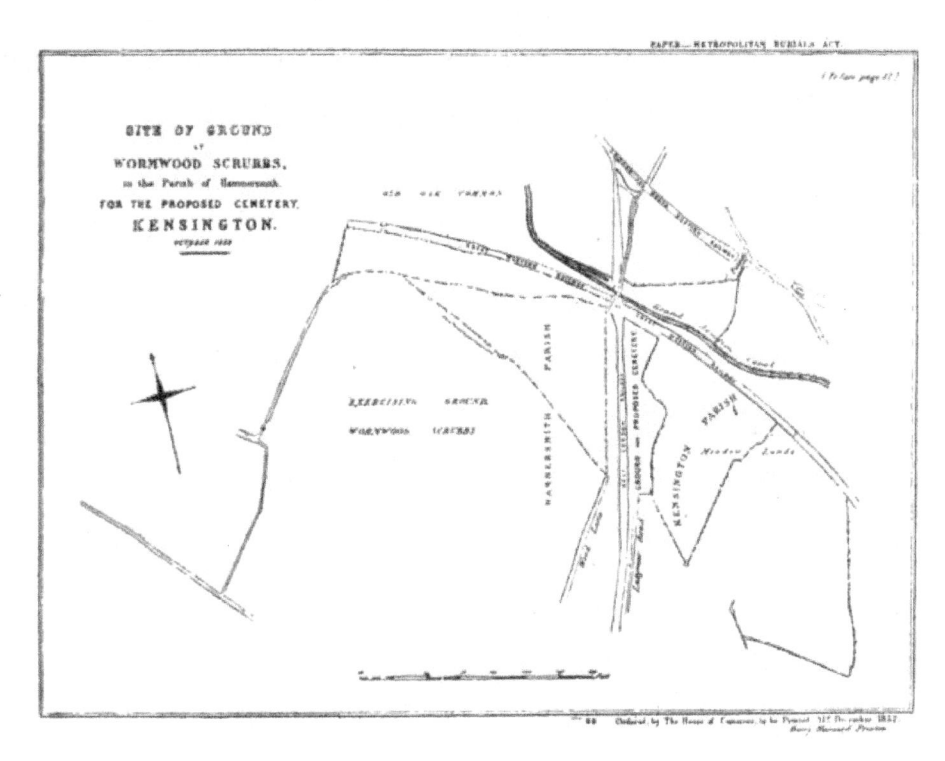

SITE OF THE GROUND at WORMWOOD SCRUBS, in the Parish of Hammersmith

    It must not be imagined that land was secured for these cemeteries without difficulty. The inhabitants of the districts in which it was proposed to place them naturally petitioned against their formation. A huge scheme for securing ninety-two acres (the Roundwood Farm Estate), between Willesden and Harlesden, for the Great Extramural Cemetery Association, was opposed by the Middlesex magistrates and others, and was not sanctioned by the Secretary of State. Part of this site is now a public park. The parish of Kensington applied for permission to form a cemetery of thirty acres at Wormwood SCRUBS, but had eventually to go as far out of London as Hanwell in order to secure a suitable plot. Unfortunately some public land was allotted. I believe that Norwood Cemetery was formerly a part of Norwood Common, and Putney and Barnes Cemeteries (the latter being just outside the boundary of London) are on Putney and Barnes Commons. The cemetery at Tooting was once meadow-land known as Baggery Mead, and for most of the others farm land and fields were taken. Happily it would now be very difficult to acquire a piece of common or lammas land for any such purpose, as we know far better than we did how to preserve our greatest treasures. How disastrous it would be if, when our village churchyards could no longer be used, the village greens were turned into burial-grounds!

NORWOOD CEMETERY ABOUT 1851.

The accompanying picture of Norwood Cemetery was published in 1851, and shows a single row of tombstones by the paths. Now there is row upon row behind these, the place seems to be entirely filled, and "yet there is room." These grounds are all much alike, but Norwood is peculiar in containing a small parochial burial-ground belonging to St. Mary at Hill, in the City (the church of the Church Army), and another belonging to the Greeks. Most dwellers in London are acquainted with one or other of the cemeteries, some people finding pleasure in walking about in them, and sitting on the seats provided for visitors among the tombs; and they are, on the whole, well looked after and neatly kept. It is rather to be regretted that the custom of putting quaint and interesting epitaphs on the stones is so entirely a thing of the past; the monotonous texts do not take their place at all.

There is a special interest attached to Kensal Green Cemetery from its having been the first, but I think it is also the worst. Mr. Loftie describes it as "the bleakest, dampest, most melancholy of all the burial-grounds of London." I doubt if it is the dampest, though the soil is a heavy clay, for I think that the Tower Hamlets Cemetery is probably far damper. Nor is Kensal Green so overcrowded or untidy as the Tower Hamlets, where gravestones are tumbling and lying about, apparently unclaimed and uncared for, amongst dead shrubs and rank grass; it has also not quite so large a proportion of "common graves" (for eight bodies or so), as there are in some of the other grounds, and the number of burials per acre has not been quite so enormous as, for instance, at Tooting, Brompton, or Abney Park. The last-named ground, when it had only been opened fifteen years, was described in an official report as being "a mass of corruption underneath," the soil being a "damp, blue clay." But Kensal Green Cemetery is truly awful, with its catacombs, its huge mausoleums, family vaults, statues, broken pillars, weeping images, and oceans of tombstones, good, bad, and indifferent. I think the indifferent are to be preferred, the bad should not be anywhere, and the good are utterly out of place. It is also the largest in the metropolis, and as the Roman Catholic ground joins it there are in this spot, or there very soon will be, ninety-nine acres of dead bodies.

THE TOMB OF PRINCESS SOPHIA.

There are many sad sights in London, but to me there are few so sad as one of these huge graveyards. Not that the idea of the numbers of dead beneath the soil produces any thoughts of melancholy, but I feel inclined to exclaim with the disciples, "To what purpose is this waste?" Can there be any more profitless mode of throwing away money than by erecting costly tombstones? They are of no use to the departed, and they are grievous burdens laid on the shoulders of succeeding generations. The only people who profit by them are a few marble and granite merchants, and a few monumental masons—and they might be better employed. The whole funeral system is an extravagant imposition, and has been for years. It may be said that the heavy trappings, the plumes, the scarves, &c., are going out of fashion; and this is true, but other things are taking their place. I saw the other day a neat little copy of the Burial Service, bound in black leather, with a cross outside. On the fly leaf was printed the name of the person to be buried, with the date of death, place of interment, &c. This book was given by the undertaker to each of those who attended the funeral, and as the ceremony was conducted by a Nonconformist minister, who arranged it in accordance with his own individual predilection, the little book was useless! I merely mention this as a specimen of the way in which the expenses of a modern funeral may be mounted up. The rich lavish their money on costly, almost indestructible coffins, which it would be far better to do without altogether, and on masses of flowers that die unseen, while the poor go into debt to buy mourning, which they often pawn before a month is over; and many a widow and family, who have a hard struggle to provide daily food, deny themselves the necessities of life, and sow the seeds of disease and want, in order to set up a tombstone or monument on a grave. And who sees it? A few people may occasionally go to Kensal Green to look at the tomb of Princess Sophia, the family mausoleum of the Duke of Cambridge, or the monuments erected to the Duke of Sussex, Thackeray, Mulready, Tom Hood, George Cruikshank (whose body has been removed to St. Paul's Cathedral), Leigh Hunt, John Leech, Hugh Littlejohn, or Sydney Smith; but they are utterly spoilt by their surroundings. It is hardly possible to appreciate such memorials when they are closely hedged in by others in all descriptions of stone, of all shapes and sizes, and in all styles of architecture. And it is appalling to think of the amount of money that has been spent on these massive monuments. How many a church or chapel might have been built in a growing district; how many a beautiful old church now falling to decay might have been restored[2]; how many missionaries might have been sent to foreign lands; how many hospital beds might have been endowed; how many struggling families, or sick members of the same, might have been given a holiday in the country or by the sea; how many open spaces might have been secured and laid out for the people; how many drinking fountains might have been erected; how many grants might have been made to voluntary schools or secular institutions for benefiting mankind; and how many objects of real beauty and antiquarian interest might have been preserved! It is impossible to give an answer to these questions—perhaps one would be sadder still if one could.

9. Four English Cathedrals are at the present time in urgent need of funds for restoration.

The Jews think a great deal of their tombstones, and erect very large ones. When one is "set up" they have a special ceremony, which they advertise beforehand, and the friends and relations gather at the grave. I have already referred to the very different custom of the Society of Friends—the Quakers—and I trust that they may long preserve the simplicity of their burial practices, for "it consorts not with our principles," said W. Beck and T. F. Ball, in their history of the London Friends' Meetings (1869), "unduly to exalt the honoured dead; their names we canonise not, and o'er their graves we raise no costly monument." It has been the dying wish of very many of our best men that their bodies might be laid to rest in quietness, and without undue expense or show. Unfortunately their wishes have not always been carried out. Sir John Morden, who founded Morden College or Almshouses for decayed Merchants, in Blackheath, left directions in his will that he should be interred in the chapel of the college "without any pomp or singing boys, but decently." I do not think the singing boys would have hurt him, but his wish to dispense with "pomp" was most praiseworthy. His funeral *was* made the occasion of a considerable ceremony, but, as it took place at 9 o'clock in the evening, perhaps it was unaccompanied by such an institution as a champagne lunch. His name and his fame have survived by reason of the noble work he did, There is a deep lesson in Sir Christopher Wren's epitaph in St. Paul's Cathedral:—

> "Si momentum requiris circumspice."

Longfellow sang the same strain in his well-known verses:—

"Alike are life and death

When life in death survives,

And the interrupted breath

Inspires a thousand lives.

Were a star quenched on high,

For ages would its light,

Still travelling downward from the sky,

Shine on our mortal sight.

So when a good man dies,

For years beyond our ken,

The light he leaves behind him lies

Upon the paths of men."

And it is reiterated still more beautifully in the touching conversation between the schoolmaster and Little Nell in Dickens' "Old Curiosity Shop," towards the close of the fifty-fourth chapter.

IN KENSAL GREEN CEMETERY.

I cannot conclude this division of my subject without an earnest appeal to those who are contemplating erecting a tombstone to the memory of a beloved relation or friend, to consider beforehand which is the wisest way of commemorating the departed,—whether the simplest memorial is not after all the best, "for sublimity always is simple," whether it may not be better still to have none at all in a cemetery already overcrowded with monuments, and whether it is well to add indefinitely to the forests of practically imperishable gravestones which are gradually surrounding London and our other large towns.

CHAPTER XIV

A FORECAST OF THE FUTURE.

"Now our sands are almost run:

More or little, and then dumb."

SHAKESPEARE.

I ACKNOWLEDGE a hesitation in writing this chapter, because there are many people who feel very strongly upon the subject of the disposal of the dead, and whose feelings I wish in no way to appear to treat with anything but the greatest consideration.

The custom of burying the body has been in practice in England ever since Christianity was established here, and so completely did burial take the place of burning that the latter expedient has never been formally forbidden, or, until 1884, even referred to, in English law. It is well that this fact should be clearly understood, viz., that it is not illegal to dispose of a dead body by other means than by burial in earth (unless it should be proved a public nuisance at common law), nor has it been illegal in England in the past, but it has merely not been the custom, "inhumation" having been systematically practised for a thousand years.

It is natural that many beautiful thoughts should have been expressed by our greatest writers in connection with the burial of the dead; it has been a theme upon which poets have loved to dwell. The mourners, the lych-gate, the weather-worn stones, the solemn stillness, the yew-tree—they all furnish subjects for reflection and for verse. Tennyson refers in terms of tenderest meaning to the yew-tree in the churchyard in his "In Memoriam," and even Tom Hood puts aside his joking mood when he thinks of it—

"How wide the yew-tree spreads its gloom,

And o'er the dead lets fall its dew,

As if in tears it wept for them,

The many human families

That sleep around its stem!"

I confess I love these associations dearly, and it would be hard indeed to give them up. But will they ever cling around our cemeteries? I think not.

On the other hand, many very curious notions have arisen in connection with this subject—notions as groundless as they are quaint. I will mention three only, which are illustrated by the two following epitaphs, the first of which is from St. Olave's, Jewry, and the second from Bermondsey, as quoted by Maitland:—

1. "Under this Tomb, the sacred Ashes hold,

The drossie Part of more celestiall Gold;

The Body of a Man, a Man of Men,

Whose worth to write at large, would loose my Pen.

Then do thy worst, Death, glut thyself with Dust,

The precious Soul is mounted to the Just.

Yet, Reader, when thou read'st, both read and weep,

That Men so good, so grave, so wise, do sleep."

2. "Where once the famous *Elton* did entrust

The Preservation of his sacred Dust,

Lyes pious *Whitaker*, both justly twined,

Both dead one Grave, both living had one Mind;

And by their dissolution have supply'd

The hungry Grave, and Fame and Heaven beside.

This stone protect their Bones, while Fame enrolls

Their deathless Name, and Heaven embrace their Souls."

In the first we are told to weep because so good a man has gone, from the second we are led to believe that the gravestone protects the body of the departed, and both contain the idea that the grave or earth is anxious to receive the mortal remains, and is more comfortable for having done so. First there is the question of the weeping. It is very usual, on gravestones and monuments, to find the order given to the reader to "drop a tear." And yet how impossible it is to carry it out. Imagine dropping a tear all along a line of graves of people of whom one has never heard, and who died 250 years ago! But happily there are quite as many injunctions to the contrary, and we are as often told not to weep:—

"Weep not for me, friends, though death us do sever,

I'm going to do nothing for ever and ever."

This epitaph to a poor overworked woman is, perhaps, flippant. Here is a more serious one, which was in the church of St. Martin Outwich:—

"Reader, thou may'st forbear to put thine Eyes

To charge For Tears, to mourn these Obsequies:

Such charitable Drops would best be given

To those who late, or never, come to Heaven.

But here you would, by weeping on this Dust,

Allay his Happiness with thy Mistrust;

Whose pious closing of his youthful Years

Deserves thy Imitation, not thy Tears."

(*In memory of John Wight*, 1633.)

Secondly there is the question of the protecting gravestone. This is also not uncommonly met with. The poet Gray's well-known "Elegy in a Country Churchyard" contains the following verse:—

"Yet e'en these bones from insult to protect

Some frail memorial still erected nigh,

With uncouth rhymes and shapeless sculpture decked,

Implores the passing tribute of a sigh."

But there could be few notions more false. Gravestones have often enough been "moved about to give more appearance of room," and oftener still cleared away altogether, while the bodies beneath have been cast out almost as soon as they were buried; and unfortunately there are many country churchyards now which are terribly overcrowded. A short time after the death of Lawrence Sterne his admirers collected money to put a monument on his grave in St. George's burial-ground, Bayswater Road. It was erected in what was supposed to be about the right position—no one could point to the exact spot where the body lay.

Thirdly we have the idea of the hungering grave, which is carried to a ridiculous point in this passage from "The Wonderful Yeare 1603, wherein is shewed the picture of London lying sicke of the Plague."—"Let us look forth, and try what consolation rises with the sun. Not any, not any; for, before the jewel of the morning be fully set in silver, hundred hungry graves stand gaping; and every one of them (as at a breakfast) hath swallowed downe ten or eleven lifeless carcases. Before dinner, in the same gulfe, are twice so many more devoured. And, before the Sun takes his rest, those numbers are doubled."

SHEEP IN THE SAVOY CHURCHYARD ABOUT 1825.

Now the grave is not hungry, and the earth does not want dead bodies; it is better without them. Yet, strangely enough, there is a certain benefit to be derived from a moderate supply, and the most advanced cremationists advocate the use of the few remaining ashes as manure for some kinds of farm lands. Sir Henry Thompson, a cremationist worthy of every honour, has referred to the great increase there would be in the fish supply if burial at sea were generally practised, a plan approved of by some *anti*-cremationists. We have seen that churchyard water has been drunk for generations, and very bad it is. Churchyard poultry and churchyard mutton are also common enough, many a poor parson being glad to earn a few pounds in the year by allowing sheep to graze among the graves. This is all very well in some country places, but it used to be practised in London, and sheep have been actually killed by swallowing with the grass the poisonous products of the overfilled ground. In the Charterhouse graveyard there are some magnificent wall fruit trees, such as are seldom seen in crowded towns; one of the Stepney pest-fields became a market-garden; while breweries and burial-grounds seem to be closely associated with each other.

But the question of paramount importance is how to stop the increase of cemeteries. Are we ever to allow England to be divided like a chess-board into towns and burial-places? What we have to consider is how to dispose of the dead without taking so much valuable space from the living. In the metropolitan area alone we have almost filled (and in some places overfilled) twenty-four new cemeteries within sixty years, with an area of above six hundred acres; and this is as nothing compared with the huge extent of land used for interments just outside the limits of the metropolis. If the cemeteries are not to extend indefinitely they must in time be built upon, or they must be used for burial over and over again, or the ground must revert to its original state as agricultural land, or we must turn our parks and commons into cemeteries, and let our cemeteries be our only recreation grounds—which Heaven forbid!

I fail to understand how any serious-minded person can harbour the idea that burning the body can be any stumbling-block in the way of its resurrection, for the body returns "earth to earth, ashes to ashes, dust to dust," whether the process takes fifty years or fifty minutes. But many people have a horror of the notion—they know it is sanitary, but they think it irreverent. There are other alternatives, worthy of careful consideration. Some have advocated burial at sea; others, and among them Sir Seymour Haden, have pressed forward the advantages of using perishable coffins, wicker baskets, and the like—a suggestion as excellent as it is economical, for the sooner the earth and the body meet the better it is. Perhaps, in this scientific generation, some one may invent a totally new method of disposing of the dead, which will commend itself both to those who advocate cremation and to those who dislike it. He would indeed be a public benefactor, deserving of the Faraday medal. But that cremation is on the increase cannot be denied. Even Kensal Green Cemetery has now a

"Columbarium," which is an elegant name for pigeon-holes for cinerary urns, built in 1892, with forty-two little cupboards. Since the decision of Mr. Justice Stephen in the case of Dr. William Price, in February, 1884, it has been recognised as legal in England, and the crematoriums at Woking and elsewhere have been frequently used. But if the practice is to become at all general it must be advocated by a different set of people. It has, to a certain extent, happened hitherto that those who have been cremated have been more or less associated (I hope I may not be misunderstood here) with the advanced school—those that consider themselves "enlightened," Radicals, or Socialists, or persons of little or no professed religious views. This was not the case with the promoters of cremation, but it has been so with some of their disciples, or at any rate many anti-cremationists think so. The Rev. H. R. Haweis is excellent in his way—I speak of him with the greatest respect—but I venture to think that cremation will not be taken up very largely until a few such men as the Archbishop of York, the Chief Rabbi, the Rev. Prebendary Webb Peploe, and Father Staunton pronounce in its favour. Then it would soon be necessary to have a crematorium in every cemetery.

THE COLUMBARIUM AT KENSAL GREEN.

It is morbid and useless to make previous preparation for death, except by life insurance, a proper will, and other business-like arrangements for the benefit of survivors. It is foolish to erect, as many have done, a tomb during lifetime (like the Miller's tomb on Highdown Hill, Sussex), to keep a coffin under the bed, or to have a picture of a skeleton always on the wall. Such eccentric practices as that of the gentleman who died in a house by Hyde Park, and, at his wish, had his body kept in a coffin under a glass case on the roof of the house, are not to be admired. We can never forget that our life here will have its ending, our friends, companions, and neighbours are constantly leaving us, our daily paper has its daily obituary column, and surely no artificial method is needed to remind us of this fact. Cowper has said:

"Like crowded forest-trees we stand,

And some are marked to fall;

The axe will smite at God's command,

And soon shall smite us all."

The utmost we need do, if we do not want our bodies to rest in the cemeteries, is to tell our friends that we wish them cremated, or buried in perishable coffins, or quietly laid in some far-off, rural spot. All else we may leave—it is in higher hands than ours; and already the Church on earth, imperfect, faulty, and divided though she be, has "mystic, sweet communion

With those whose rest is won."

A few words in closing about the future of the disused burial-grounds in London. I think they are tolerably safe now. I have attempted to show how many there still are, closed and idle, or being used for a totally wrong purpose, between Hampstead and Plumstead, Hammersmith and Bow; but they are surely, if but slowly, being reclaimed and changed, one by one, into places of rest and recreation for the living. The public mind has so far awaked to the necessity of securing all the breathing-spaces which may be had, that the smallest corner of land in which interments can have been said to have taken place now forms a subject of litigation if attempts are made to build upon it. Preservation is the first step upon the ladder, acquisition the next, while conversion crowns them all.

I can foresee no better fate for the disused graveyards than that they should become gardens or playgrounds. The churchyards must be gardens, as green and bright and neat as they can be made, for the older people; and the unconsecrated grounds, detached from places of worship, will serve as playgrounds, many of them having to be reclaimed from their present use as builders' yards, cooperages, &c. Spa Fields, Clerkenwell, a burial-ground to the history of which I have already referred, is a typical London playground, in the very centre of the town, although surrounded by courts and streets with such rural names as Rosoman Street, Wood Street, Pear-tree Court and Vineyard Walk—grim reminders of what the district was like a hundred years or more ago. Exmouth Street, behind which this open space is situated, is worth a visit. I was there recently, one Monday afternoon. Trucks and stalls with wares of all kinds lined the narrow road, and there seemed scarcely a square yard without a person on it. One woman was selling old garments, of which she had only about six, and these were spread out on the road itself—in the mud. A little farther on I noticed a stall, where two women were making purchases of "freshly-boiled horse-flesh at 2d. a lb." This was not cut up as for cat's meat, but was in large, dark brown, shapeless-looking joints. In the middle of the street is the Church of the Holy Redeemer, a huge structure in imitation of an Italian church. It stands on the site of the Spa Fields Chapel, an old round building, removed a few years ago, belonging to the Lady Huntingdon Connexion, which had a stone obelisk in front of it to the memory of Lady Huntingdon, who lived in a neighbouring house. Behind the church is the open space, which is nearly two acres in extent. Originally taken for a tea-garden the speculation failed, and the ground was used as a burial-ground, slightly lower fees being charged than in the neighbouring churchyards. After being grossly overcrowded it was closed for interments in 1853. For several years the space has been used as a drill-ground by the 3rd Middlesex Artillery and the 39th Middlesex Rifles; and in 1885 the Metropolitan Public Gardens Association entered into negotiations with the owner, the Marquis of Northampton, and he generously handed it over at a nominal rental for the purposes of a children's playground, and subsequently added to it half an acre of adjoining land. The association drained it and carted a large amount of soil and gravel into it, and put up some gymnastic apparatus in the additional piece, which was not a part of the burial-ground. The entrance is from Vineyard Walk, Farringdon Road. When I last visited the playground, although it was a chilly afternoon, a great many children were enjoying themselves, and some women were swinging their little ones. But after or between school-hours is the proper time to see it. Then it is crowded, and every swing, rope, pole, bar, ladder, and skipping-rope is in use, and children are running about all over the open part of the ground.

SPA FIELDS PLAYGROUND.

It is a strange-looking place. On the north-west side is the unfinished apse of the Church of the Holy Redeemer, and on the south side is the parish mortuary, the presence of which does not seem to have any sobering effect upon the children. I watched four boys on the giant's stride, and when they had vacated it a little girl of about eight years, who had been sitting on a seat with a baby on her lap, and was knitting a long strip with odd bits of coloured wools, beckoned to another sad-looking little girl sitting on my seat, and off they went to take the boys' places. The baby was deposited on yet another seat, and it wept copiously. But the children did not heed its cries; they had a silent and vigorous turn at the giant's stride, each holding on to two ropes. They neither spoke nor smiled, and, when they had finished, the one returned to her baby and her knitting and the other clambered on to the back of the long-suffering and well-worn vaulting-horse. They are very strong, some of these poor children, and it is wonderful what they can do. The shabbiest often seem the most active. I noticed one little lad, whose clothes were literally dropping to pieces—shoes, stockings, knickerbockers, and blouse all in tatters—and he twisted himself about on the handle swings, putting his toes through the handles, and performing all sorts of gyrations which many a well-fed boy, clad in the best of flannels, would have given his all to be able to accomplish.

A playground such as Spa Fields is about as different from an ordinary village green, where country boys and girls romp and shout, as two things with the same purpose can well be. For the soft, green grass, you have gritty gravel; for the cackling geese who waddle into the pond, you have a few stray cats walking on the walls; for the picturesque cottages overgrown with roses and honeysuckle, you have the backs of little houses, monotonous in structure, in colour, and in dirt; and instead of resting "underneath the shadow vast of patriarchal tree," you must be content with a wooden bench close to the wall, bearing on its back the name of the association which laid out the ground. But it is only necessary to have once seen the joy with which the children of our crowded cities hail the formation of such a playground, and the use to which they put it, to be convinced that the trouble of acquiring it, or the cost of laying it out, is amply repaid. They are so crowded at home, so crowded at school, so crowded in the roads, that it seems hard to lose one opportunity of securing a piece of ground, however small, where they can be free to stretch their arms, their legs, and their lungs, away from the dangers and the sad sights of the streets, under the charge of a kindly caretaker,

"And where beadles and policemen

Never frighten them away."

And can the dead beneath the soil object to the little feet above them? I am sure they cannot. Even Gray, in describing Stoke Pogis Churchyard, which is surrounded by meadows, rejoiced to see the "little footsteps lightly print the ground." Such a space as Spa Fields may never have been consecrated for the use of the dead, but perchance the omission is in part redeemed by its dedication to the living.

APPENDIX A.

BURIAL-GROUNDS WITHIN THE METROPOLITAN AREA, WHICH STILL EXIST, WHOLLY OR IN PART. ABRIDGED FROM THE RETURN PREPARED FOR THE LONDON COUNTY COUNCIL IN THE SPRING OF 1895, AND CORRECTED UP TO DATE.

HAMPSTEAD.

1. *St. John's Churchyard.*—1½ acres in extent. It is full of tombstones, but very neatly kept, and although not handed over to any public authority, nor provided with seats, the gates are usually open.

2. *Burial-ground in Holly Lane.*—1¼ acres. This is still used for interments, and new graves are occasionally dug here. It was consecrated in 1812. It is tidily kept, and the gates are open whenever the gardener is on the ground.

3. *Hampstead Cemetery.*—19½ acres. First used in 1876. Open daily. It is well kept, except the part nearest to Fortune Green.

4. *The Tumulus, Parliament Hill Fields.*—Excavated in 1894 by the London County Council, and said to be an ancient British burial-place of the early bronze period. Railed round for its protection.

N.B.—There are tumuli in Greenwich Park, and evidences of Roman cemeteries and other ancient burial-places in several parts of London.

ST. MARYLEBONE.

5. *St. Marylebone Episcopal Chapel-ground*, High Street.—⅓ acre

This chapel was the parish church until 1816. The churchyard is full of tombstones, closed and fairly neat.

6. *St. Marylebone Burial-ground*, Paddington Street, north side.—¾ acre. A mortuary was built in it a few years ago. The ground was consecrated in 1772. It is closed to the public, but neatly kept and used as a garden for the inmates of the adjoining workhouse.

7. *St. Marylebone* (also called *St. George's*) *Burial-ground*, Paddington Street, south side.—2¼ acres. Consecrated in 1733, and very much used. Since 1886 it has been maintained as a public garden by the vestry, and is well kept.

8. *St. John's Wood Chapel-ground.*—An additional burial-ground for the parish of Marylebone. 6 acres. The tombstones have not been moved, but the Marylebone Vestry maintains the ground as a public garden. It has a few seats in it, and is neatly kept.

PADDINGTON.

9. *St. Mary's Churchyard.*—1 acre. The tombstones have not been moved, but the ground has been neatly laid out, and is kept open by the vestry.

10. *The Old Burial-ground*, Paddington.—3 acres. This adjoins St. Mary's Churchyard, and was laid out and opened as a public garden by the vestry in 1885. It contains the site of an older church, dedicated to St. James.

KENSINGTON.

11. *St. Mary Abbots Churchyard.*—About 1¼ acres. The graveyard is smaller than it was 20 years ago because the present church is far larger than the original one, and recently a long porch or cloister has been added. It is neatly laid out but closed to the public.

12. *Holy Trinity Churchyard*, Brompton.—3½ acres. There are public thoroughfares through this ground, but they are railed off, and the churchyard is closed and has a neglected appearance.

13. *Brompton Cemetery*, also called West London Cemetery and London and Westminster Cemetery.—38 acres. First used in 1840. By 1889 upwards of 155,000 bodies had been interred there. It is crowded with tombstones, and is in the midst of a thickly populated district.

14. *All Souls Cemetery*, Kensal Green, partly in Hammersmith.—69 acres. Open daily and neatly kept. This cemetery has been in use since 1833, and it is crowded with tombstones and contains catacombs and numerous vaults and mausoleums.

15. *Burial-ground of the Franciscan Convent of St. Elizabeth*, Portobello Road.—This is a triangular grass plot, not above ¼ acre in size, in the garden behind the convent. It is surrounded by trees and neatly kept. It was sanctioned by the Home Secretary in 1862, and is only used for the interment of nuns, of whom five have been buried here, the first in 1870 and the last in 1893.

HAMMERSMITH.

16. *St. Paul's Churchyard.*—1 acre. This is smaller than it used to be, the present church being larger than the old one, and a piece of the ground having been taken in 1884 to widen the road. It is neatly laid out and often open, but not a public recreation ground. It was consecrated in 1631, and frequently enlarged.

17. *St. Peter's Churchyard*, Black Lion Lane.—1,800 square yards. Closed and untidy.

18. *New West End Baptist Chapel-ground*, King Street.—¼ acre. This is north and south of the chapel, the northern part having been encroached upon. Closed and neatly kept.

19. *Wesleyan Chapel Burial-ground*, Waterloo Street.—The chapel has been supplanted by a Board School, and the playground is the site of the burial-ground. It is tar-paved, has a few trees in it, and is about 500 square yards in size.

20. *Friends Burial-ground*, near the Creek.—300 square yards. This is on the north side of the Friends meeting-house, and is closed, but very neat. There are a few flat tombstones, and burials took place until about 1865.

21. *St. Mary's Roman Catholic Cemetery*, Kensal Green.—30 acres. The first interment was in 1858, and it is now crowded with vaults, tombstones, &c. It is open daily and neatly kept.

22. *The Cemetery of the Benedictine Nunnery*, Fulham Palace Road.—This is a small burial-ground in the garden. According to a report from the Home Office it is about 14 by 12 yards in extent. It was in use before 1829, but was closed for interment some years ago.

23. *The Cemetery of the Convent (Nazareth Home)*, in Hammersmith Road.—This is at the extreme end of the garden, under the wall of Great Church Lane. It is not more than 12 yards

by 9 yards, and is used for the interment of the sisters, burials only taking place at considerable intervals. This ground has been in use for upwards of 40 years.

FULHAM.

24. *All Saints' Churchyard.*—Two acres or more. This is kept open during the summer months, and has seats in it, but the gravestones have not been moved, nor has the ground been handed over to any public authority for maintenance. It is neatly kept. No new graves are dug in it, but where the rights can be proved certain old vaults are still occasionally used.

25. *St. Mary's Churchyard*, Hammersmith Road.—Size ½ acre. This ground is closed, but fairly tidy. Several of the tombstones have been moved.

26. *St. John's Churchyard*, Walham Green.—½ acre. There are only a few tombstones on the north side of the church and none on the south side, and the ground is closed and appears neglected.

27. *St. Thomas's Roman Catholic Churchyard*, Fulham.—2,600 square yards. This ground was closed by order in Council in 1857, but only partially, for new graves are still dug in it, in the midst of a densely-populated district of new streets. The gate is usually open.

28. *Lillie Road pest-field* (the orchard of Normand House).—The site of this orchard, then 4 acres in extent, was used extensively for burials at the time of the Great Plague. Lintaine Grove now occupies part of it, and a row of houses in Lillie Road. Only about ¾ acre is still unbuilt upon, at the corner of Tilton Street, and this is offered for sale.

29. *Fulham Cemetery.*—12½ acres. First used in 1865. Open daily.

30. *Hammersmith Cemetery*, in Fulham Fields.—16½ acres. First used in 1869. Open daily.

CHELSEA.

31. *St. Luke's Churchyard* (the old church on the Embankment).—¼ acre. This ground is closed and neglected.

32. *St. Luke's Churchyard* (the new church in Robert Street).—2¼ acres. This ground was consecrated in 1812, and contains vaults and catacombs. It was laid out as a public garden and is maintained by the Chelsea Vestry.

33. *Old Burial-ground*, King's Road.—¾ acre. Given to the parish of Chelsea by Sir Hans Sloane, consecrated in 1736, and enlarged in 1790. A mortuary has been built in it. It is laid out as a garden for the use of the inmates of the adjoining workhouse. Fragments of an old chapel and graveyard have been found here.

34. *Chelsea Hospital Graveyard*, Queen's Road.—1⅓ acres. This ground was used for the interment of the pensioners. It is closed, but neatly kept.

35. *All Souls Roman Catholic Burial-ground*, Cadogan Terrace.—1½ acres. The adjoining chapel (St. Mary's) was consecrated in 1811. The ground is closed and full of tombstones.

36. *Moravian Burial-ground*, Milman's Row.—The part actually used for interments is fenced in and closed. It is neatly kept, the tombstones being very small flat ones. It belongs to the Congregation of the Moravian Church in Fetter Lane, E.C., and was closed by order in Council about 8 years ago.

37. *Jewish Burial-ground*, Fulham Road.—½ acre. It belongs to the Western Synagogue, St. Alban's Place, S.W., and was first used in 1813. It is closed to the public except between 11 and 4 on Sundays.

ST. GEORGE'S, HANOVER SQUARE.

38. *St. George's Burial-ground*, Mount Street.—1¼ acres. Laid out as a public garden, and beautifully kept by the vestry. The ground dates from about 1730, but there are very few tombstones.

39. *St. George's Burial-Ground*, Bayswater Road.—Laid out by the vestry, the gravestones having been placed round the walls. The approaches to this ground are its chief drawback, and it is not visible from any public road. One entrance is through the chapel facing Hyde Park, and the other is in a mews. It is about 5 acres in extent.

WESTMINSTER (ST. MARGARET AND ST. JOHN).

40. *The Churchyard of Westminster Abbey.*—What remains of the extensive burial-ground which once occupied this site is the piece of land on the north side of the Abbey, and the cloisters. (See *St. Margaret's*.)

41. *St. Margaret's Churchyard.*—This was laid out as a public garden, and forms one ground with the Abbey churchyard. It is well kept up by the burial board of the parish. The size of the churchyard, with the ground used for interments which belongs to the Abbey, is about 2¼ acres.

42. *Christ Church Churchyard*, Victoria Street (also called St. Margaret's burying-ground).—This church was a chapel of ease to St. Margaret's. The adjoining graveyard has had a vicarage built in it. What remains is 7,000 square yards in size, closed, with flat tombstones and grass.

43. *St. John the Evangelist Churchyard*, Smith Square.—This churchyard used to extend, at the beginning of the century, for some distance on the south side of the church, but was thrown into the road. Now all that remains is a very small bare enclosure, not ¼ acre in size, railed in round the church.

44. *Additional ground for St. John's Parish*, Horseferry Road.—Walled in in 1627, and very much used, especially for the burial of soldiers. It is 1½ acres in size, and has been laid out as public garden. It is neatly kept by the vestry, and much frequented.

45. *Vincent Square.*—8 acres. This is what remains of the Tothill Fields pest-field. It is the playground of Westminster School, and some buildings have been erected in it. A stone-paved yard in Earl Street is said to be the site of the plague-pits.

46. *Millbank Penitentiary Burial-ground.*—432 square yards in size. In 1830-33 there were an average of 14 interments per annum, but at times it was more used. The site of this graveyard will be preserved when the space which used to be occupied by the prison is built upon.

47. *Knightsbridge Green.*—Victims of the plague from the leper hospital and elsewhere were buried here. A grassy, closed triangle opposite Tattersalls.

ST. MARTIN'S IN THE FIELDS.

48. *St. Martin's Churchyard.*—⅓ acre. This is stone-paved, has trees and seats in it supplied by the Metropolitan Public Gardens Association, and is maintained by the vestry.

49. *Additional ground in Drury Lane.*—Less than ¼ acre. Laid out as a public garden, and now maintained by the vestry. It is well kept, and contains some gymnastic apparatus for the use of the children. Also called the Tavistock burial-ground.

ST. JAMES'S, WESTMINSTER.

50. *St. James's Churchyard*, Piccadilly.—½ acre. This is a dreary ground, and might be made very attractive. The part where most burials took place is considerably raised above the rest. The yard on the north side of the church is entirely paved with stones, amongst which are many tombstones. In the upper part tombstones form the walks, the walls, &c. One gate is often unlatched.

51. *St. James's Workhouse Ground*, Poland Street.—The workhouse was built upon a "common cemetery" where, at the time of the plague, many thousands of bodies were interred. A small part of it was kept as the workhouse burial-ground, but this has now disappeared, and all that is left of the original ground used for interments is the garden or courtyard of the workhouse. It is a pleasant recreation ground for the inmates, and is well supplied with seats, being about ¼ acre in extent.

THE STRAND.

52. *St. Mary le Strand Churchyard.*—At the west end of the church, about 200 square yards in size, closed and not well kept.

53. *Additional ground, Russell Court, Catherine Street.*—430 square yards. It is probable that few grounds in London were more overcrowded with bodies than this one, which was entirely surrounded by the backs of small houses. When closed in 1853 it was in a very disgusting and unwholesome condition, and it continued to be most wretched until the Metropolitan Public Gardens Association asphalted it in 1886. It is maintained as a children's playground by the London County Council. This is the scene of "Tom all alone's" in "Bleak House." There are 6 gravestones against the wall.

54. *St. Clement Danes Churchyard.*—This is now ¼ acre in extent, having been curtailed when the Strand was altered. It is closed.

55. *Additional ground, Portugal Street.*—This was called the "Green-ground," and was crowded with bodies. A corner of King's College Hospital was built upon the ground. The remaining piece is nearly ½ acre in size, between the hospital and Portugal Street. It is now the entrance drive and a grass plot. It is neatly kept, with some trees and seats in it, and is used solely by the hospital.

56. *St. Paul's Churchyard*, Covent Garden.—¾ acre. Given by the Earl of Bedford in 1631. It is closed and very neat, the tombstones forming a flat paved yard round the church, while the rest of the ground is turfed.

57. *St. Ann's Churchyard*, Soho.—½ acre. It is estimated that in this small ground and the vaults under the church 110,240 bodies were interred during 160 years. It was laid out by the Metropolitan Public Gardens Association in 1892, and is maintained as a recreation ground in very good order by the Strand District Board of Works.

58. *The Churchyard of the Chapel Royal (St. Mary's)*, Savoy.—¼ acre. This ground was much used for the internment of soldiers. It belongs to Her Majesty the Queen, as Duchess of Lancaster, and was laid out as a public garden at the cost of the Queen, the Earl of Meath, and others. It is well maintained by the parish.

ST. GILES IN THE FIELDS.

59. *St. Giles' Churchyard.*—Nearly an acre. This ground being originally consecrated by a Roman Catholic, was much used by the poor Irish. It was enlarged in 1628, and at various subsequent dates, and was very much overcrowded, and it occupies the site of an ancient graveyard attached to a leper hospital. It has been laid out as a public garden, and is

maintained by the St. Giles' District Board of Works. The brightest part of the ground is north of the church, and this is only opened at the discretion of the caretaker.

HOLBORN.

60. *Additional ground for St. John's, Clerkenwell*, in Benjamin Street.—This land, which is nearly ¼ acre in extent, was consecrated in 1775. It was laid out as a public garden ten years ago, and is maintained by trustees with help from the Holborn District Board of Works and the Clerkenwell Vestry. Very well kept.

61. *Charterhouse Square.*—This garden is a part of the site of a burial-ground dating back to 1349, when Sir Walter de Manny purchased from St. Bartholomew's Hospital 13 acres of land, known as the Spittle Croft, for the burial of those who died in the plague of that time. In 20 years 50,000 bodies were interred there. In 1371 the Carthusian Monastery was built upon it. This Pardon Churchyard was a space of three acres acquired a year earlier, to which the plague-ground was added. This Pardon Churchyard survived longer, being used for suicides and executed people. Charterhouse Square is 1¼ acres.

62. *The old Charterhouse Graveyard.*—In 1828 to 1830, when the present Pensioners' Court and other buildings were erected, part of this ground was built upon; but part exists in the courtyard on each side of the Pensioners' Courts, being about ⅓ acre in extent. All the open land has been used at one time or another for burials.

63. *The new Charterhouse Burial-ground.*—When the above ground was done away with, a smaller piece to the north was set aside for the interment of the pensioners. This remains still, and is very neatly kept. There are a few gravestones on the wall and splendid fruit trees. It is about ¼ acre in extent.

CLERKENWELL.

64. *St. James's Churchyard.*—¾ acre. This ground was purchased in 1673, enlarged in 1677, and is now laid out as a public garden and maintained by the vestry.

65. *Additional ground, Bowling Green Lane* (called St. James's middle ground).—This was leased by the parish, with the adjoining "Cherry Tree" public-house, in 1775 for 99 years. It is ¼ acre in size, situated at the corner of Rosoman Street and Bowling Green Lane. The London School Board secured it when the lease ran out, and it is now the playground of the Bowling Green Lane School.

66. *The Burial-ground of St. James's*, Pentonville Road.—This was formed as an additional ground for the parish of St. James, Clerkenwell. It is nearly an acre in extent, full of tombstones and very untidy, but the Metropolitan Public Gardens Association has undertaken to convert it into a public garden.

67. *St. John's Churchyard.*—What exists of this is between the church and St. John Street, a narrow strip, about 320 square yards in extent, closed and paved with tiles and tombstones. Its laying out by the Metropolitan Public Gardens Association is in hand.

68. *Spa Fields Burial-ground*, Exmouth Street.—Originally a tea-garden, afterwards a burial-ground, managed by a private individual. It is the property of the Marquis of Northampton, is about 1¾ acres in extent, and in the evenings is occasionally used as a volunteer drill-ground. In 1885 the Metropolitan Public Gardens Association laid it out as a playground, and the London County Council maintains it.

ST. PANCRAS.

69. *St. Pancras Burial-ground*, Pancras Road.

70. *St. Giles in The Fields Burial-ground*, Pancras Road.—These two grounds now form one garden, about 6 acres in extent, maintained with much care for the use of the public by St. Pancras Vestry. St. Giles' ground dates from 1803, but the other is much older. In 1889 part of St. Pancras ground was acquired under a special Act by the Midland Railway Company. This part was, in 1791, assigned to the French *Émigrés*, and many celebrated Frenchmen and Roman Catholics were buried there. Part of it has not actually been built upon, as the railway goes over it on arches. There are many high stacks of tombstones in the garden, and a "trophy" and a "dome" of headstones, numbering 496, which were taken from the part acquired by the railway.

71. *St. Martin's in the Fields Burial-ground* in Pratt Street.—1¾ acres. This was consecrated in 1805. It is now a well-kept public garden under the control of the St. Pancras Vestry. A part appears to have been appropriated as a private garden for the almshouses and as a site for a chapel and other buildings.

72. *St. James's Burial-ground*, Hampstead Road.—This belongs to the parish of St. James, Piccadilly. It was laid out as a public garden in 1887, and is maintained by the St. Pancras Vestry, a large slice at the east end having been taken off for public improvements. The remaining portion measures about 3 acres.

73. *St. Andrew's Burial-ground*, Gray's Inn Road.—1¼ acres. This ground belongs to the parish of St. Andrew, Holborn, adjoins the church of Holy Trinity, and is maintained as a public garden by the St. Pancras Vestry. It is well kept, except a railed-off piece south of the church, which is a sort of lumber-room.

74. *The Burial-ground of St. George's*, Bloomsbury.

75. *The Burial-ground of St. George the Martyr*, Bloomsbury.—These are out of Wakefield Street, Gray's Inn Road, and together form one public garden maintained by the St. Pancras Vestry, and very well kept. A part of the latter, which was consecrated in 1714, is still closed. Each ground is 1¼ acres in extent. There are vaults under the church in Hart Street.

76. *Whitfield's Tabernacle Burial-ground*, Tottenham Court Road.—Somewhat less than ½ acre. The London County Council opened it as a public garden in February, 1895. It is said that in 97 years upwards of 30,000 bodies were interred in this ground.

77. *Wesleyan Chapel-ground*, Liverpool Street, King's Cross.—An untidy little closed yard at the west end of the chapel containing two tombstones and much rubbish, and measuring about 225 square yards.

78. *St. James's Cemetery*, Highgate.—38 acres. First used in 1839. In 50 years 76,000 interments had taken place. It is in two portions and situated on a steep slope. Open daily.

ISLINGTON.

79. *St. Mary's Churchyard.*—1⅓ acres. This ground was enlarged in 1793, and was laid out as a public garden in 1885. It is maintained by the vicar and churchwardens.

80. *Additional ground round the Chapel of Ease in Holloway Road.*—4 acres. This is also laid out as a public garden, and is beautifully kept by the Islington Vestry.

81. *Burial-ground of St. John's Roman Catholic Church*, Duncan Row.—½ acre. A strip at the northern end of this ground is railed off with some tombstones in it, the remainder being tar-paved and used as a playground for the boys' Roman Catholic school.

82. *Islington Chapel-ground*, Church Street (also called Little Bunhill Fields).—The original chapel was built in 1788, and had a small graveyard. In 1817 the Rev. Evan Jones bought the

garden of 5, Church Row, and added it to this graveyard, the whole ground being nearly 1 acre in extent. It is now in several divisions, part is a yard belonging to the General Post Office, and the other parts are let and sold as builders' yards, or are vacant.

83. *Maberley Chapel-ground*, Ball's Pond Road.—Now called Earlham Hall. The ground is about 270 square yards, between the chapel and the road. It is closed and bare.

84. *Jewish Burial-ground*, Ball's Pond.—1¼ acres. This belongs to the West London Synagogue, is very neatly kept, and is still in use. It is full of very large tombstones.

ST. LUKE'S.

85. *St. Luke's Churchyard*, Old Street.—In two parts. Size of the whole ground, nearly 1¾ acres. The piece round the church is closed, and full of large altar tombs, ivy being planted most profusely. There is a great deal of rubbish in it. The part on the north side was laid out as a public garden in 1878, and is maintained by the vestry.

86. *The Poor ground*, Bath Street.—¼ acre. This was originally larger than it is now. It was consecrated in 1662 for the parish of St. Giles, Cripplegate, and called the pest-house ground. After 1732, when St. Luke's parish was formed, it was used by that parish. Now it is neatly laid out and used as a recreation ground by the patients of the St. Luke's Asylum. It is ¼ acre in extent.

87. *Wesleyan Chapel-ground*, City Road.—½ acre. The part in front of the chapel is neatly kept, but the part behind is closed and not so tidy. Wesley himself was buried in a vault here.

88. *Bunhill Fields*.—5 or 6 acres. This was originally two grounds, the southern part having been intended for burials in the Great Plague, but not being used was let by the Corporation to a Mr. John Tyndall, who carried it on as a private cemetery. Subsequently the northern part was added, and the whole ground extensively used for the interment of Dissenters. The Corporation maintain it as a public garden, but the tombstones have not been moved, and only the gates at the eastern end are generally open.

89. *The Friends Burial-ground*, Bunhill Row.—Acquired in 1661, many times added to, and chiefly used by the Friends of the Peel and Bull-and-Mouth divisions. In 1840 a school was built in it. The existing portion is about ½ acre in size, and is neatly kept as a private garden; but the remainder was used as the site for a Board School, a coffee palace, houses and shops, including the Bunhill Fields Memorial Buildings, erected in 1881.

90. *St. Bartholomew's Hospital Ground*, Seward Street.—⅓ acre. This was used for the interment of the unclaimed bodies. After being closed it was let as a carter's yard until it was laid out as a public playground by the Metropolitan Public Gardens Association in 1891. It is maintained by St. Luke's Vestry.

91. *Cripplegate Poor ground*, Whitecross Street.—It was called the "upper churchyard" of St. Giles, and was first used in 1636. It was very much overcrowded, the fees being low. A part of the site is occupied by the church and mission-house of St. Mary, Charterhouse, erected in 1864, and only a very small courtyard now exists between these buildings, with a large vault.

92. *The City Bunhill (or Golden Lane) Burial-ground*.—¼ acres. This was the site of a brewery, and set aside for burials in 1833. About one-third of it is in the City. It is now divided. One part is in the occupation of Messrs. Sutton and Co., carriers, and is full of sheds and carts, the greater part being roofed in, and the southern part has the City mortuary and coroner's court on it. What is unbuilt upon is a neat, private yard between these two buildings. It was closed for burials in 1853.

SHOREDITCH.

93. *St. Leonard's Churchyard.*—1½ acres. Maintained as a public garden by the Shoreditch Vestry. It is, I believe, partly in Bethnal Green.

94. *Old Burial-ground*, Hackney Road.—½ acre. This has an ancient watch-house in it, which was subsequently used as a cholera hospital. In 1892 the Metropolitan Public Gardens Association laid it out as a public playground, and it is maintained by the Burial Board.

95. *Holywell Mount Burial-ground.*—Behind St. James's Church, Curtain Road, which occupies the site of a theatre of Shakespeare's time. The ground is very old, and was much used at the time of plagues, and many actors are buried there. There is only about ⅓ acre left, the greater part having been used as the site for a parish room, and this is a timber-yard approached from Holywell Row.

96. *St. Mary's Churchyard*, Haggerston.—1⅓ acre. This is maintained by the Shoreditch Burial Board as a public garden, open during the summer. It was laid out by the Earl and Countess of Meath in 1882.

97. *St. John's Churchyard*, Hoxton.—1¼ acres. Also maintained by the Shoreditch Burial Board, and laid out by the Earl and Countess of Meath.

98. *Jewish Burial-ground*, Hoxton Street.—¼ acre. This belongs to the United Synagogue, and was used from 1700 till 1795. There is no grass, but many tombstones, and some one is sent four times a year to clear away the weeds, &c. It is not a tidy ground.

HACKNEY.

99. *St. John at Hackney Churchyard.*—6 acres. This includes an older ground, attached to the original church of St. Augustine, of which the tower still remains. Part of the churchyard is laid out as a public garden, and is neatly kept by the Hackney District Board of Works, but the newer part to the south of the church is still full of tombstones and rather untidy grass. The newest part of all, "the poor ground," which is at the extreme southern end, is laid out for the use of children.

100. *West Hackney Churchyard*, Stoke Newington Road.—Nearly 1½ acres. This was consecrated in 1824, and laid out as a public garden in 1885. It is maintained by the Hackney District Board of Works.

101. *St. Barnabas's Churchyard*, Homerton.—¾ acre. This ground is not open, but a good deal of care is shown in its management. In 1884 the Easter offerings were devoted to its improvement, and many tombstones were then laid flat.

102. *St. John of Jerusalem Churchyard*, South Hackney.—About ¾ acre. This was consecrated in 1831. It is full of tombstones, and the grass is not well kept, but it is usually open for people to pass through. It was closed for burials in 1868.

103. *Wells Street Burial-ground.*—This contains the site of the original South Hackney Church. It was laid out as a public garden in 1885, and is very neatly kept by the Hackney District Board of Works. Nearly ¾ acre.

104. *Independent Chapel-ground*, Mare Street (also called St. Thomas' Square Burial-ground).—⅔ acre. Laid out in 1888, and maintained by the Hackney District Board of Works, who paid, £100 for a passage to join this ground with No. 103, one caretaker managing both of them. It is very bright and neat. The ornamental shelter occupies the site of a previous building.

105. *Baptist Chapel-ground*, Mare Street.—About 500 square yards at the back of the chapel. There are several tombstones tumbling about, and the ground is very untidy.

106. *New Gravel Pit Chapel-ground*, Chatham Place, attached to the Unitarian Church.—¾ acre. This is full of tombstones and fairly tidy. The gate is usually open, the chapel-keeper living behind the chapel, and having a green-house and fowl-house, &c., in the ground.

107. *Retreat Place*.—A garden in front of 12 almshouses, founded in 1812 "for the widows of Dissenting ministers professing Calvinistic doctrines." Samuel Robinson, the founder, and his wife, are buried in the middle of the garden.

108. *Jewish Burial-ground*, Grove-street.—2¼ acres. This belongs to the United Synagogue, and was purchased in 1788. It is closed and full of erect tombstones, and has some trees and flower-beds near the entrance.

STOKE NEWINGTON.

109. *St. Mary's Churchyard*, Stoke Newington.—¾ acre. A very pretty ground round the old church, but not laid out or opened.

110. *Friend's Burial-ground*, Park Street, Stoke Newington, adjoining the meeting-house.—¾ acre. This was bought in 1827, and enlarged in 1849. It is still in use and neatly kept, but not open to the public.

111. *Abney Park Cemetery*.—32 acres. First used in 1840. Neatly kept and open daily, being chiefly used by Dissenters. It is crowded with tombstones.

BETHNAL GREEN.

112. *St. Matthew's Churchyard*.—About 2 acres. This was consecrated in 1746, and was much overcrowded. A mortuary was built in it some years ago. There are vaults under the schools as well as the church. It is closed, but negotiations are on foot respecting its conversion into a garden.

113. *St. Peter's Churchyard*, Hackney Road.—¼ acre. This churchyard is maintained as a public garden by the vicar, who opens it during the summer months. There are not many tombstones.

114. *St. Bartholomew's Churchyard*, near Cambridge Road.—Nearly an acre. This was laid out by the Metropolitan Public Gardens Association in 1885, and is maintained by the London County Council. It is immensely appreciated.

115. *St. James the Less Churchyard*, Old Ford Road.—Over an acre. Closed and considerably below the church. It contains about 10 tombstones, and several cocks and hens live in it. It is bare and damp.

116. *Providence Chapel Burial-ground*, Shoreditch Tabernacle, Hackney Road, was built on the site of the chapel. Part of the graveyard exists as a tar-paved yard or passage by the Tabernacle, with 4 tombstones against the walls.

117. *Victoria Park Cemetery*.—11 acres. This is maintained as a public garden by the London County Council, having been laid out in 1894 by the Metropolitan Public Gardens Association. It was formed in 1845, and used for 40 years. Before being laid out it was a most dreary, neglected-looking place; the soil is a heavy clay, and there used to be large wet lumps lying about all over the ground. At a burial in 1884 the clerk brought a handful of earth out of his pocket to throw upon the coffin. Now it is a bright, useful, little park, and is called Meath Gardens.

118. *Peel Grove Burial-ground* (also called North-East London Cemetery, Cambridge Heath or Road Burial-ground and Keldy's Ground). According to a return in 1855 it was 4 acres in extent, but now there is hardly one acre. It is in the occupation of J. Glover and Sons, dealers in building materials, and is full of wood, pipes, &c. There are some sheds in it. It was a private ground, formed 100 years ago, and was very much crowded. The late Metropolitan Board of Works saved the existing part from being built over. Before its present use it was often let out for shows, fairs, &c.

119. *Gibraltar Walk Burial-ground*, Bethnal Green Road.—Another private ground, formed about 100 years ago. It belongs to a lady who lives in the house which opens into it, and who has let pieces of it as yards for the shops and houses round. It is full of shrubs, trees, and weeds, and covered with rubbish, and is about ¾ acre in size.

120. *Jewish Burial-ground*, Brady Street.—This existed 100 years ago, and belongs to the United Synagogue. I believe it is about 4 acres. It is crowded with upright gravestones, and there are no properly made paths, but it is covered with neglected grass. Part of it is higher than the rest, the soil having been raised and the ground having been used a second time. This was the "Strangers'" portion.

WHITECHAPEL.

121. *St. Mary's Churchyard.*—¾ acre. This is a very old churchyard, and was much overcrowded. It is maintained by the rector as a garden, but a charge of 1d. is made for entrance. It is neatly laid out.

122. *Additional ground, Whitechapel Road*, entrance in St. Mary's Street.—This was called the workhouse burial-ground, the workhouse having been built in 1768 upon a former graveyard, and this piece to the north of it having then been set aside for interments and consecrated in 1796. The workhouse site was built upon some years ago, and the burial-ground became the playground of the Davenant Schools, one of which, the one facing St. Mary's Street, was built in it. In the order for closing it, dated May 9, 1853, it is called the Whitechapel Workhouse and Schools Ground. It is difficult to say exactly how far east the burial-ground extended, but from the Ordnance map and some older plans it would appear that the recent addition to the school in Whitechapel Road has been built in the burial-ground. In 1833 the size was given as 2,776 square yards, but it was stated that in 1832 196 cholera cases were interred in an adjoining piece of ground. This is probably what is now used as a stoneyard, with carts in it.

123. *Christ Church Churchyard*, Spitalfields.—1¾ acres. Laid out as a public garden by the Metropolitan Public Gardens Association in 1892, the association having undertaken to maintain it for 5 years.

124. *St. Peter and Vincula Churchyard*, in the Tower.—This, with the vaults under the church, was used for the interment of distinguished prisoners. It is a part of the great courtyard, and is about 525 square yards in extent.

125. *Holy Trinity Churchyard*, Minories.—A burial-ground possibly dating back to 1348. It has been added to the roadway of Church Street, some posts showing its boundaries. It was about 302 square yards in extent. Part has been built upon.

126. *Aldgate Burial-ground*, Cartwright Street.—This belongs to the parish of St. Botolph, Aldgate, and was consecrated in 1615. At the beginning of this century it was covered with small houses, the Weigh House School being built on it in 1846. The rookery was cleared by the Metropolitan Board of Works, and Darby Street was made, gravestones and remains being then discovered. The Metropolitan Public Gardens Association informed the Board of the

former existence of a burial-ground, with the result that what remained of the burial-ground was not built upon, but was made into an asphalted playground, about ⅛ acre in extent, for the children of the adjoining block of tenements.

127. *German Lutheran Church*, Little Alie Street.—A small yard exists at the back of the church. Closed.

128. *Friends Burial-ground*, Baker's Row.—Very nearly an acre. This belonged to the Friends of the Devonshire House division, who acquired it in 1687. It is leased by the society to the Whitechapel District Board of Works, who maintain it as a public recreation ground. It is well laid out and well kept, being chiefly used by children.

129. *Mile End New Town Burial-ground*, Hanbury Street.—This adjoined the chapel, and extended from Hanbury Street to Old Montague Street. A school and other buildings have been erected in it, and all that is left is a paved yard, about 250 square yards in size, on the west side of the chapel.

130. *Sheen's Burial-ground*, Church Lane.—A private ground, immensely used. It seems to have been at one time used by the congregation of the Baptists in Little Alie Street, and was then called "Mr. Brittain's burial-ground." If so it existed in 1763. After being closed for burials it was used as a cooperage, and now it is Messrs. Fairclough's yard, and full of carts and sheds, &c. A new stable was built in 1894, but the London County Council declined to prevent its erection. The size of the ground is about ½ acre.

131. *The London Hospital Burial-ground*.—In a plan of 1849 the whole of the southern part of the enclosure is marked as a burial-ground, which would be 1½ acres in extent. It was closed on November 25, 1853, but at the hospital it is stated that bodies were interred there after 1859, though not after 1864. Since then the medical school, the chaplain's house, and the nurses' home have been built in it. The remaining part of the ground is used as a garden and tennis-lawn for the students and nurses.

ST. GEORGE'S IN THE EAST.

132. *St. George's Churchyard.*—Dates from about 1730. The wall between this ground and the next one was taken down in 1875, and the two grounds were laid out as a public garden. They are maintained by the vestry, and, although in a densely crowded district, are beautifully kept. The size of the whole garden, consisting of the two graveyards, is about 3 acres.

133. *St. George's Wesleyan Chapel-ground*, Cable Street.—This forms one garden with the above.

134. *New Road Congregational Chapel-yard*, Cannon Street Road, between Lower and Upper Chapman Streets.—This was a much-used burial-ground, part of which has been covered with sheds and houses. What is left is about ⅓ acre in extent. The chapel was bought in 1832, and became Trinity Episcopal Chapel, and was subsequently removed and its site used for the new building of Raine's School. The burial-ground is in three parts, viz., the playground of the school, a cooper's yard, belonging to Messrs. Hasted and Sons, and a carter's yard of Messrs. Seaward Brothers.

135. *Danish Burial-ground*, Wellclose Square.—The Danish (or Mariners') Church has been supplanted by the Schools of St. Paul's, London Docks, and the whole of the garden is neatly laid out, and used as a private ground for the people who look after the schools, the crèche, &c. There are no tombstones now, and it is possible that only an enclosure round the church was used, like the railed-in enclosure in Prince's Square.

136. *Swedish Burial-ground*, Prince's Square.—Round the Eleanora Church, over ½ acre in size. It is very neatly laid out and well kept, and contains many tombstones.

137. *Ebenezer Chapel Burial-ground*, St. George's Street.—This was described in 1839 as being very much overcrowded. The chapel has been used us a school, but is now deserted, the small yard on the south side of it is used as a timber-yard and closed. About 220 square yards.

138. *Congregational Chapel-ground*, Old Gravel Lane.—140 square yards. Closed, bare, and untidy, with two gravestones against the wall.

139. *Baptist Burial-ground*, Broad Street, Wapping.—Mentioned by Maitland in 1756, and shown on Rocque's plan. The chapel has gone, but part of the adjoining yard exists as a small yard belonging to a milkman. Before he bought it it was the parish stoneyard. It is about 200 square yards in size. I have little doubt that this is a burial-ground.

140. *Roman Catholic Burial-ground*, Commercial Road.—The tombstones are flat and the ground is used as a private garden for the priests. It is about ½ acre in extent.

LIMEHOUSE.

141. *St. Anne's Churchyard.*—3 acres. Consecrated 1730, and since enlarged, but in 1800 a piece was cut of for Commercial Road, the bodies being removed south of the church. Laid out as a public garden by the Metropolitan Public Gardens Association in 1887, and now maintained by the London County Council. It is nearly kept, except the private passage to the mortuary.

142. *St. Paul's Churchyard*, Shadwell.—¾ acre. Consecrated in 1671, but used before that as a pest-field for Stepney. Laid out by the Metropolitan Public Gardens Association in 1886, and now maintained and kept in good order by the London County Council.

143. *St. James's Churchyard*, Ratcliff.—Nearly 1 acre. Laid out as a public garden by the Metropolitan Public Gardens Association in 1891, and maintained by the vicar.

144. *St. John's Churchyard*, Wapping.—600 square yards. Consecrated in 1617. This ground used to be very low and full of water. It is closed and fairly tidy, having many large altar tombs in it.

145. *Additional ground opposite St. John's Church.*—Rather over ½ acre. This was one of the Stepney pest-fields. It is closed, but tidy. There are quantities of tombstones in this ground, many of which seem to be falling to pieces, and an unusual number of trees and flowering shrubs.

146. *Friends Burial-ground*, Brook Street. Ratcliff.—800 square yards. This is approached through the house on the south side of the meeting-house. It was acquired by the Society of Friends in 1666 or 1667, the land being originally copyhold, but enfranchised in 1734 for £21. It is neatly kept, and has four small upright stones.

147. *Brunswick Wesleyan Chapel-ground*, Three Colt Lane.—Approached by a passage at the back of the chapel. It is about 450 square yards in size, and is used as a private garden. There are vaults under the chapel and three tombstones. It is said that about 1,000 bodies were buried here, the last interment taking place in 1849.

MILE END OLD TOWN.

148. *St. Dunstan's Churchyard Stepney.*—About 6 acres, or rather more. At the time of the Great Plague about 150 bodies were interred here daily, and several extra grounds were provided for the parish. It was laid out as a public garden in 1887 by the Metropolitan Public

Gardens Association. It is a most useful and shady ground, and is very neatly kept by the London County Council.

149. *Stepney Meeting-House Burial-ground*, White Horse Street (also called the Almshouse ground and Ratcliff Workhouse ground).—There are many tombstones and the ground is fairly tidy. The gate is generally open, as the entrance to the almshouses is through it. Size ½ acre.

150. *Holy Trinity Churchyard*, Tredegar Square.—¾ acre. Laid out by the Metropolitan Public Gardens Association in 1887, and maintained by the London County Council. The gravestones have not been moved, and some of the graves are still occasionally used, though no new ones are dug.

151. *Wycliffe Chapel Burial-ground*, Philport Street, Stepney.—¾ acre. This dates From 1831, and is behind the chapel and the Scotch church. It is full of tombstones, closed and untidy. Chadwick divides it into a part belonging to the chapel and a larger part belonging to the Scotch church, but it appears to be all one now, and is in the hands of the elders of Wycliffe Chapel.

152. *Globe Road Chapel Burial-ground*, also called Mile End Cemetery.—The chapel is now Gordon Hall, and belongs to Dr. Stephenson of the Children's Homes. The burial-ground is in private hands. The ground was very much overcrowded, and there were vaults under the chapel, the schools and the sexton's house, but all the part south of the chapel was taken by the Great Eastern Railway Company. The existing piece is about 670 square yards in extent, is closed and most untidy, quantities of rubbish lying about amongst the tombstones.

153. *East London Cemetery*, Shandy Street, also called the Beaumont Burial-ground.—2¼ acres. This was much crowded. It was laid out as a playground by the Metropolitan Public Gardens Association in 1885, and is maintained by the London County Council.

154. *Burial-ground of the Bancroft Almshouses*, Mile End Road.—The People's Palace is on the site of the almshouses, and part of the burial-ground has been merged into the roadway on the east side of the palace. St. Benet's Church, Hall and Vicarage were built in this ground, the church being consecrated in 1872. Three pieces still exist, in all less than ½ acre; one is the vicarage garden, another is open to the road, and the northern point is closed and roofed over, forming a little yard where flag-staffs, &c., are stored. The open part is also a store-yard, having heaps of stones in it, besides much rubbish. There are gravestones against the wall.

155. *Stepney Pest-field.*—Many acres to the south of the London Hospital were used for interments at the time of the plague, and the Brewers' Garden and the space by St. Philip's Church are, according to some authorities, part of the site originally called Stepney Mount. At the Home Office it is believed that there have been no burials in the ground round St. Philip's, nor have there since it was St. Philip's churchyard; but I think there were long before the first St. Philip's Church or the Brewers' Almshouses existed. The Brewers' Garden is open to the public at a charge of 1d.

156. *Jewish Burial-ground*, 70, Bancroft Road.—About 1,650 square yards. This ground belongs to the Maiden Lane Synagogue, and is crowded with upright gravestones. The grass is neglected. Burials still take place. It is in a densely-populated district.

157. *Jewish Burial-ground*, Alderney Road.—1 acre. Formed in 1700, enlarged in 1733. Belongs to the United Synagogue. The tombstones are upright, and they are not so thick as in most of the Jewish grounds, while the grass is kept more neatly.

158. *Jewish Burial-ground*, Mile End Road.—This ground is nearly ¾ acre in extent, and is at the back of the Beth Holim Hospital. It belongs to the Spanish and Portuguese Jews, the tombstones are flat, there are several trees, and the ground is very neatly kept. Part of the graveyard (where it is said that there have been no interments) has some seats in it, and is used by the patients of the hospital as a garden.

159. *Jewish Cemetery*, Mile End Road.—4¾ acres. This belongs to the Spanish and Portuguese Jews, and is still in use. The gravestones are flat ones and low altar tombs, and the ground is neatly kept, although very bare.

POPLAR.

160. *All Saints' Churchyard.*—Size, with that part which was used for the burial of cholera victims, on the other side of the road, 4 acres. The northern part of the churchyard was laid out by the Metropolitan Public Gardens Association in 1893, the rector having undertaken to maintain it for a few years. It is much appreciated and well kept.

161. *St. Matthias's Churchyard.*—(This church was the chapel of the East India Dock Company, and is sometimes called Poplar Chapel.) 1¼ acres. It is in the middle of the Poplar Recreation Ground, closed and fairly tidy. There are many tombstones.

162. *St. Mary's Churchyard*, Bow.—2,716 square yards. This is in two portions, the eastern one is closed, but the western one has been laid out by the Metropolitan Public Gardens Association and provided with seats, the rector maintaining it.

163. *St. Mary's Churchyard*, Bromley-by-Bow, or Bromley St. Leonard.—This churchyard is 1¼ acres in size and is closed, but very neatly kept up by the parish, and has some tombstones of artistic value in it. Its opening as a public garden is under consideration.

164. *Baptist Chapel-ground*, Bow.—⅓ acre. Part of this ground is railed off as a private garden, the rest is used as a thoroughfare by the school-children. There are several tombstones, some of which have been put against the walls.

165. *Trinity Congregational Chapel-ground*, East India Dock Road.—⅓ acre. This was laid out in 1888 as a public garden, the minister of the chapel maintaining it. On his removal from the district it was closed and has not been re-opened.

166. *Roman Catholic ground*, Wade's Place.—1,300 square yards. This belonged to St. Mary's Roman Catholic Church in Finsbury Circus, Moorfields, and was chiefly used for the poor Irish. It was a very damp, unwholesome ground. It is now used as a playground for the adjoining Roman Catholic school.

167. *City of London and Tower Hamlets Cemetery* (partly in Mile End).—33 acres. First used in 1841. By 1889, 247,000 bodies had been interred here, many being buried in common graves. It is still in use and open daily, a regular ocean of tombstones, many of which are lying about, apparently uncared for and unclaimed; in fact, most of the graves, except those at the edges of the walks, look utterly neglected, and parts of the ground are very untidy. It is situated in a densely-populated district.

WANDSWORTH.

168. *All Saints' Churchyard*, High Street.—¼ acre. This is closed, and is much more tidy at the eastern end than the western end.

169. *East Hill Burial-ground*, Wandsworth Road.—½ acre. This was consecrated in 1680, and many French Huguenots were buried in it. It is closed and fairly tidy.

170. *Garratt Lane Cemetery*, South Street, Wandsworth.—1¾ acres. This was consecrated in 1808. It is closed to the public, and closed for interments with the exception of widows, widowers, and parents of deceased persons already interred there. It is maintained by the Wandsworth Burial Board.

171. *Friends Burial-ground*, High Street, Wandsworth.—400 square yards. This is attached to the meeting-house, is closed and very neatly kept. There are a few upright tombstones.

172. *Baptist Burial-ground*, North Street, Wandsworth.—An untidy little closed yard with no tombstones in it and neglected grass. The chapel now belongs to the Salvation Army. I doubt if it was much used for burials, but, at any rate, there was one interment in 1854. It is about the same size as the Friends' ground.

173. *Independent Burial-ground*, Wandsworth.—This is now a small tar-paved yard adjoining Memorial Hall, which was built on the site of an old chapel or school-house. There are a few trees.

174. *St. Mary's Churchyard*, Putney.—½ acre. Closed and neatly kept.

175. *Putney Burial-ground*, Upper Richmond Road.—1 acre. This was a gift to the parish from the Rev. R. Pettiwand, and consecrated in 1763. It was laid out in 1886, but the tombstones were not moved, and many of them are dilapidated brick altar tombs. It is maintained for the public by the Putney Burial Board.

176. *St. Nicholas Churchyard*, Lower Tooting.—2 acres. This is still in use. It is open daily and kept in good order.

177. *Lower Tooting Chapel-ground.*—231 square yards behind the chapel (Congregational in High Street) and about 30 square yards in front. Some tombstones. Chapel dates from 1688, and was founded by Daniel Defoe.

178. *St. Leonard's Churchyard*, Streatham.—1¼ acres. The present church dates from 1831, but the churchyard is at least 100 years older. It is closed for burials and well planted with flowers, grass, and trees. The gates are sometimes open.

179. *St. Paul's Churchyard*, Clapham, in the Wandsworth Road.—1½ acres. This is closed, and very full of tombstones. It is maintained by the Clapham Burial Board, but it is in a rather jungly condition.

180. *Union Chapel-ground*, Streatham Hill.—About 500 square yards. This is a neat little garden between the chapel and the schools, both of which have been rebuilt, the schools in 1878. There is a row of tombstones against the walls. It is generally closed.

181. *Wandsworth Cemetery.*—12 acres. First used in 1878. Open daily.

182. *Lambeth Cemetery*, Tooting Graveney.—41 acres. First used in 1854. Open daily.

183. *Putney Cemetery.*—3 acres. First used in 1855. This is an encroachment on a common.

BATTERSEA.

184. *St. Mary's Churchyard.*—¾ acre. Closed. The laying out of this ground is under consideration.

185. *St. George's Churchyard*, Battersea Park Road.—¾ acre. This is closed, and in a very neglected condition. There are not many gravestones.

186. *Battersea Cemetery*, Bolingbroke Grove.—8½ acres. First used in 1860. Open daily.

LAMBETH.

187. *St. Mary's Churchyard.*—½ acre. A very old ground, enlarged in 1623 and 1820. It is very neatly laid out and the gates are left open, though there are no seats in it.

188. *Additional ground in High Street* (also called Paradise Row burial-ground).—1½ acres. Given to the parish by Archbishop Tenison, and consecrated in 1705. It was laid out in 1884 by the Lambeth Vestry, who maintain it efficiently.

189. *St. John's Churchyard*, Waterloo Bridge Road.—An acre in size. This was laid out as a garden and playground in 1877, and is well kept up by the Lambeth Vestry.

190. *St. Mark's Churchyard*, Kennington.—1¾ acres. This is closed and full of tombstones, but neatly kept.

191. *Regent Street Baptist Chapel-ground*, Kennington Road.—A little ground at the back of the chapel, with a few tombstones and one great vault in it.

192. *Esher Street Congregational Chapel-ground*, Upper Kennington Lane.—About 480 square yards, closed, and very untidy.

193. *St. Matthew's Churchyard*, Brixton.—2 acres. This dates from 1824. It is closed, but neatly kept.

194. *Denmark Row Chapel-ground*, Coldharbour Lane.—This has been partly built upon, and there is now only a small yard behind the chapel.

195. *Stockwell Green Congregational Chapel-ground.*—¼ acre, or rather more. This is behind the chapel, and is a particularly neglected and untidy graveyard.

196. *St. Luke's Churchyard*, Norwood.—1 acre. This dates from 1825. It is tidily kept, except the part near the station. The gate is generally open. The gravestones are in situ.

197. *Congregational Chapel-ground*, Chapel Road, Lower Norwood.—About ⅓ acre behind the chapel. It is closed, and has grass and a few tombstones in it.

198. *Norwood Cemetery*, 40 acres.—First used in 1838. Open daily, and fairly well kept. It is crowded with tombstones, and it includes a Greek cemetery and a burial-ground belonging to the parish of St. Mary at Hill, each about 550 square yards in size.

CAMBERWELL.

199. *St. Giles's Churchyard.*—3¼ acres. Enlarged in 1717, 1803, and 1825. Closed, full of tombstones, and not well kept.

200. *St. George's Churchyard*, Well Street, Camberwell.—The church was consecrated in 1824, the ground being given by Mr. John Rolls. The churchyard measures about an acre, and was laid out in 1886 by the Metropolitan Public Gardens Association. It is maintained by the vestry. A mortuary has been built on it.

201. *Dulwich Burial-ground*, Court Lane, the graveyard of God's Gift College.—Size, 1½ roods. This ground dates from about 1700. It is closed and very neatly kept. There are several large altar tombs in it, and it is a most rural and picturesque spot.

202. *Wesleyan Chapel-ground*. Stafford Street, Peckham.—336 square yards. The chapel in now a school, the burial-ground being the playground, a paved yard.

203. *Friends Burial-ground*, Peckham Rye.—About 470 square yards. This ground was purchased in 1821, it is behind the meeting-house in Hanover Street, has some small flat gravestones in it, and is closed. It is most beautifully kept with neatly mown grass and a border of flowers.

204. *Camberwell Cemetery*, Forest Hill Road.—29½ acres. First used in 1856. Open daily.

205. *Nunhead Cemetery* (All Saints').—50 acres. First used in 1840. Open daily.

NEWINGTON.

206. *St. Mary's Churchyard.*—1¼ acres. This was enlarged in 1757 and 1834, and is now maintained as a public garden by the burial board, the freehold being vested in the rector. It is well laid out.

207. *St. Peter's Churchyard*, Walworth.—1¼ acres. This is also maintained as a public garden by the Newington Burial Board, having been laid out by the Metropolitan Public Gardens Association, at the sole cost of the Goldsmiths' Company, and opened in May, 1895.

208. *Sutherland Congregational Chapel-ground*, Walworth.—This is close to St. Peter's, about 300 square yards in size, and closed. It has been somewhat encroached on by the school, which was enlarged in 1889. A few tombstones exist in the passage on the north side of the chapel and in the ground at the back. It is fairly tidy.

209. *York Street Chapel-ground*, Walworth.—About 700 square yards at the rear of the chapel and not visible from the street. It is closed and full of tombstones, but is to be laid out.

210. *East Street Baptist Chapel-ground*, Walworth.—About 400 square yards, with one tombstone in it. It is closed and very untidy.

211. *St. John's Episcopal Chapel-ground*, Walworth.—In 1843 it was estimated at 6,400 square yards. The chapel is in Penrose Street, and is now the workshop of a scenic artist, the front wall having been heightened for the purpose of advertising the *South London Press*. The burial-ground is approached from Occupation Road, Manor Place, the railway line going across it on arches, and it is now the vestry depôt for carts, manure, gravel, &c. An adjoining plot is the site for the baths and washhouses. This ground is in danger of being encroached upon, and new bays for dust and other erections of the sort are often built in it.

212. *New Bunhill Fields*, Deverell Street, New Kent Road (also called Hoole and Martin's).—¾ acre. This was a private speculation, and was most indecently crowded. Between 1820 and 1838 10,000 bodies were buried here, the vault under the chapel containing 1,800 coffins. The ground was closed in 1853, and it then became a timber-yard. The chapel now belongs to the Salvation Army, but the burial-ground is still "Deverell's timber-yard," and is covered with high stacks of timber. There are many sheds in it, and iron bars, &c.

ST. GEORGE THE MARTYR.

213. *St. George's Churchyard*, Borough.—This is about an acre in size, and is maintained as a public garden by the rector and churchwardens, having been laid out in 1882. It is much used.

214. *St. George's Recreation ground*, Tabard Street (the Lock burial-ground).—Rather over ¼ acre. This was originally the burial-ground of the Lock Hospital, which was pulled down in 1809, a portion of the site of the hospital and ground having been before then consecrated as a parish burial-ground. It was chiefly used for pauper burials, and was crowded with bodies. It is now a neat public garden, laid out by the vestry in 1887, and in the possession of the rector and churchwardens of St. George's.

215. *Chapel Graveyard*, Collier's Rents, Long Lane.—This is about 620 square yards in extent, and is on the north side of an old Baptist chapel, which now belongs to the Congregational Union. The ground dates from before 1719, and is closed. There are a few tombstones and grass, but it is not very well kept.

ST. SAVIOR'S, SOUTHWARK.

216. *St. Saviour's Churchyard.*—This ancient ground has been often enlarged and curtailed, and at times was used as a marketplace. What now exists is about ½ acre on the south side of the church, which is at present under restoration.

217. *Additional ground for St. Saviour's,* called the College Yard or St. Saviour's Almshouse Burial-ground, Park Street.—This existed before 1732. Size, ¼ acre. The London, Brighton and South Coast Railway goes over it on arches, and it is now the store-yard of Messrs. Stone and Humphries, builders. Most of it is roofed in, but it is not actually covered with buildings.

218. *Additional ground for St. Saviour's,* called the Cross Bones, Redcross Street.—This was made, at least 250 years ago, "far from the parish church," for the interment of the low women who frequented the neighbourhood. It was subsequently used as the pauper ground, and was crowded to excess. Nevertheless two schools were built in it. The remaining piece is about 1,000 square yards. It has frequently been offered for sale as a building site, and has formed the subject for much litigation. It is made a partial use of by being let for fairs, swings, &c. It was sold as a building site in 1883, but, not having been used by 1884, the sale was declared (under the Disused Burial-grounds Act) null and void.

219. *Christ Church Churchyard,* Blackfriars Bridge Road.—1½ acres. This dates from about 1737, and has been enlarged. An infant school was built in it. It is closed, and not laid out.

220. *Deadman's Place Burial-ground.* Deadman's Place is now called Park Street.—This ground was originally used for the interment of large numbers of victims to the plague. Then it became the graveyard of an adjoining Independent chapel, and was extensively used for the interment of ministers, being a sort of Bunhill Fields for South London. Now it is merely one of the yards over which trucks run on rails, in the middle of the large brewery belonging to Messrs. Barclay and Perkins, about ½ acre in extent. It existed as a burial-ground in 1839, but not, I believe, in 1843.

221. *Baptist Burial-ground,* Bandy Leg Walk (subsequently called Guildford Street).—There was such a ground in 1729. In 1807 there existed the St. Saviour's Workhouse, with a burial-ground on the east side of it which, from its position, may have coincided with the Baptists' ground, and what is now left of the burial-ground is a garden or courtyard, about 1,000 square yards in size, between the new buildings of the Central Fire Brigade Station, Southwark Bridge Road, and the old house behind them. It is entered through the large archway.

ST. OLAVE'S.

222. *St. Olave's Churchyard,* Tooley Street.—A stone-paved yard, 634 square yards in extent, between the church and the river. Closed.

223. *Additional ground to St. Olave's and to St. John's,* Horselydown, near St. John's Church.—About ½ acre, with a few tombstones in it. This was laid out in 1888, being chiefly asphalted, and is maintained as a recreation ground by the Board of Works For the St. Olave's District. It is well used and neatly kept.

224. *St. John's Churchyard,* Horselydown.—Nearly 2 acres. Laid out as a public garden in 1882, and maintained by the St. Olave's Board.

225. *St. Thomas's Churchyard.*—This does not adjoin the church, but is behind the houses opposite. Size about 787 square yards. It belongs to St. Thomas's Hospital, and is used as a private garden by a house in St. Thomas' Street.

226. *St. Thomas's Hospital Burial-ground,* St. Thomas' Street.—Part of this has been covered by St. Olave's Rectory and Messrs. Bevington's leather warehouse. The remaining piece

measures about 1,770 square yards, and is an asphalted tennis-court and garden for the students of Guy's Hospital, the building in it being the treasurer's stables. It belongs to St. Thomas's Hospital, and is leased to Guy's.

227. *Butler's Burial-ground*, Horselydown.—This was made about 1822, the entrance being in Coxon's (late Butler's) Place, and was 1,440 square yards in size. It is now Zurhoorst's cooperage and is full of barrels. A small piece, which I believe was a part of the burial-ground, is a yard belonging to a builder named Field. There were vaults running under four dwelling-houses. These still exist, and are under the houses next to the entrance to Mr. Field's yard.

BERMONDSEY.

228. *St. Mary Magdalene's Churchyard*.—Rather over 1½ acres. This was enlarged in 1783 and 1810, and contains the remains of an ancient cemetery belonging to Bermondsey Abbey. It is maintained as a public garden by the vestry, the rector reserving certain rights. It is well laid out, and forms a most useful and attractive garden.

229. *St. James's Churchyard*, Bermondsey, Jamaica Road.—1¾ acres. It was extensively used for a drying-ground for clean clothes when the Metropolitan Public Gardens Association secured it in 1886, and laid it out as a garden. It is maintained by the vestry.

230. *Roman Catholic Ground*, Parker's Row.—The land was given for the purpose in 1833 or 1834. The ground between the church and the road measures about 300 square yards, and was very much overcrowded. It is closed and untidy, with no tombstones. Burials also took place in the garden, which is used as a recreation ground for the schools, and is neatly kept.

231. *Southwark Chapel Graveyard (Wesleyan)*, Long Lane.—900 square yards. This is on the west side of the chapel, which dates from 1808. It is closed, and contains a few gravestones and a hen-coop.

232. *Guy's Hospital Burial-ground*, Nelson Street.—This is nearly 200 years old, and is rather over ½ acre. Since being closed for burials it has been let as a builder's yard. The Bermondsey Vestry is now negotiating for its purchase as a recreation ground.

233. *Friends Burial-ground*, Long Lane.—¼ acre. This was bought in 1697 for £120. It was closed in 1844, but in 1860 a large number of coffins, &c., were brought there and interred when Southwark Street was made and the Worcester Street burial-ground annihilated. It is being laid out for the public, and will be maintained by the Bermondsey Vestry, who have it on lease from the Society of Friends. There are no gravestones in it.

234. *Ebenezer Burial-ground*, Long Lane.—This adjoins the above ground, and it is hoped that it may eventually be added to the garden. It was formed about 100 years ago. It originally belonged to the Independent Chapel in Beck Street, Horselydown, and subsequently to the trustees of Ebenezer Baptist Chapel. There is a "minister's vault" in the centre. It is closed and untidy, 220 square yards in extent.

ROTHERHITHE.

235. *St. Mary's Churchyard*.—¾ acre. This is closed, except on Sundays. It is full of tombstones and kept in good order.

236. *Additional ground in Church Street*.—1¼ acres. This is also only open on Sundays, and is fairly tidy.

237. *Christ Church Churchyard*, Union Road.—700 square yards. This is closed, and there are no tombstones on the north side of the church. The south side is rather untidy, except

round the grave of General Sir William Gomm, who gave the ground for the church (being Lord of the Manor), where there is a patch of good grass and flowers.

238. *All Saints' Churchyard*, Deptford Lower Road.—Nearly 1 acre. This land was given by Sir William Gomm in 1840, and was used for 17 years. It is closed, and wooden palings separate it from the ground in front of the church. It is not well kept.

239. *Holy Trinity Churchyard*, near Commercial Docks Pier.—About 1 acre. Consecrated in 1838. This ground was also only used for 20 years; a part of it is railed of for the vicarage garden, where probably no interments took place. It was laid out by the Metropolitan Public Gardens Association in 1885, and taken over by the London County Council in 1896. It is a very attractive, shady garden.

GREENWICH.

240. *St. Alphege Churchyard.*—Enlarged in 1716, 1774, and 1808. Size 2,740 square yards. This was laid out by the Metropolitan Public Gardens Association in 1889, and is maintained by the Greenwich District Board of Works. There are no seats in it.

241. *Additional ground*, separated from the above by a public footpath.—This is 2½ acres, and was consecrated in 1833. It was laid out in 1889 by the Metropolitan Public Gardens Association, and is maintained by the Greenwich District Board of Works. There are plenty of seats in it, and it is well used and neatly kept.

242. *St. Nicholas Churchyard*, Deptford.—¾ acre. This is closed and full of tombstones, but fairly tidy.

243. *Additional ground*, Wellington Street.—¾ acre. This ground, belonging to the parish of St. Nicholas, was laid out in 1884 by the Kyrle Society, and is very well kept up by the Greenwich District Board of Works, who have lately acquired a piece of adjoining land to be added to the recreation ground.

244. *St. Paul's Churchyard*, Deptford.—2½ acres. This is vested in the rector, and maintained by the Deptford Burial Board. The gravestones are not moved, but there are a few seats in the ground, which is open to the public.

245. *Baptist (Unitarian) Chapel Burial-ground*, Church Street.—This touches the above, and is about ¼ acre. It is closed, the railings and gravestones are broken, and there is a quantity of rubbish lying about.

246. *Friends Burial-ground*, High Street, Deptford.—About 360 square yards. This is behind the meeting-house and closed. It is neatly kept and only contains one gravestone.

247. *Congregational Chapel Burial-ground*, High Street, Deptford.—About 400 square yards. This is closed, but neatly laid out, and there are gravestones against the walls.

248. *Congregational Chapel-ground*, Greenwich Road.—¼ acre, or rather less. This dates from 1800. The gate is often open, and the gravestones are flat or against the walls, but it is a bare, uninteresting-looking ground.

249. *Congregational Chapel-ground*, Maze Hill, Greenwich.—A rather neglected-looking ground in Park Place, with several flat tombstones, about 500 square yards in size.

250. *Greenwich Hospital Burial-ground.*—This adjoins the Royal Naval Schools, and measures about 4 acres. An inner enclosure is full of tombstones, but the outer part has only some monuments in it. It is very well kept, with splendid trees and good grass, and the gate from the school playground is generally open.

251. *Greenwich Hospital Cemetery.*—In Westcombe. This is nearly 6 acres in size, and was first used in 1857.

LEWISHAM.

252. *St. Mary's Churchyard.*—2 acres. Laid out as a public garden in 1886, and maintained by the Lewisham District Board of Works.

253. *St. Bartholomew's Churchyard*, Sydenham.—¾ acre. Closed for interments. This is beautifully kept and is a very pretty ground. The gates are generally open, but there are no seats.

254. *Deptford Cemetery.*—17 acres. First used in 1858. By 1889, 50,000 bodies had been interred there.

255. *Lewisham Cemetery.*—15½ acres, of which 4 are reserved and let as a market-garden. First used 1858.

256. *Lee Cemetery.*—In Hither Green. 10 acres, of which 4 are in reserve. First used 1873. These are open daily.

PLUMSTEAD.

257. *St. Nicholas's Churchyard.*—Still in use for burials, but under regulation. It is open daily, and measures about 4 acres.

258. *Woolwich Cemetery*, Wickham Lane. (Partly outside the boundary of Plumstead.)—32 acres. First used in 1856. Open daily.

259. *Plumstead Cemetery*, Wickham Lane.—32¼ acres. First used 1890. Open daily.

LEE.

260. *St. John the Baptist Churchyard*, Lee, Eltham.—3 acres. This is also in use, but under regulation, and is open daily.

261. *St. Margaret's Churchyard*, Lee.—Still in use, open daily, and very neatly kept. It is about 1½ acres in size.

262. *The Old Churchyard*, Lee.—This is opposite St. Margaret's, and contains the ruins of the old church. It is full of tombstones and neatly kept. It is generally open, but has no seats in it.

263. *St. Luke's Churchyard*, Charlton.—½ acre. This is full of tombstones and closed, but very neatly kept. Burials occasionally take place in existing vaults, but in each case permission has to be obtained from the Home Secretary.

264. *St. Thomas's Churchyard*, Charlton.—On the borders of Woolwich. Nearly an acre. This churchyard was in use for burials in 1854 when it was put under regulation.

265. *Morden College Cemetery*, Blackheath.—¼ acre. Closed. Neatly kept. Contains about 80 tombstones. The college was founded about 1695.

266. *Charlton Cemetery.*—8 acres. First used in 1855. Open daily.

267. *Greenwich Cemetery.*—15 acres. Open daily.

WOOLWICH.

268. *St. Mary's Churchyard.*—Over 3 acres. In a fine situation overlooking the river. Laid out as a public garden by the Metropolitan Public Gardens Association, at the cost of Mr. Passmore Edwards, and opened in May, 1895. It is maintained by the Woolwich Local Board.

269. *Enon Chapel-yard*, High Street.—112 square yards. A tar-paved and closed yard, with some tombstones against the walls.

270. *Union Chapel Graveyard*, Sun Street.—⅓ acre. This is closed. There is a very bad fence round it, and it looks uncared for. Negotiations are on foot to secure it for the public.

271. *Salem Chapel-yard*, Powis Street.—300 square yards. Eighteen or twenty years ago the London School Board took the chapel and adapted it as a school. It is now the infant school, other buildings having been added, and the graveyard is a tar-paved passage used as a playground.

272. *Wesleyan Chapel-yard*, William Street.—¼ acre. Here a school building has evidently encroached upon the burial-ground. There are several gravestones, and it is fairly tidy, the gate being often open.

273. *Roman Catholic Ground*, New Road.—This also has probably been encroached upon. What now exists is a yard, ¼ acre in size, between the school and the Roman Catholic church, with three graves in one enclosure in the middle. The gate is open during school hours.

THE CITY.

I. Burial-grounds which are laid out as public recreation grounds—

274. *St. Paul's Cathedral Churchyard.*—Used as a burial-place since Roman times. It includes the Pardon Churchyard, the burial-grounds for the parishes of St. Faith and St. Gregory, and a piece allotted to St. Martin, Ludgate. Size, 1½ acres. Maintained by the Corporation. Laid out in 1878-1879.

275. *St. Botolph's Churchyard*, Aldersgate Street.

276. *Additional ground for Christ Church*, Newgate Street.

277. *Additional ground for St. Leonard's*, Foster Lane.—These three form together one public garden, rather more than ½ acre in extent. Very neatly kept up with parochial funds.

278. *St. Olave's Churchyard*, Silver Street.—Site of the burned church.

279. *Allhallows' Churchyard*, London Wall.

280. *St. Katharine Coleman Churchyard*, Fenchurch Street.

281. *St. Botolph's Churchyard*, Aldgate.—¼ acre.—Four grounds laid out by the Metropolitan Public Gardens Association.

281. *St. Botolph's Churchyard*, Bishopsgate. Size nearly ½ acre.

283. *St. Botolph's*, Billingsgate, upper burial-ground, Botolph lane.

284. *St. Mary Aldermanbury Churchyard.*

285. *St. Sepulchre's Churchyard*, Holborn.

286. *St. Bride's Churchyard*, Fleet Street.—Five small grounds laid out with the assistance of the Metropolitan Public Gardens Association. No. 282 was laid out by the Association, but the entire cost was borne by the parish.

287. *Additional ground for St. Dunstan's in the West*, in Fetter Lane. Asphalted and used as a playground for the Greystoke Place Board School. Some tombstones remain in an enclosure at the edge. 4,750 square feet in area.

II. Burial-grounds that are not laid out as open spaces for the public use, although most of them are neatly kept, while a few are used as store-yards, &c., and others are open at times—

288. *The Temple Churchyard.*—Partly public thoroughfare, partly closed.

The churchyards of—

289. *St. Andrew*, Holborn.

290. *Christ Church*, Newgate Street.—On the site of the western end of the church of the Greyfriars.

291. *St. Ann*, Blackfriars.—Two grounds. The western one is the site of the burned church.

292. *St. Andrew by the Wardrobe*, Queen Victoria Street. Very little left.

293. *St. Bartholomew the Great.*—On the site of the ancient nave, the *Green-ground* on the site of the south transept, and a remnant of the *Poor ground* on the north side.

294. *St. Dionys Backchurch*, Lime Street.

295. *St. Bartholomew the Less.*—In the hospital. At one time it extended further south.

296. *St. Giles*, Cripplegate, with the *Green-ground*, an extension to the south. Often Open. Neatly kept.

297. *St. Alphege*, London Wall.—The churchyard does not adjoin the church. It contains a portion of the old wall.

298. *St. Ann and St. Agnes*, Gresham Street.

299. *St. John Zachary*, Gresham Street.—Site of burned church.

300. *St. Mary Staining*, Oat Lane.—Site of burned church.

301. *St. Alban's*, Wood Street.

302. *St. Peter Cheap*, Wand Street.—Site of burned church.

303. *St. Vedast*, Foster Lane.

304. *St. Mildred*, Bread Street.—Yard full at ladders.

305. *St. Mary Somerset*, Thames Street.—Store-yard for old iron, behind the tower. Most of this ground has gone.

306. *St. Peter*, Paul's Wharf.—Site of burned church.

307. *St. Martin Vintry*, Queen Street.—No church.

308. *St. Thomas the Apostle*, Queen Street.—Little left except a large vault.

309. *St. Mary Aldermary*, Watling Street.

310. *St. Antholin*, Watling Street.—Very little left except one great vault.

311. *St. Pancras*, Pancras Lane.—Site of burned church.

312. *St. Benet Sherehog*, Pancras Lane.—Site of burned church.

313. *St. Martin Pomeroy* (St. Olave, Jewry), Ironmonger Lane.—The site of St. Martin's Church, used as St. Olave's Churchyard, when that became a private garden.

314. *St. Stephen*, Coleman Street.

315. *St. Mildred*, Poultry.—Given by Thomas Morsted 1420. Almost lost in 1594. Abridged before 1633, and enlarged 1693.

316. *St. Matthew*, Friday Street.

317. *St. John*, Watling Street.—Site of burned church.

318. *St. Michael*, Queenhithe.—Private garden for St. James's Rectory.

319. *St. Martin*, Ludgate.—Stationers' Hall Court. The vaults are under the ground.

320. *St. Christopher le Stocks*.—Garden of the Bank of England since 1780.

321. *St. Michael*, Cornhill.—Some shops were built in this ground in 1690.

322. *St. Peter*, Cornhill.

323. *St. Stephen*, Walbrook.—Encroached upon in 1693.

324. *St. Margaret*, Lothbury.—Improved and planted at the expense of Dr. Edwin Freshfield, F.S.A.

325. *St. Martin Outwich*, Camomile Street.—The burial-ground of the priory of St. Augustine Papey. Given by Robert Hyde 1538.

326. *St. Michael Paternoster Royal*, College Hill.

327. *St. James*, Garlickhithe.

328. *St. Nicholas Cole Abbey*, Queen Victoria Street.—Very little left.

329. *St. Swithin*, Cannon Street.—Additional ground. One adjoining the church has gone.

330. *Allhallows the Great*, Upper Thames Street.

331. *Allhallows the Less*, Upper Thames Street.—Site of burned church.

332. *St. Lawrence Pountney*, Cannon Street.—Two grounds. One is the site of the burned church.

333. *St. Martin Orgar*, Cannon Street.—Site of burned church.

334. *St. George*, Botolph Lane.

335. *St. Mary at Hill*, Eastcheap.—Saved by the City Church and Churchyard Protection Society 1879.

336. *St. Andrew Undershaft*, Leadenhall Street.

337. *St. Catherine Cree*, Leadenhall Street.—A part of the cemetery of Holy Trinity Priory, Aldgate.

338. *St. Helen*, Bishopsgate.—This is very often open, but not provided with seats.

339. *St. Ethelburga*, Bishopsgate.

340. *St. Clement*, Eastcheap.

341. *St. Leonard*, Fish Street Hill.—Site of burned church.

342. *St. Magnus the Martyr*, London Bridge.

343. *St. Mary Woolnoth*, Lombard Street.—In danger at the present time.

344. *St. Nicholas Acons*, Lombard Street.

345. *St. Edmund King and Martyr*, Lombard Street. The property of the Salters' Company. Laid out as a garden with seats.

346. *Allhallows*, Lombard Street.—Closed in the cholera year, 1849.

347. *St. Gabriel*, Fenchurch Street.—The gift of Helming Legget.

348. *Allhallows, Staining*, Mark Lane.—Church destroyed in 1870 except the tower. The property of the Clothworkers' Company.

349. *St. Olave's*, Hart Street.

350. *Allhallows, Barking*, Town Hill.

351. *St. Dunstan's in the East*, Lower Thames Street.—Its opening is under consideration.

352. *The Burial-ground of Christ's Hospital.*—This has been almost covered with buildings, but a small piece remains as a yard near the great hall.

353. *The Burial-ground of the Greyfriars.*—This is a courtyard, surrounded by the cloisters, in Christ's Hospital, used as a playground by the boys.

354. *St. James's Churchyard*, Duke Street.—This is used as a playground for the Aldgate Ward Schools.

355. *Additional ground for St. Bride's*, Fleet Street.—This is off Farringdon Street, is about 750 square yards in extent, and used as a volunteer drill-ground. There are no tombstones, and the ground is untidy. Consecrated 1610. Given by the Earl of Dorset.

356. *St. Mary's Roman Catholic Church ground*, Finsbury Square.—Very little left.

357. *Bridewell Burial-ground.*—This is about 900 square yards in size, and is at the corner of Tudor and Dorset Streets. It was the burial-ground of the hospital, which has been removed. It is now a very untidy yard, boarded up with a rough advertisement hoarding, in the occupation of H. S. Foster, builder, 7, Tudor Street. It would make a good public playground.

III. Burial-grounds which have been paved and added to the public footway, but are still traceable. The churchyards of—

358. *St. Mary*, Abchurch Lane.—This was thrown into the pavement about 160 years ago, with posts round it.

359. *St. Margaret Pattens*, Rood Lane.

360. *St. Lawrence Jewry*, by the Guildhall.

361. *St. Michael Bassishaw*, Basinghall Street.—Two good trees.

362. *St. Benet Fink*, Threadneedle Street.—Railed in, with Peabody's statue in it.

363. *The Cloisters of the Augustine Friars.*—Lately discovered on the north side of the Dutch Church, Austin Friars Square forming part of the site.

IV. Burial-ground still in use—

364. *Newgate Burial-ground.*—A passage in the prison, used for the interment of those who are executed; 10 feet wide and 85 feet long.

APPENDIX B.

BURIAL-GROUNDS IN LONDON WHICH HAVE BEEN ENTIRELY DEMOLISHED FOR NEW STREETS, RAILWAY LINES, PUBLIC BUILDINGS, PRIVATE HOUSES, &C.

THE CITY.

Name of Churchyard or Burial-ground. What occupies the Site.

1.	There were Roman Cemeteries in various parts of the City.
2.	Sepulchral remains have been found in Newgate Street,
3.	Ludgate, Camomile Street, St. Mary at Hill, St. Dunstan's
4.	in the East, St. Paul's Churchyard, and Bishopsgate
5.	Churchyard (the last named being very ancient, possibly of
6.	British origin). See also Whitechapel, Limehouse, Bermondsey,
7.	and Lewisham.

Name of Churchyard or Burial-ground   What occupies the Site

8. Burial-grounds of St. Martin le Grand and St. Lennard, Foster Lane   The General Post Office.

9. Jews original Burial-ground   Jewin St. and neighbourhood.

10. St. Nicholas Shambles   Newgate Street.

11. St. Benet, Paul's Wharf   Thrown into St. Benet's Hill.

12. The Workhouse Ground, Shoe Lane, belonging to St. Andrew's, Holborn   The Farringdon Market occupied the site, and a street has now taken its place

13. Allhallows', Honey Lane   The Old City of London School was built on its site.

14. St. Mary le Bow   Warehouses and street full of vans, called Bow Churchyard.

15. St. John, Cloak Lane   Taken by District Railway in 1879 for Cannon Street Station, &c.

16. St. Mary Bothaw   Cannon Street Station, S.E.R.

17. St. Mary Mounthaw   Taken for Queen Victoria St.

18. St. Nicholas Olave   Taken for Queen Victoria St.

19. St. Mary Magdalen   Taken for Queen Victoria St.

20. Elsing Spital Priory   Warehouses, London Wall.

21. St. Peter le Poer, Broad St.   Houses in Broad Street.

22. St. Thomas Acons   Mercer's Hall.

23. St. Bartholomew's Priory, Smithfield   This had a cemetery attached, which is covered by the buildings near the south transept of the church.

24. St. Bartholomew's Hospital Burial-ground West wing of hospital.

25. St. Swithin, Cannon Street   Roadway on north side of church.

26. St. Dunstan in the West, Fleet Street   Probably north end of present church.

27. St. Michael le Querne   Cheapside.

28. Additional ground to Christ Church, Moorgate Street   Southern end of St. Bartholomew's Hospital.

29. St. Mary Colechurch   Old Jewry.

30. St. Margaret Moses, Friday Street Cannon Street.

31. Garden in Hosier Lane, used for St. Mary le Bow   Built upon about 1560.

32. Holy Trinity the Less, Trinity Lane   Mansion House Station.

33. St. Mary Axe, Leadenhall Street   Houses on west side of the street called St. Mary Axe.

34. St. Mary Woolchurch Haw   Mansion House.

35. St. Bartholomew by the Exchange   Threadneedle Street.

36. Bethlem Burial-ground (also called Rowe's)   Liverpool Street Station.

37. St. Benet, Gracechurch St.   Corner of Fenchurch Street.

38. St. Margaret, New Fish St.   Metropolitan Railway.

39. St. Andrew Hubbard   Houses between Botolph Lane and Love Lane. The old King's Weigh House Chapel was on the site.

40. St. Botolph, Billingsgate (Lower Ground)   Warehouse in Lower Thames Street, with terra cotta heads on the frontage.

41. Garden of Hundsdon House, Blackfriars (French Embassy)   95 bodies buried in two pits here in 1623 after an accident. Site now disappeared.

42. Pest-field, Hand Alley   New Street, Bishopsgate Street.

43. The Churchyard of the Dutch Church, Austin Friars   This Burial-ground was on the south side of the Dutch Church, now built over.

44. St. Michael, Crooked Lane   King William Street.

45. St. James' Hermitage Burial-ground   Houses south of the postern and the south wall of St. Giles' Churchyard, Cripplegate.

46. Cemetery of the Crutched Friars   South of Fenchurch Street.

ST. MARYLEBONE.

47. Churchyard of Old Tyburn Church   Marylebone Court House, Stratford Place.

48. Burial-place for those executed at Tyburn   Corner of Upper Bryanston Street and Edgware Road.

PADDINGTON.

49. Pest-field, Craven Hill Probably never used.   Craven Hill Gardens.

HAMMERSMITH.

50. Convent Burial-ground, King Street   Part of the buildings of the Convent of the Sacred Heart, rebuilt by Cardinal Manning.

ST. MARGARET AND ST. JOHN, WESTMINSTER.

51. Buckingham Chapel, Palace Street   Brewery on south side.

ST. MARTIN'S IN THE FIELDS.

52. St. Martin's additional ground   Part of the buildings of the National Gallery.

53. Burial-ground for the Friends of the Westminster Division   Castle Street, Long Acre.

54. Burial-ground of St. Mary Rounceval Convent   Northumberland Avenue.

ST. JAMES'S, WESTMINSTER.

55. Pest-field   Golden Square and district round.

THE STRAND.

56. Additional ground for St. Martin's in the Fields   French Chapel, Crown Street, Soho, now Charing Cross Road.

57. German Burial-ground, Savoy   Medical Examination Hall and Savoy Chambers.

58. Old Somerset House Cemetery   Somerset House.

59. Westminster Convent Burial-Ground   Part of Covent Garden Market.

60. Almshouse Ground, Clemens Lane   New Lane Courts.

61. Burial-ground by the Workhouse, St. Paul's, Covent Garden   Possibly the Floral Arcade.

62. Cemetery of old St. Mary le Strand   Somerset House, &c.

ST. GILES' IN THE FIELDS.

63. The Workhouse Burial-ground   Part of the Workhouse in Shorts

HOLBORN.

64. St. Sepulchre's Additional Ground, Durham Yard   Great Northern Goods Depôt.

65. St. Sepulchre's Workhouse Ground, Durham Yard   Ditto. This was the larger of the two.

66. Pardon Churchyard, Charterhouse,   Wilderness Row, subsequently Clerkenwell Road.

67. Baptist Chapel-ground, Glasshouse Yard   Goswell Road, just to the south of St. Thomas's, Charterhouse.

CLERKENWELL.

68. Nun's Burial-ground   Houses west side of St. James' Walk.

69. St. James's Additional Ground, Ray Street   Farringdon Road and the Railway.

70. Corporation Row Burial-pit   Artisans' dwellings on north side.

71. Priory Cemetery   St. John's Square, &c.

ST. LUKE'S.

72. Thomas', Golden Lane   Factory on west side of St. Mary's Church, Charterhouse, Playhouse Yard.

73. Pest-field, Old Street   Bath Street, and many acres to the north

74. Pest-field, Mount Mill   Seward Street, Goswell Road, north side.

75. Cupid's Court Ground, Golden Lane   Offices, &c., north of Brackley Street.

SHOREDITCH.

76. Gloucester Street Chapel-ground Gas Light and Coke Company's premises.

77. Shoreditch Burial-ground, Hoxton   Wing of the Workhouse built in 1884.

78. Burial-ground by the Goldsmiths' Almshouses   New block of Artisans' Dwellings west side of Goldsmith Row.

79. Worship Street Baptist Chapel-ground   London and North Western Goods Depôt.

STOKE NEWINGTON.

80. Abney Congregational Chapel, Church Street   School buildings.

BETHNAL GREEN.

81. Roman Catholic Ground, Bethnal Green   Cambridge Road.

82. Pest-field, belonging to Stepney   South of Lisbon Street and Collingwood Street.

WHITECHAPEL.

83. Roman Cemetery   Goodman's Fields.

84. Burial-ground, Whitechapel Road   Whitechapel Workhouse.

85. St. Katharine, near the Tower   St. Katharine's Docks.

86. Additional Ground to St. Katharine   St. Katharine's Docks.

87. Bone Yard, Gower's Walk   Houses.

88. Zoar Chapel, Great Alie St.   Warehouses, shops, and a forge.

89. Pest-field, Spital Square St. Mary's Church, &c.

90. Pest-field, east of the Mint, and Cemetery of the Convent of St. Mary of Grace   The Royal Mint.

91. Pest-field, Petticoat Lane   Built over.

92. Tower Burial-ground (outside the wall)   Demolished for Tower Bridge.

93. St. Mary Spital Priory   Spital Square and district.

94. Pest-field or Plague-Pit in Gower's Walk   Messrs. Kinloch's new buildings.

95. Mill Yard Sabbatarian Chapel   Railway by Leman St. Station.

96. German Church, Hooper Square. Railway.

LIMEHOUSE.

97. Roman Cemetery   Sun Tavern Fields, Shadwell.

98. Friends' Burial-ground   Wapping Street.

MILE END OLD TOWN.

99. Rose Lane Chapel-ground   East London Railway, public house and shops close to Stepney Station.

ST. GEORGE THE MARTYR, SOUTHWARK.

100. London Road Chapel-ground   Tailor's Shop in London Road, east side.

101. Baptist Chapel-ground, Sheer's Alley   Wilmott's Buildings.

102. Zion Chapel, Borough Artisans' Dwellings, Chapel Court.

ST. SAVIOR'S.

103. Friends' Burial-ground, Worcester Street London Bridge and Charing Cross Railway.

104. Chapel Burial-ground, Ewer Street   London Bridge and Charing Cross Railway.

105. Baptist Chapel-ground, Pepper Street (Duke Street Park)   Houses at corner of Pepper Street.

106. St. Margaret, Southwark   Borough High Street and Market

ST. OLAVE'S.

107. St. Olave, Additional Ground   St. Thomas Street.

108. Flemish Burial-ground, Carter Lane   Approach to London Bridge Station.

109. Mazepond Baptist Chapel   Guy's Hospital Medical School.

110. Baptist Chapel, Dipping Alley   Fair Street or Charles Street, Horselydown

BERMONDSEY.

111. Roman Cemetery   Snow Fields, Union Street, and Deverell Street (Newington).

GREENWICH.

112. Roman Cemetery   Neighbourhood of Blackheath.

WOOLWICH.

113. Bethlem Chapel-ground, Charles Street   Club House.

APPENDIX C.

CHURCHES AND CHAPELS WITH VAULTS UNDER THEM THAT HAVE BEEN USED FOR INTERMENTS, BUT WITH NO GRAVEYARDS ATTACHED.

The Foundling Chapel, W.C.

Lincoln's Inn Chapel and Cloisters, W.C.

Gray's Inn Chapel, E.C.

Ely Place Chapel, E.C.

Lambeth Palace Chapel, S.E.

St. Pancras New Church, W.C.

Camden Chapel, St. Pancras, N.W.

Christ Church, Marylebone, N.W.

Holy Trinity, Marylebone, N.W.

Holy Trinity, Islington, N.

St. John's, Upper Holloway, N.

St. John's, Paddington, W.

St. Barnabas, Kensington, W.

All Saints, Islington, N.

Aske's Hospital Chapel, Hoxton, N.

St. Barnabas, King Square, E.C.

St. Thomas', Charterhouse, E.C.

St. Mark's, Clerkenwell, E.C.

St. Mark's, North Audley Street, W.

Grosvenor Chapel, South Audley Street.

Hanover Chapel, Regent Street, W. (About to be destroyed.)

St. Peter's, Pimlico, S.W.

St. Stephen's, Westminster, S.W.

St. James's, Clapham, S.W.

St. Anne's, Wandsworth, S.W.

Holy Trinity, Newington, S.E.

St. Mary Magdalene's, Peckham, S.E.

Holy Trinity, Little Queen Street, W.C.

Wesleyan Chapel, Great Queen Street, W.C.

Mission Chapel, Little Wyld Street, W.C.

Elim Chapel, Fetter Lane, E.C.

Baptist Chapel, Blandford Street, N.W.

Roman Catholic Chapel, Grove Road, N.W.

Congregational Chapel, Kentish Town, N.W.

Brunswick Chapel, Mile End Road, E. (Now connected with Charrington's Assembly Hall.)

Baptist Chapel, Romney Street, S.W.

Surrey Chapel, Blackfriars Road, S.E. (Now a machine manufactory.)

Queen Street Chapel, Woolwich, S.E.

Some vaults, such as those under the Guildhall Chapel, the Rolls Chapel, and the notorious Elton Chapel, Clements Lane, have disappeared with the buildings; and it must be remembered that the City churches that have lost their churchyards have vaults underneath them, and so have other buildings, such as the Charterhouse Chapel and cloisters, the burial-ground there being of much later date, and detached from the chapel.

APPENDIX D.

STEPS TO BE TAKEN FOR LAYING OUT AND THROWING OPEN TO THE PUBLIC A DISUSED CHURCHYARD OR BURIAL-GROUND, AND FOR ITS MAINTENANCE BY THE LONDON COUNTY COUNCIL, OR THE LOCAL AUTHORITY. (REPRINTED FROM THE ANNUAL REPORT OF THE METROPOLITAN PUBLIC GARDENS ASSOCIATION, 83, LANCASTER GATE, W.)

1. Decide how much assistance is to be sought from the London County Council, or the Local Authority, that is the Vestry or District Board, if in London, or the Urban or Rural Sanitary Authority, if in the provinces, in the carrying out of the scheme. Thus, in approaching any of these bodies, it should be considered—

(*a*) Whether they are to be asked to lay out the ground, or only to take it over for maintenance after it has been laid out by others, *e.g.*, the Association.

(*b*) Whether they may require, or can have the freehold, or only a limited interest, such as a lease of the ground.

2. The Incumbent or Owner will, when the consent of the Local Authority or London County Council has been obtained, be required to execute a Deed transferring the Ground to the Local Authority, or the Council, upon the terms and conditions that have been mutually arranged.

3. Consecrated Grounds require a Faculty. In the case of a Consecrated Ground, a Faculty must be obtained from the Bishop of the Diocese by the Local Authority, or the London County Council, as the case may be, permitting such body to exercise powers of management over it; and should it be needful to move tombstones, such Faculty must also contain a license to do so, otherwise they cannot be moved (*vide* para. 5).

4. The Consistory Court of the Diocese usually requires the following preliminary steps to have been taken, before it will hear an application for a Faculty:—

(*a*) The preparation of a plan and detailed statement of what it is proposed to do to the ground, and of an estimate of the expense involved.

(*b*) The submission of plan, statement, and estimate, to a meeting of the Vestry of the Parish, and the passing of a resolution (which should be carefully prepared) by the Vestry approving the plan, statement, estimate, and application for a Faculty.

(*c*) The approval of plan, statement, and estimate, by the Local Authority or the London County Council, as the case may be.

(*d*) The presentation of a petition for a Faculty to the Bishop or his Consistory Court, by the Local Authority or the Council, as the case may be, setting out the scheme, accompanied by the plan, statement, and resolutions.

(*e*) This petition should in the ordinary course have the concurrence of the Incumbent, and he may be, and it is usually desirable that he should be, a party to it.

5. Removal of Tombstones in consecrated and unconsecrated grounds. In the case of any disused churchyard, cemetery, or burial-ground, whether consecrated or not, if tombstones are to be moved, at least three months before any tombstone or monument is moved the following steps have to be taken:—

(*a*) A statement shall be prepared sufficiently describing by the name and date appearing thereon the tombstones and monuments standing or being in the ground, and such other particulars as may be necessary;

(*b*) Such statements shall be deposited with the clerk of the County Council or Local Authority, and shall be open to inspection by all persons;

(*c*) An advertisement of the intention to remove or change the position of such tombstones and monuments shall be inserted three times at least in some newspaper circulating in the neighbourhood of the burial-ground, and such advertisement shall give notice of the deposit of such statement, as is hereinbefore described, and of the hours within which the same may be inspected;

(*d*) A notice in terms similar to the advertisement shall be placed on the door of the church (if any) to which such churchyard, cemetery, or burial-ground is attached, and shall be delivered or sent by post to any person known or believed by the County Council or Local Authority to be a near relative of any person whose death is recorded on any such tombstone or monument.

Ditto in consecrated grounds only. In the case of any consecrated ground a Faculty is also required (*vide* page 3), but no application for a Faculty can be made until the expiration of one month at least after the appearance of the last of such advertisements.

Provided that on any application for a Faculty nothing shall prevent the Bishop from directing or sanctioning the removal of any tombstone or monument, if he is of opinion that reasonable steps have been taken to bring the intention to effect such removal to the notice of some person having a family interest in such removal.

Ditto in unconsecrated grounds only. In the case of an unconsecrated burial-ground, no Faculty is requisite either for management or for moving tombstones.

N.B.—Faculties, which only emanate from the Courts of Diocesan Bishops, cannot apply to burial-grounds, unless consecrated by Bishops of the Established Church.

6. Playing of Games. The playing of any games or sports is not allowed in any churchyard, cemetery, or burial-ground in or over which any estate, interest, or control is acquired under section five of the Metropolitan Open Spaces Act, 1881.

Provided that—

(*a*) In the case of consecrated ground, the Bishop, by any license or Faculty granted under the Metropolitan Open Spaces Act, 1881, or this Act (Open Spaces Act, 1887), and

(*b*) In the case of any churchyard, cemetery, or burial-ground, which is not consecrated, the body from which any such estate, interest, or control as aforesaid is acquired may expressly sanction any such use of the ground, and may specify such conditions as to the extent or manner of such use.

If an Incumbent or owner wishes to lay out a Disused Churchyard or Burial-ground, and to maintain it himself directly or by his agents, *e.g.*, the Association, no application to the Local Authority, or London County Council, is required, and if it is a consecrated ground but no tombstones are moved, no Faculty or consent of any other person is required. Any arrangement of this nature *an Incumbent* may make is not, however, binding on his successor. In unconsecrated grounds no Faculties are needed.

APPENDIX E.

The Disused Burial-Grounds Act, and Amending Clauses in Subsequent Open Spaces Acts.

A.D. 1884. 47 & 48 Vict. [Ch. 72.]
Disused Burial grounds Act, 1884.

An Act for preventing the erection of Buildings on Disused Burial grounds. [14th August, 1884.]

Whereas an Act was passed in the session of Parliament holden in the fifteenth and sixteenth years of Her Majesty, chapter eighty-five, to amend the laws concerning the burial of the dead in the metropolis, and an Act was passed in the session holden in the sixteenth and seventeenth years of Her Majesty, chapter one hundred and thirty-four, "to amend the laws concerning the burial of the dead in England, beyond the limits of the metropolis, and to amend the Act concerning the burial of the dead in the metropolis": And whereas, in pursuance of the provisions of the above recited Acts, numerous Orders in Council have been made for the discontinuance of burials in certain burial-grounds within the metropolis and elsewhere: And whereas it is expedient that no buildings should be erected on any burial-ground affected by any of such Orders in Council:

Be it therefore enacted by the Queen's most Excellent Majesty, by and with the advice and consent of the Lords Spiritual and Temporal, and Commons, in this present Parliament assembled, and by the authority of the same as follows:

Short title. 1. This Act may be cited as the Disused Burial-Grounds Act, 1884.

2. Interpretation clause Amended by 50 & 51 Vict. c. 32. In this Act a "disused burial-ground" shall mean a burial-ground in respect of which an Order in Council has been made for the discontinuance of burials therein in pursuance of the provisions of the said recited Acts.

3. Amended by 50 & 51 Vict. c. 32. After the passing of this Act No buildings to be erected upon disused burial-grounds for enlargement, etc. it shall not be lawful to erect any buildings upon any disused burial-ground, except for the purpose of enlarging a church, chapel, meeting-house, or other place of worship.

4. Saving for buildings already sanctioned. Nothing in this Act shall prevent the erection of any building on a disused burial-ground, for which a Faculty has been obtained before the passing of this Act.

5. Saving of burial-grounds already sold by Act of Parliament. Nothing in this Act contained shall apply to any burial-ground which has been sold or disposed of under the authority of any Act of Parliament.

[48 & 49 VICT.] [Ch. 167.]

Metropolitan Board of Works (Various Powers) Act, 1885.

And whereas it is expedient to confer further powers upon the Board for enforcing the due observance in the metropolis of the provisions of the Disused Burial Grounds Act, 1884:

PART IV.

Miscellaneous (Disused Burial-grounds).

56. A.D. 1885.

Board to be the authority to enforce the Disused Burial-Grounds Act, 1884. The Board shall be and they are hereby constituted the authority for preventing the violation and for enforcing the due observance of the provisions of the Disused Burial-grounds Act, 1884, within the metropolis, and they may from time to time institute and prosecute all such legal proceedings and do all such acts, manners, and things as may in the opinion of the Board be necessary or expedient for preventing the violation by any person and for enforcing the due observance by all persons of the provisions of the said Act within the metropolis.

A.D. 1887. [50 & 51 VICT.] *Open Spaces Act, 1887.*
CHAPTER 32

An Act for extending certain Provisions of the Metropolitan Open Spaces Acts, 1877 and 1881, with Amendments, to Sanitary Districts throughout England, Wales, and Ireland; and for other purposes. [23rd August, 1887.]

40 & 41 Vict. c. 35. 44 & 45 Vict. c. 34. WHEREAS by the Metropolitan Open Spaces Acts, 1877 and 1881 (herein called the principal Acts), certain facilities were provided for making available the open spaces and burial-grounds in the metropolis for the use of the inhabitants thereof for exercise and recreation, and it is expedient to provide facilities for making available open spaces and burial-grounds in all sanitary districts in England, Wales, and Ireland, for the like use of the inhabitants thereof, and to make other provisions for the 47 & 48 Vict. c. 72. purpose aforesaid, and also to amend the Metropolitan Open Spaces Act, 1881, and the Disused Burial-grounds Act, 1884:

Be it therefore enacted by the Queen's most Excellent Majesty by and with the advice and consent of the Lords Spiritual and Temporal, and Commons, in this present Parliament assembled, and by the authority of the same, as follows:

---

4. Amendment of 47 & 48 Vict. c. 72. In the Disused Burial-grounds Act, 1884, and this Act, the expression "burial-ground" shall have the same meaning as in the Metropolitan Open Spaces Act, 1881, as amended by this Act, and the expression "disused burial-ground" shall mean any burial-ground which is no longer used for interments, whether or not such ground shall have been partially or wholly closed for

burials under the provisions of any statute or Order in Council, and the expression "building" shall include any temporary or movable building.

---

11. Power over open spaces already vested in sanitary authority. The Metropolitan Board[10] or the sanitary authority may exercise all the powers given to them by the Metropolitan Open Spaces, 1881, or this Act respecting open spaces, churchyards, cemeteries, and burial-grounds transferred to them in pursuance of the said Act or of this Act in respect of any open spaces, churchyards, cemeteries, and burial-grounds transferred to them in pursuance of the said Act or of this Act in respect of any open spaces, churchyards, cemeterie, and burial-grounds of a similar nature which are or shall be vested in them in pursuance of any other statute, or of which they are otherwise the owners.

10. Read London County Council.

N.B. Clauses 2 and 3 in this Act, which also refer to burial-grounds, are incorporated in Appendix D.

SCHEDULE.

Portions of the Metropolitan Open Spaces Act, 1881, repealed.

In section one, the following words occurring in the definition of an "open space," viz., "but shall not include any enclosed land which has not a public road or footpath completely round the same."

In the same section, the following words occurring in the definition of a "burial-ground," viz., "and in which interments have taken place since the year 1800."

In the second paragraph of section five, the words, "but such Metropolitan Board,[11] vestry, or district board shall not allow the playing of any games or sports therein."

11. Ibid.

Note from the Editor

Odin's Library Classics strives to bring you unedited and unabridged works of classical literature. As such, this is the complete and unabridged version of the original English text unless noted. In some instances, obvious typographical errors have been corrected. This is done to preserve the original text as much as possible. The English language has evolved since the writing and some of the words appear in their original form, or at least the most commonly used form at the time. This is done to protect the original intent of the author. If at any time you are unsure of the meaning of a word, please do your research on the etymology of that word. It is important to preserve the history of the English language.

Taylor Anderson

Printed in Great Britain
by Amazon